The Politics of Hope

THE ORIGINS OF SOCIALISM
IN BRITAIN 1880 – 1914

Edited and introduced by Edmund and Ruth Frow

PLUTO  PRESS

First published 1989 by Pluto Publishing Ltd
11-21 Northdown Street, London N1 9BN

Distributed in the USA by
Unwin Hyman Inc
8 Winchester Place
Winchester
MA 01890, USA

Typesetting 'The Works', Exeter, Devon.

Printed in Hungary by Interpress

British Library Cataloguing in Publication Data
The Politics of hope : the origins of
  socialism in Britain
  1. Socialism—Great Britain—History
  —Sources
  I. Frow, Edmund   II. Frow, Ruth
  335′ .00941   HX243

ISBN 1-85305-063-6

Contents

Preface   ix
Introduction   xi

1. THE DEMOCRATIC FEDERATION   1
   Socialism Made Plain
2. JAMES LEIGH JOYNES   7
   The Socialist Catechism
3. ANNIE BESANT   32
   Why I am a Socialist
4. SIDNEY JAMES WEBB   41
   What Socialism Means
5. GEORGE BERNARD SHAW   53
   What Socialism Is
6. WILLIAM MORRIS   59
   How I Became a Socialist
7. TOM MANN   70
   The Socialists' Program
8. ROBERT BLATCHFORD   85
   Real Socialism
9. WILLIAM MORRIS   102
   Monopoly or, How Labour is Robbed
10. THE SOCIALIST GROUP OF THE LONDON SOCIETY   114
    OF COMPOSITORS
    Socialism and Trade Unionism
11. HENRY MAYERS HYNDMAN   125
    Social Democracy

12. ISABELLA FORD   155
    Women and Socialism
13. H. G. WELLS   177
    This Misery of Boots
14. JAMES CONNOLLY   192
    Socialism Made Easy

Appendix: Organisations and Publications   219
Index   227

SOUVENIR of the S.D.P. CONFERENCE. HELD AT BRISTOL EASTER 1909.

HAIL! DAWN of LIBERTY DAY of EQUALITY

Preface

The pamphlets in this collection represent just a fraction of the vast quantity of socialist literature published in the 30 years spanning the period 1880 to the outbreak of the First World War. The selection of these particular examples has been made in order to present a cross-section of views and styles as well as to cover the whole of this key period in British history. The authors have been chosen because of their important contribution to the socialist cause, and almost all of them are household names.

The pamphlets are presented in chronological order according to the dates when they first appeared, and they are published here exactly as in the originals, unedited apart from a few alterations in spelling. Each pamphlet is introduced by a short biography of the author, and is followed by a Notes section compiled by the editors to help the present-day reader through some of the more obscure references in the text.

Brief histories of some of the most important socialist organisations and publications of the period are included in the Appendix.

The Politics of Hope has been chosen as the title of this volume to convey the mood of the period, when the ideas of Marx and Engels were just beginning to gain acceptance, and when working people in Britain began to believe that a genuinely socialist society could be achieved by means of the parliamentary system.

The introductory biographies are important in contextualising the message contained in each of the pamphlets and explain the various splits and debates occurring within the labour movement at the time.

The focus of political debate has now changed, but many of the problems of that period, particularly with regard to divisions within the trade union movement, socialist organisations and political parties, are still with us. It is hoped therefore that the revival of these pamphlets will throw light upon our present difficulties and strengthen the resolve of those engaged in the struggle for a more just society.

SOCIALIST LEAGUE

HAMMERSMITH BRANCH

BRANCH
SECRETARY

TREASURER

Introduction

EDMUND AND RUTH FROW

From the earliest days of the Industrial Revolution when the structure of domestic-based work was replaced by the extreme exploitation of the factories, working people looked forward with hope to a future in which their personal problems would become bearable. As workers developed a class consciousness, such hopes were perceived in wider terms and the aspirations of the individual became immersed in those of the class.

It has been the aim of the ruling class and their apologists to suppress revolutionary tendencies and to maintain the illusion not only that change can be brought about by reforms but that there is no need to change the capitalist system if a way can be found to make it work so that the majority of people are satisfied. They believe that while the hopes of individuals can be met to some extent, the hopes of the workers as a class can be contained and fears of a revolutionary change averted.

Although the Chartists in 1840 formed the first working-class political party in the National Charter Association, and employed all forms of struggle against the ruling class, from peaceful petitioning to armed insurrection, neither the moral force nor the physical force sections of the movement had a revolutionary programme. The pikes that were forged and the pistol shots that punctuated mass meetings were intended to bring forward the day when workers would participate in the capitalist system, not change it.

It was not until the *Communist Manifesto* by Karl Marx and Frederick Engels was published in 1848 that for the first time the working class had a revolutionary theory explaining the dialectics of the development of society and the transient nature of the capitalist system.

In Britain, scientific socialism fell on barren ground. By 1850 Britain had become the workshop of the world and the centre of a vast colonial empire. This enabled the ruling class to bribe a stratum of skilled workers with conditions of work and wages which were an improvement on those they had experienced previously. Moreover, as the century proceeded, the vote was extended to more males and an apparent increase in democracy was obtained. British capitalism was able to keep its workers quiescent and ostensibly satisfied through intense exploitation of the colonial workers.

As the hopes of the Owenites for a new moral world, based on the rights of all to the produce of their labour, and the Chartist aspirations for male enfranchisement, faded into the 1850–80 period of an apparent lull in activity, the ideas formulated by Marx and Engels slowly gained acceptance and gave renewed hope.

During that period, the working class had no political party. It still formed 'the tail of the "Great Liberal Party"'.[1] The trades unions acted as the custodians of the welfare and interests of their own members, who for the most part were skilled males sufficiently powerful to maintain a position of supremacy in terms of wages and conditions.

Beneath the surface there was plenty of evidence that individual workers were becoming aware that as a class they were immobile. Unskilled men, the increasing numbers of working women, and the army of sweated, poverty-stricken workers, began to demonstrate their understanding that 'who would be free, themselves must strike the blow.'[2] There was an ever increasing realisation that although the problems of wages and hours were omnipresent, it was the basic structure of society that needed changing if the hopes of all for a better life were to be fulfilled.

The strong radical tradition reaching back to the early struggles for a reform of Parliament and the freedom of the press, which developed out of the ferment of ideas formulated by Thomas Paine, Thomas Spence and the 'Utopian' socialists still lingered among politically minded workers. Although the concept of the equality of man had been superseded, workers still gathered in radical clubs where the ideas of political and industrial democracy were exchanged and disseminated. Gradually the theory of socialism re-entered the British labour movement and the Owenite dream of a different order of things was replaced by a scientific theory which gave hope of a revolutionary change. The understanding that socialism was a superior system to capitalism, economically, politically, morally, ethically and in every sphere of human endeavour, raised the sights of the workers.

It was the politics of hope that sustained the pioneers in their daily struggles to win converts to the socialist cause. This vision of a society in which there would no longer be exploitation of man by man, poverty nor wars, but instead a brotherhood of men and women, was seductive.

During the late 1870s and early 1880s there was a growing ferment of social criticism and a development of socialist ideas which gave rise to the formation of political groupings determined to change the system. By the 1880s, Britain's industrial supremacy was being challenged by the US and Germany. There was a severe depression and considerable misery which became the seeds of revolt. The ideas of socialism gained fresh impetus, and when Henry Mayers Hyndman's Democratic Federation adopted an avowedly socialist programme and changed its name to the Social Democratic Federation in 1883, the modern socialist movement can be said to have been born.

But it was a different brand of socialism from that formulated by the early socialists, such as Owen, Bray, Thompson and Gray. The work of Marx and Engels now provided a scientific basis to their ideas.

Marxism, as enunciated by the Social Democratic Federation, emphasised Historical Materialism and the Theory of Value. Historical Materialism showed that the growth of productive forces leads to one social system being displaced by its successor on a higher level of production. Just as capitalism replaced feudalism, so socialism would in time replace capitalism.

In *Capital,* Marx explained how labour power became a commodity. The wage worker sells his labour power to the capitalist and spends part of the working day creating values sufficient to maintain himself and his family. But the rest of the day he spends creating surplus values which are appropriated by the capitalist. From this surplus, the capitalist obtains his profit, the wealth of the ruling class. Understanding these concepts gave the newly formed socialist groups evangelical fervour. They felt that the message of hope was so potent that it had to be passed on. To understand would be to agree.

However, although hope permeated the socialist movement from the time of the formation of the Social Democratic Federation (SDF), differences of emphasis and approach became apparent. As a federation, the SDF contained different strands and several variations on the central socialist theme. Important among them were the trade unionists whose activity was to be decisive in building the modern labour movement. But the differences predominated over their cohesive interest in the ideas of socialism, and, in 1884, the majority of the Federation's Council resigned and formed a new organisation, the Socialist League. Among those who left were William Morris, Eleanor Marx-Aveling and her husband, Edward.

The new organisation shared the basic weakness of the Federation. It failed to find a way to integrate theory and practice and saw its function as being mainly educational. In spite of this weakness, it was socialists who spearheaded the action that won considerable advances during the last 20 years of the century.

In 1885, it was the arrest of socialists in Dodd Street, Limehouse, that led to a mass protest of such proportions that the crowd filled the street and the police had to give way. The right to free speech was won. A year later, in 1886, a socialist demonstration in Trafalgar Square provoked jeers and sneers from the wealthy onlookers in the clubs around the square. Stones were thrown and arrests made. At the subsequent trial John Burns made a speech in his own defence which was then published in a pamphlet entitled *The Man with the Red Flag*. A second demonstration at which between 80,000 and 100,000 people marched on to Trafalgar Square with bands and banners was confronted by 4,000 police, later joined by a detachment of the Grenadier Guards and two squadrons of the Life Guards. The struggle for possession of the square continued far into the evening. One demonstrator was fatally injured, and William Morris made the occasion a call to battle by composing his *Death Song*.

It was the Socialists Eleanor Marx and Annie Besant who answered the cry of the Match girls in 1888, when the exploitation and ill-treatment they endured were exposed in an article entitled 'White Slavery in London'. When the firm tried to force the girls to sign a denial of the content of the article, they appealed to Annie Besant for help. She and a number of socialists answered the call. Mrs Besant recalled later, 'a pretty hubbub we created; we asked for money, and it came pouring in; we registered the girls to receive strike pay, wrote articles, roused the club; held public meetings, got Mr Bradlaugh to ask questions in Parliament, stirred up constituencies in which the shareholders were members, till the whole country rang with the struggle.'[3]

The success of the Matchgirls in forming a strong trade union, and in partially improving their conditions, led to the dock strike the following year. Inspired and guided by the socialists Tom Mann, John Burns and Ben Tillett, who were joined by many other members of the SDF and Socialist League, 10,000 dockers went on strike for a wage of 6*d* per hour, special payment for overtime and the abolition of piecework. The strike lasted a month, by which time nearly £50,000 had been raised and almost all of the demands met.

By 1890 it was clear that greater working class unity and organisation was needed in order to obtain working class representation in Parliament, particularly after the Liberal Party had so patently failed to answer the increasingly vociferous demands already made. Following the largest demonstrations of working people in Britain since the Chartist meetings, on May Day 1890 Frederick Engels delivered a report to German workers concerning the day's events as follows:

What the numerous onlooking bourgeois politicians took home with them as the overall effect was the certainty that the English proletariat, which for fully 40 years had trailed behind the big Liberal Party and served it as voting cattle, had awakened at last to new, independent life and action.

Engels recognised that the 'grandchildren of the old Chartists' were 'stepping into the line of battle'.[4]

In 1891 the Independent Labour Party (ILP) was formed in the provinces; it rapidly spread from Yorkshire and Lancashire to London and then to the rest of the country.

By the turn of the century it must have looked as if socialism was an idea whose time had come. The trade unions' determination to obtain representation in Parliament; the formation of the Labour Representation Committees; the first elections of working men in 1900 and their increase to 29 in the 1906 general election, when the Labour Party was formed; together with the huge increase in trade union membership following the formation of general unions; all raised the aspirations of working people so that socialism appeared a desirable and possible goal.

It was not only men who were given hope and dignity in the proposals for a socialist change in society. Women, who had been doubly exploited since the days of the Industrial Revolution, doing the meanest work and receiving paltry wages for it, began to realise that under a socialist state they would achieve full status as citizens and be expected to take their share in the affairs of state and society. Slowly such ideas penetrated among women, from both the working and middle classes, and the Suffrage Movement became the focal point.

The 1906 Liberal victory, however, proved to be hollow. Instead of improved wages and conditions, the reverse took place. Real wages dropped by 8 per cent between 1900 and 1911. Despite the demagogy of Lloyd George, the introduction of National Insurance and a number of other long-awaited reforms, the two Parliamentary contests in 1910 with their Liberal victories were marked by general apathy.

As a result of the Liberal government's reforming Trade Board Act and the National Insurance Act, 4,000–5,000 new administrative posts with salaries of up to £1,000 a year were created. Hundreds of active trade unionists, most of them officials, were among those appointed to these posts. This discredited the labour leaders and enhanced the appeal of socialism.

The four years prior to the outbreak of the First World War became known as 'The Great Unrest'. It was marked by strikes and industrial strife of unprecedented ferocity. There was an obvious need for coordinated leadership which the socialists appeared to have lost to the syndicalists. The Social Democratic Party called a conference in Manchester in 1911 at which the British Socialist Party was formed. Among the groups that attended were 32 Clarion Clubs, 41 Independent Labour Party branches, 68 delegates from the Social Democratic Party and 48 from other socialist organisations. The total number of socialists represented was estimated at 35,000. This new party developed the activity of the rank and file and played a significant part in the industrial struggles of the stormy years, 1910–14. During the 1912–13 transport strike, the party was particularly active attempting to give a socialist perspective to the struggle and to rally support for those involved.

The drive for socialist unity was frustrated only by the outbreak of the war in 1914.

The need to feed the growing army of socialists with suitable propaganda to use as ammunition exercised the minds of all the socialist groups. It was not a new problem. The 1837 congress of the Owenite organisation, the Association of All Classes of All Nations, established a Social Missionary and Tract Society, which by 1840 had 62 branches and a series of Social Tracts. These were issued in large numbers. An unsympathetic source, the Bishop of Exeter, asserted in the House of Lords in 1840 that the sale of tracts the previous year had been 500,000. At a time when literacy was by no means universal, this must be considered a large sale.

Among the activists who considered their primary work as the dissemination of ideas through pamphlet sales was George Jacob Holyoake, who wrote about 60 pamphlets between 1841 and 1903. He published both in his own name and under at least eight pseudonyms. Some of his pamphlets were reprinted in many editions, including one which was reprinted 11 times. The subjects he covered ranged from freethought to trade unionism, biography, grammar and mathematics.

Many of the Socialist pamphlets enjoyed several reprints. There were nine editions of William Morris's *Monopoly or How Labour Is Robbed*; Peter Kropotkin's *Appeal To The Young* was published in six editions between 1886 and 1914; and J.L. Joynes' translation of *Wage Labour and Capital* by Karl Marx ran through six editions between 1893 and 1913.

A major difficulty was that books on socialist theory were few. 'Our available literature consisted of the *Communist Manifesto*, the Kerr edition of Marx's *Capital*, the Social Science Library (also published in America), the Daniel de Leon pamphlets, and that was about all.'[5]

The socialist ideal inspired the pioneers to self-sacrifice and devotion to the cause. Socialists organised innumerable branch meetings, public outdoor meetings, debates and conferences, building or hiring halls and meeting places and adapting them to serve as the centre for their activities. Many towns had a market place where traditionally public meetings had taken place, and some large towns had a number of recognised meeting places where large crowds assembled to listen to speakers on a variety of subjects. In London there was Hyde Park; in Glasgow, the Green, in Birmingham, the Bull Ring and in Manchester Stevenson's Square.

At such meetings the essential ingredients were a chair-person, a speaker, a comrade who carried the platform, and those who sold literature – mainly socialist pamphlets. Regular literature-sellers equipped themselves with a wooden case which held their stock, and in addition to a carrying handle there was a strap that went round the neck to support the open case when it was used to display wares.

All demonstrations would be accompanied by literature-sellers, at the assembly point, along the route and at the meeting which was the focal point of the march. Pamphlets were sold at literature stalls in socialist halls, and at every meeting the parting cry of the chair-person was always, 'Don't forget the literature, Comrades.' Harry Pollitt wrote, 'I have as my clearest recollection the importance we placed on penny pamphlets and socialist literature generally. There never was a finer literature stall than that to be found at Margaret Street, Openshaw, at the time I write of. It was the first place we made for on entering the hall.'[6]

The influence of these socialist pamphlets was considerable. They were read by many men and women who were already or were to become the lay officers and officials of the trade union, labour and socialist movements, and from them they obtained a grounding in theory and practice. They led the reader on to study larger and more substantial works.

The basic tenet of these pamphlets was that socialism would cure the ills of capitalist society. It is therefore pertinent, at this time when capitalism in Britain is in deep crisis and the labour movement in urgent need of renewing its socialist conviction, that these pamphlets should be reprinted. In the words of Samuel Johnson nearly two and a half centuries ago, 'Since the advantages of preserving these small Tracts are so numerous; our attempt to unite them in volumes cannot be thought either useless or unreasonable; for there is no other method of securing them from accidents; and they have already been so long neglected, that this design cannot be delayed, without hazarding the loss of many pieces, which deserve to be transmitted to another age.'[7]

The pamphlet war has been waged in England for hundreds of years. At one time intellectual controversy on matters of State and Church was often conducted solely through the means of pamphlets. Progressive ideas and theories have often been aired initially through the publication of a pamphlet; and the establishment, recognising the influence of the written word, has used Star Chambers, fines, imprisonment, suppression and legislation to try to prevent the spread of 'small tracts and fugitive pieces'.[8]

Radicals and reformers were well aware of the value of pamphlets. They extolled the power of the printing press 'in spite of new Acts, and attempts to restrain it'.[9] Their courageous defiance of the authorities frequently resulted in printers, authors and publishers being imprisoned and their publications suppressed. John Milton recognised that censorship would be 'primely to the discouragement of all learning, and the stop of Truth...'[10] and to quote Samuel Johnson once again, 'Controversies cannot be long continued, nor frequently revived, where an inquisitor has a right to shut up the disputants in dungeons.'[11]

The socialists were faced with more subtle opposition. Their message was directed at the working class, whose members were often ill-educated, living in poverty and degradation and working long hours in appalling conditions. Workers were subject to the powerful influence of the dominant ruling class ideology disseminated through the Church and the State, and socialist ideas often fell on stony ground.

However, some of the pamphlets enjoyed a wide circulation and were influential in converting the electorate to socialism. In the period in question pamphlets were an important means of disseminating ideas and stimulating debate. Samuel Johnson himself had recognised the importance of pamphlets a century earlier: 'Pamphlets', he said, 'are yet to be considered as Sparks of Truth, which when united, may afford Light in some of the Darkest Scenes of state.'[12]

The selection of pamphlets in this volume together cover the main strands in the labour movement at the turn of the century, and were written by some of the most able exponents of socialism, such as H.G. Wells, Robert Blatchford, George Bernard Shaw and Annie Besant.

Only two of the pamphlets were written by women: during the period of the socialist revival women concentrated their energy and skills on securing the vote and freeing themselves from the restrictions that had been imposed on them.

Several of the struggles in which working people were engaged in the period 1880–1914 continue as we approach the twenty-first century. The questions of workers' alienation from the labour process, or equal rights for women, for example, are as pertinent today as they were in the early 1900s, and the messages contained in these pamphlets serve to illuminate the history of the labour movement to date, and particularly present crises within the trade union movement.

Notes

1. Frederick Engels in *The Labour Standard*, no. 12, 23 July 1881.
   Marx and Engels, *Articles On Britain*, Moscow 1975, p. 378.
2. Lord Byron, *Childe Harold's Pilgrimage*, Canto II, Verse LXXVI:
   Hereditary bondsmen! know ye not
   Who would be free themselves must strike the blow?
   By their own right arms the conquest must be wrought?
3. Annie Besant, *An Autobiography*, 1893, p. 336. 'White Slavery In London' was written by Annie Besant and published as an article in the *Link*, 23 June 1888.
4. Frederick Engels in *Arbeiter-Zeitung*, 23 May 1890; Marx and Engels, *Articles On Britain*, pp. 405–6.
5. Harry Pollitt, *Serving My Time*, Lawrence & Wishart, 1940, p. 46.
6. Ibid., p. 55.
7. Samuel Johnson, *An Essay On The Origin and Importance of Small Tracts and*

Fugitive Pieces; A.C. Ward, *A Miscellany of Tracts and Pamphlets*, OUP 1927, p. 389.

8. Ibid., p. 385.
9. William Hone, *The Political House That Jack Built*, 1819.
10. John Milton, *Areopagetica and Other Tracts*, Dent and Sons 1925, p. 7.
11. Samuel Johnson as n. 7, p. 386.
12. Samuel Johnson as n. 7, p. 388.

EDUCATE! AGITATE! ORGANIZE!

The Socialist League.

All who look forward to the Inevitable Change, and desire to work for its realization, are urged to sign this Application for Membership, and send it in to the Central Office, or to a Branch.

"I accept the principles of THE SOCIALIST LEAGUE, as stated in its Manifesto. I will do my utmost to uphold its principles, and will adhere to its rules."

188

xx

1
Socialism Made Plain
THE DEMOCRATIC FEDERATION

Introduction

The formation of the Democratic Federation in June 1881 was the result of Henry Mayers Hyndman's attempts to find allies in a campaign against British government abuse of the rights of the Irish people. The campaign at the time centred around the Irish Coercion Bill, which had been introduced by the newly elected Liberal government to deal with disturbances arising from tenant evictions in Ireland.

At the Federation's inaugural conference, Hyndman took the Chair, calling for unity among the various organisations of Democrats and workers throughout Great Britain and Ireland to secure equal rights for all. The programme included four points of the People's Charter which had yet to be granted, as well as a call for the nationalisation of the land, abolition of the House of Lords as a legislative body, and independence for Ireland.

In its first year, the Federation succeeded in forming six provincial groups at Manchester, Liverpool, Edinburgh, Glasgow, Nottingham and Dulwich. The membership was largely middle class, and the programme not avowedly socialist. But from the time of the second annual conference, a full socialist programme was adopted based on six lectures that Hyndman had given earlier in the year. The programme was published as the pamphlet *Socialism Made Plain*. The declaration of principles contained in the pamphlet included a list of immediate demands and ended with the well known call:

Educate! We shall need all our intelligence
Agitate! We shall need all our enthusiasm
Organise! We shall need all our force.

The outcome of the new socialist programme presented in the pamphlet was that the Democratic Federation was renamed the Social Democratic Federation (SDF) a year later in 1884.

Then in 1885, complaints arose against Hyndman's allegedly autocratic methods, and a split developed. Under the leadership of William Morris, the 'left' tendency cut itself off from the Federation and formed the Socialist League with its own paper *The Commonweal*. The two organisations continued to operate for four years until the Socialist League disintegrated in 1888.

In 1911 the SDF incorporated itself into the newly formed British Socialist Party (BSP) largely as a result of the industrial unrest of the pre-1914 period. Hyndman himself left the BSP during the war as he opposed the party's anti-war stand. The BSP went on to become one of the components in the formation of the British Communist Party in 1920.

Socialism Made Plain was published by the Modern Press, set up by Henry Hyde Champion and J.C. Foulger in 1883. Between 1883 and 1889 the press published a series of socialist pamphlets, of which *Socialism Made Plain* was the most successful, selling 100,000 copies.

Sources

Society For The Study Of Labour History Bulletin 31, Autumn 1975, pp. 62–5.
R. and E. Frow, *The Modern Press and The Social Democratic Federation*.

★   ★   ★

Fellow Citizens

The time has come when it is absolutely necessary that the mass of the people should seriously take in hand their own business unless they are content to find themselves in the near future worse off than they have ever yet been. At present, social and political power is monopolised·by those who live upon the labour of their fellows; and Tories or Conservatives, Whigs, Liberals or Radicals strive only to keep the workers ignorant of the truths which most nearly concern them. After the Reform Bill of 1832[1] the capitalists entered into alliance with the landlords except on one question, and from the repeal of the Corn Laws[2] in 1846 to this day the lords of the money-bag and the lords of the soil have together been absolute masters of the millions who labour throughout the United Kingdom. So complete has been their control that since the year 1848 no vigorous attempt has even been made to overthrow it. But what has been the result to the workers of this supremacy of the luxurious classes? During fifty years our labourers have competed against one another for wages which barely suffice to keep them alive. Whilst the realised wealth and the annual income of the country have more than trebled, those who create these riches remain a wage-slave class, overworked and underfed, at the mercy of every crisis and the victims of each succeeding depression. The improved machinery, the extension of railways, the great steam and electric communications – that vast increase of the power of man over nature which has been the main feature of our epoch, has brought luxury for the few, misery and degradation for the many. Even in the past ten years what have we seen? The interests of Great Britain utterly neglected,

Ireland shamefully misgoverned, India ruined and South Africa estranged. In 1874 the Liberals were dismissed for incapacity and Conservatives ruled in their stead for six years. Not a single measure did they introduce during that long tenure of office which could in any way lighten the lot of the millions who toil. The Conservatives having been turned out in disgust the Liberals again try their hand, and once more not a single measure is before Parliament, not a single measure is proposed for future legislation, which can benefit the working men and women who are really the source of all our wealth.

Fellow-Citizens, the further success of this pitiful trickery depends upon your ignorance and will last as long as your apathy. Landlords and capitalists, who own the House of Lords and fill the House of Commons, wish nothing better than to protect their interests under the pretence of looking after yours. Take up then your own heritage, push aside these wealthy hucksters of both factions who trade upon your labour, and trust for the future in your own strength alone.

Consider the figures below.

Total Production of the United Kingdom	£1,300,000,000
Taken by Landlords, Capitalists and Profitmongers	1,000,000,000
Left for the Producers	300,000,000

Study these figures all who toil and suffer that others may be lazy and rich; look upon the poverty, the starvation, the prostitution around you, ye who labour and return the value of your entire day's wages to your employers in the first two or three hours of your day's work. Ponder on these facts, reflect upon these figures, men and women of England, and then ask yourselves, whether it is worth while for such a result as this to bow down in slavish subjection before your 'governing classes,' whether you will not rather demand and obtain the full fruits of your labour and become your own governing class yourselves. Submit then no longer to a system of Parliamentary Government which is maintained in the interests of those who rob and oppress you – which has proved itself for generations to be alike a failure and a fraud.

Educate! Agitate! Organise!

Fellow Citizens, we of the *Democratic Federation* demand complete adult suffrage for every man and woman in these islands, because in this way alone can the whole people give free expression to their will; we are in favour of paid delegates and annual Conventions because by this means alone can the people control their representatives; we stand up for the direct reference of all grave issues to the country at large, and for the punishment as felony of every species of corruption, because thus only can tyranny be checked and bribery uprooted; we call for the abolition of all hereditary authority, because such authority is necessarily independent of the mass of the people. But all these reforms when secured mean only that the men and women of these islands will at length be masters in their own house. Mere political machinery is worthless unless used to produce good social conditions.

All wealth is due to labour; therefore to the labourers all wealth is due.

But we are strangers in our own country. Thirty thousand persons own the land of Great Britain against the 30,000,000 who are suffered to exist therein. A long series of robberies and confiscations has deprived us of the soil which should be ours. The organised brute force of the few has for generations robbed and tyrannised over the unorganised brute force of the many. We now call for Nationalisation of the Land. We claim that land in country and land in towns, mines, parks, mountains, moors should be owned by the people for the people, to be held, used, built over and cultivated upon such terms as the people themselves see fit to ordain. The handful of marauders who now hold possession have and can have no right save brute force against the tens of millions whom they wrong.

But private ownership of land in our present society is only one and not the worst form of monopoly which enables the wealthy classes to use the means of production against the labourers whom they enslave. Of the £1,000,000,000 taken by the classes who live without labour out of a total yearly production of £1,300,000,000, the landlords who have seized our soil, and shut us out from its enjoyment, absorb little more than £60,000,000 as their direct share. The few thousand persons who own the National Debt, saddled upon the community by a landlord Parliament, exact £28,000,000 yearly from the labour of their countrymen for nothing; the shareholders who have been allowed to lay hands upon our great railway communications take a still larger sum. Above all, the active capitalist class, the loan-mongers, the farmers, the mine-exploiters, the contractors, the middle-men, the factory-lords – these, the modern slave-drivers, these are they who, through their money, machinery, capital, and credit turn every advance in human knowledge, every further improvement in human dexterity, into an engine for accumulating wealth out of other men's labour, and for exacting more and yet more surplus value out of the wage-slaves whom they employ. So long as the means of production, either of raw materials or of manufactured goods are the monopoly of a class, so long must the labourers on the farm, in the mine or in the factory sell themselves for a bare subsistence wage. As land must in future be a national possession, so must the other means of producing and distributing wealth. The creation of wealth is already a social business, where each is forced to co-operate with his neighbour; it is high time that exchange of the produce should be social too, and removed from the control of individual greed and individual profit.

As stepping-stones to a happier period, we urge for immediate adoption: –

The *compulsory construction* of healthy artisans' and agricultural labourers' dwellings in proportion to the population, such dwellings to be let at rents to cover the cost of construction and maintenance alone.

Free compulsory education for all classes, together with the provision of at least one wholesome meal a day in each school.

Eight hours or less to be the normal *working day* in all trades.

Cumulative taxation upon all incomes above a fixed minimum not exceeding £300 a year.

State appropriation of railways, with or without compensation.

The establishment of *National banks*, which shall absorb all private institutions that derive a profit from operations in money or credit.

Rapid extinction of the *National Debt*.

Nationalisation of the land, and organisation of agricultural and industrial armies under State control on co-operative principles.

By these measures a healthy, independent, and thoroughly educated people will steadily grow up around us, ready to abandon that baneful competition for starvation wages which ruins our present workers, ready to organise the labour of each for the benefit of all, determined, too, to take control finally of the entire social and political machinery of a State in which class distinctions and class privileges shall cease to be.

Do any say we attack private property? We deny it. We attack only that private property for a few thousand loiterers and slave-drivers, which renders all property in the fruits of their own labour impossible for millions. We challenge that private property which renders poverty at once a necessity and a crime.

Fellow-Citizens, we appeal to every man and woman among you who is weary of this miserable huckster's society, where poverty and prostitution, fraud and adulteration, swindling and jobbery, luxury and debauchery reign supreme, we appeal to you to work with us in a never-ceasing effort to secure a happier lot for our people and their children, and to hold up a high ideal of national greatness for those who come after. Such an ideal of true greatness, and glory, needs but intelligence, enthusiasm, and combination, to make it a reality even in our own day. We, at least, will never falter. We stretch out our hands for help, co-operation, and encouragement, to all creeds and all nationalities, ready ourselves to render assistance in every struggle against class injustice and individual greed. The land of England is no mean heritage; there is enough and to spare for all; with the powers mankind now possess wealth may easily be made as plentiful as water at the expense of trifling toil. But today the worn-out wage-slaves of our boasted civilisation look hopelessly at the wealth which they have created to be devoured only by the rich and their hangers-on. To the abject poor patriotism is but a mockery, all talk of happiness, of beauty, of morality, is a sneer. We call, then, upon every lover of freedom to support us in our endeavour to form a real party of the people, which shall secure a noble future for our own and other lands.

The aims and objects of the *Democratic Federation* are before you. Success can only be achieved by organised effort.

Educate. We shall need all our intelligence.
Agitate. We shall need all our enthusiasm.
Organise. We shall need all our force.

Educate! Agitate! Organise!

The Executive Committee of the Democratic Federation: –

HERBERT BURROWS, Treasurer,
JOHN CLARK,
PATRICK HENNESSY,
J.L. JOYNES,
JAMES MACDONALD,
JAMES MURRAY,
ANDREAS SCHEU,

H.H. CHAMPION, Hon. Secretary,
A.J. DADSON,
H.M. HYNDMAN, Chairman,
TOM. S. LEMON,
WILLIAM MORRIS,
H.W. ROWLAND, Hon. Secretary,
HELEN TAYLOR,
JOHN WILLIAMS.

Membership of the Democratic Federation is open to all who agree with its objects and subscribe not less then One Shilling a year. Clubs and Associations are cordially invited to co-operate. Those ready to form Branches should communicate with the Hon. Secretaries.

Notes

1. The Reform Bill of 1832 was passed in spite of strong opposition from the Tories. It gave the vote to people with property qualifications and enfranchised the new industrial towns. The Rotten and Pocket Boroughs were abolished.
2. There had been laws restricting the trade in grain from very early times, at least as far back as 1360. The object was to prevent the price of grain rising too high. Supporters of the Corn Laws claimed that protecting grain brought poor land into use and therefore employed men; that it freed the country from foreign dependence; that it enabled the landed proprietors to patronise manufacturing industry. Cobden and Bright with the Anti-Corn Law League opposed the Laws and advocated free trade.

2

The Socialist Catechism

JAMES LEIGH JOYNES (1853 – 93)

Introduction

James Leigh Joynes was the son of a master at Eton College, and in turn was a pupil and master there himself. He was shy, retiring and silent by nature, and as a boy seldom took part in the games of his fellow students at Eton.

He left Eton for King's College, Cambridge in 1871, and gained a first class degree in the classical tripos. The college's petty restrictions and veneer of respectability irked him, however, and he developed a strong sense of the ridiculous. He soon turned towards free thought.

After Cambridge he became an assistant master at Eton and was an exemplary tutor. Yet he was always under suspicion, for being a radical and a free-thinker. He was a vegetarian, which in the climate of Eton at that time was regarded as dangerous and immoral, and he rode a tricycle, yet another eccentricity.

A crisis arose when Joynes accompanied Henry George, the author of *Progress and Poverty* on a tour of Ireland. The two of them became involved in a misunderstanding with the local police, and were arrested. They were rapidly discharged, but the story was eagerly seized upon by the press. Then when a forthcoming book was announced entitled *Adventures of a Tourist in Ireland* by Joynes, the headmaster at Eton gave him a choice: to stop the publication of the book or lose his job. Joynes abandoned his academic career.

The change gave Joynes a new lease of life. He became involved in the socialist cause through the Social Democratic Federation, throwing himself into committee work. He was soon working alongside activists such as William Morris and H.M. Hyndman. He founded the *Christian Socialist* and *Today*, of which he became co-editor. He contributed to *Justice*, *The Commonweal*, *Progress* and *Our Corner*. The pamphlet *The Socialist Catechism*, published in 1885, was one of the most successful pamphlets ever issued by the socialist press.

In addition to his support for socialist causes, Joynes contributed to organisations such as the vegetarian Wheatsheaf restaurant in Rathbone Place which he frequented in the company of George Bernard Shaw. He wrote for the *Food Reform Magazine*, and his literary output consisted of both poetry and prose. At one time he was contributing a poem a day for the *Pall Mall Gazette*. His other achievements included translating Marx's *Wage Labour and Capital* from the German, and setting

CAPITAL AND LABOUR.
Why don't they drop him?

a number of songs to music.

When William Morris and others left to form the Socialist League, Joynes refused to take sides and remained on good terms with all concerned.

In 1887 he enrolled as a medical student at the Middlesex Hospital, having long been interested in scientific and medical matters. The intense study that this involved may have been a crucial factor in the subsequent breakdown of his health. From 1889 to his death in 1893 he remained confined to his Sussex cottage. His last letter was to his friend William Morris, whose genius he admired greatly.

The Socialist Catechism demonstrates that Joynes's attempt at a popular exposition of socialism as advocated by Karl Marx was conceived in terms of the ideas of the Social Democratic Federation (SDF). Like H.M. Hyndman, the founder of the SDF, Joynes had failed to understand certain elements of Marx's ideas, and the result was a distorted, almost mechanistic version of the scientific socialism formulated by Marx and Engels.

For example, in describing the relation between labour and capital, Joynes wrote that wages for labourers tend to be at subsistence level. He called this the 'iron law of wages'. But in *Capital* Marx had shown that the laws governing wages are very complicated; that they could not be described as 'iron' nor incorporated into a rigid formula; rather that they were elastic.

Sources

Henry S. Salt, 'James Leigh Joynes, Some Reminiscences', *The Social Democrat*, no. 8, August 1897, p. 232.

H. M. Hyndman, Obituary of J. L. Joynes, *Justice*, 21 January 1893.

*   *   *

Division Of Toil

Q. Why is it necessary that any work should be done in the world?

A. Because men require food, clothing, and shelter: and these cannot be obtained without work.

Q. Is the work which must be done in order to produce these necessaries either very hard or very long? *A.* It is neither the one nor the other. After all the necessary work has been done, there is ample opportunity for the enjoyment of leisure and the production of beautiful things.

Q. Then why do immense numbers of men spend their whole lives in doing work which gives them no pleasure, while the enjoyment of leisure is an impossibility for them? *A.* Because there is another large class of men who keep all the available leisure and pleasure for themselves.

Q. How may these two sets of persons be roughly distinguished? *A.* As employers and employed; idlers and workers; privileged and plundered; or, more simply still, as rich and poor.

Q. Cannot the poor provide the rich with food, clothing, and shelter, and yet have enough time for leisure even after they have done this?

A. Certainly; but the rich are not content with exacting simple necessaries from the poor.

Q. What more do they compel them to contribute? *A.* Luxuries; and there is no end to the amount of labour which may be wasted in the painful production of useless things.

Q. Why do the poor consent to produce by their labour all these necessary and unnecessary things for persons who do nothing for them in return? *A.* Simply because they cannot help themselves.

Q. But how does it happen that they are in this helpless position? *A.* It is due to the fact that society is at present organised solely in the interests of the rich.

Q. Why cannot the poor organise society on a system which will prevent their being robbed of their own production? *A.* Because the existing organisation itself keeps them ignorant of its own causes, and consequently powerless to resist its effects.

Q. What is the first step towards a better state of things? *A.* The education of the poor to understand how it is that their own excessive work enables the rich to live in idleness upon its fruits.

Q. What is the most hopeful sign that they are ready for enlightenment on this point? *A.* Discontent with the disagreeable and degrading conditions of their own lives.

Q. What is the first principle to which they may appeal for relief from these conditions? *A.* The principles of justice, since it is manifestly unfair that those who do all the work should obtain the smallest share of the good things which it produces.

Q. What is the alternative to the present unequal distribution of work and good things? *A.* That all should be obliged to do their fair share of the work, and to content themselves with a fair share of the good things.

Q. Are those who insist upon the practical enforcement of this principle Conservatives or Radicals? *A.* They are neither, since they are necessarily opposed to all political parties.

Q. What then are they called? *A.* From the fact that they wish to displace the present system of competition for the bare means of subsistence, where each man is for himself, and to establish in its stead the principle of associated work and common enjoyment, where each is for all and all is for each, they are called Socialists.

The Capitalist System

Q. What is wealth? *A.* Everything that supplies the wants of man, and ministers in any way to his comfort and enjoyment.

Q. Whence is wealth derived? *A.* From labour usefully employed upon natural objects.

Q. Give instances of labour usefully employed? *A.* Ploughing, sowing, spinning, weaving, etc.

Q. Give instances of useless employment of labour? *A.* Digging a pit for the purpose of filling it up again, making a road that leads nowhere, supporting people in absolute idleness by presenting them with food and clothing for doing nothing, etc.

Q. What do we mean when we say that an article has value? *A.* That it is useful or agreeable to human beings.

Q. When is an article said to have an 'exchange value' in addition to its usefulness or 'use value'? *A.* When it embodies a certain amount of generally useful labour.

Q. Are the two sorts of value ever identical? *A.* They cannot be compared at all.

Q. Explain by an instance what you mean by this? *A.* The hunger of a starving man who enters a baker's shop does not affect the exchange-value of a loaf, which is measured by the amount of labour which has been expended in making and baking it.

Q. What is its use-value to him? *A.* Its use-value is infinitely great, as it is a question of life and death with him to obtain it.

Q. What is its use-value to another man? *A.* Its use-value is nothing at all to a turtle-fed alderman, sick already with excessive eating, but its exchange-value remains the same in all cases.

Q. Is there no exception to this rule? *A.* If the baker has a monopoly of baking, and no other loaves are anywhere obtainable, he can charge a much higher price than the amount of his expended labour entitles him to demand.

Q. Is this often done? *A.* Every monopolist does it, as a matter of course.

Q. Who are the chief monopolists? *A.* There are two great classes. The landlords monopolise the land, and the capitalists the machinery.

Q. What is capital? *A.* Capital is the result of past labour devoted to present production – machinery and factories for example.

Q. How does the landlord secure his profit? *A.* By extorting from the labourer a share of all that he produces, under threat of excluding him from the land.

Q. How does the capitalist act? *A.* He extorts from those labourers who are excluded from the land a share of all that they produce, under threat of withholding from them the implements of production, and thus refusing to let them work at all.

Q. On what terms does the capitalist allow the labourers to work? *A.* The capitalist agrees to return to them as wages about a quarter of what they have produced by their work keeping the remaining three quarters for himself and his class.

Q. What is this system called? *A.* The capitalist system.

Q. What is it that regulates the amount returned to the labourer? *A.* The amount that is necessary to keep him and his family alive.

Q. Why does the capitalist care to keep him alive? *A.* Because capital without labour is helpless.

Q. How is this amount settled? *A.* By competition among the labourers and the higgling of the labour market.

Q. Is it invariable? *A.* It varies with all the variations of trade and locality, and the different degrees of skill of the different labourers, but it constantly tends to a bare subsistence for the mass of the labourers.

Q. By what name is this law known? *A.* The iron law of wages.

Q. How can it be proved? *A.* By reckoning up the amount of food and clothing consumed by those who produce them.

Q. Is there any independent testimony to its truth? *A.* The witness of all doctors who have studied the subject.

Q. What evidence do they give upon it? *A.* They declare that diseases arising from insufficient nourishment are constantly present throughout the labouring classes, and that 'the poor are permanently afflicted with one disease – starvation.'

Q. What remedy for this do Socialists propose? *A.* Simply that the labouring classes should become their own employers.

Q. What effect would this have? *A.* The classes who live in idleness on the fruits of the labour of other people would be improved off the face of the earth, every one being obliged to take his share of honest work.

Q. On what compulsion? *A.* The alternative of starvation would stare them in the face, as soon as the labourers ceased to supply them gratis with food, clothing, shelter, and luxuries.

Q. Are not the 'upper classes' useful as organisers of labour? *A.* Those who organise labour are always worthy of their hire, though the hire may be fixed too high at present; but it is only the absolutely idle, and those whose work, however hard it may be, consists in perfecting and organising the arrangements for plundering the labourers of their reward, who are simply the enemies of the workers.

Q. Are shareholders in companies, for instance, useful in organising labour? *A.* As a rule they employ others to organise labour, and the work done by the company would go on just as well if the shareholders disappeared.

Surplus Value

Q. In whose interest is present production carried on? *A.* In that of the employing classes.

Q. Explain this. *A.* The labourers produce the machinery, which the employers take away from them as soon as it is made. The labourers are then employed to work it, in order to produce profit for their masters at a faster rate.

Q. What interest have the labourers in the continuance of capitalism, that is, the capitalist system? *A.* Manifestly none.

Q. Is capital, therefore, useless? *A.* Certainly not. The way in which it is used is attacked by Socialists, not the thing itself.

Q. How is it possible that it should be used in the labourer's interest? *A.* Only by means of a democratic State, acting in the interest of the producers.

Q. In what way would the State effect this? *A.* By taking into its own hands all the land and capital, or 'means of production,' which are now used as monopolies for the benefit of the possessing class.

Q. Is there any precedent for this? *A.* As the State has already taken over the Post Office and the Telegraphs, so it might take over the Railways, Shipping, Mines, Factories, and all other industries.

Q. Is the Post Office worked on Socialist principles? *A.* Certainly not. There is no pretence that the interests of its labourers, the postmen, are considered at all.

Q. What principle regulates their employment? *A.* That which regulates the employment of all other labourers, competition, reducing their wages to the lowest possible point, except in the case of the higher officials, who are paid much more than would willingly be accepted by equally capable men.

Q. Cannot the workers combine together by co-operation to defeat this principle of competition? *A.* Co-operative societies cannot defeat this principle, unless the whole body of workers are included in one society, and that is simply Socialism.

Q. Why cannot different societies defeat competition? *A.* Because they are compelled to compete against each other, to exploit those labourers who are not members of their body, and to be exploited by others in their turn.

Q. What do you mean by the word 'exploit'? *A.* To exploit is to get more than one gives in a bargain.

Q. To what extent is the exploitation of the labourers commonly carried? *A.* The employers give them a bare subsistence, and take from them all the rest of the fruits of their labour.

Q. What is the difference between the two called? *A.* Surplus-value.

Q. What proportion expresses its amount? *A.* The proportion between the two or three hours of necessary labour, and the ordinary ten, twelve, or more hours' work.

Q. What do you mean by necessary labour? *A.* That which would feed and clothe and keep in comfort the nation if all took their part in performing it.

Q. Is any individual employer responsible for the exploitation of the labourers? *A.* No, the blame applies to the whole class. Individual employers may be ruined, but the employing class continue to appropriate the surplus-value.

Q. How do you account for this? *A.* Because competition is as keen among the capitalists as among the labourers.

Q. How does it act with them? *A.* It determines the division of the spoil, different sets of people struggling to get a share in the surplus-value.

Q. How does this competition above affect the labourers below? *A.* It does not affect them at all. It is assumed that the plunder is to be shared among the 'upper classes,' and the only question is in what proportion this shall be done.

Q. How do the upper classes label this plunder? *A.* By many names, such as rent, brokerage, fees, profits, wages of superintendence, reward of abstinence, insurance against risk, but above all, interest on capital.

Q. Are all these deducted from the labourers' earnings? *A.* There is no other fund from which they could possibly come.

Q. Is surplus-value paid for at all? *A.* By no means. It is the produce of unpaid labour, and is simply taken for nothing, just as a thief accumulates his stolen goods.

Q. Does not the progress of civilisation decrease the amount of the surplus-value? *A.* On the contrary it largely increases it.

Q. How is this? *A.* Improvements in agriculture, method, and machinery, which civilisation renders possible, multiply manifold the productiveness of the labourer's toil; but competition among the labourers prevents them from reaping the benefit.

Q. Does not competion among capitalists in the same way lower the rate of interest? *A.* Certainly it does, but the rate of interest has nothing whatever to do with the rate of exploitation or of surplus-value.

Q. What is interest? *A.* Interest is a fine, paid by the private organiser of labour out of the surplus-value which his labourers supply, to the idle person from whom he borrows his capital.

Q. What is the tendency of the two rates of interest and surplus-value? *A.* The rate of interest falls, while the rate of surplus-value rises.

Q. Why is this? *A.* Because with the storing up of the increased surplus-value by the capitalists, or in other words, with the accumulation of capital, the competition among capitalists who are anxious to lend on interest becomes keener, and each individual is obliged to be content with less.

Q. Does not this lessening of the rate of interest benefit the labourer? *A.* No; since it is only due to the multiplication of those who share in his surplus-value, the result being the same as it would be if he were allowed to pay a penny to six people instead of sixpence to one.

Q. How do the capitalists adjust their own conflicting claims? *A.* It is a question of division of spoil among plunderers. If the surplus-value is high, there is more to divide among the capitalists, but if the capitalists are numerous there is so much less for each individual among them.

Q. Explain this by an example. *A.* Take the case of Belgium. The labourers are there exploited to the uttermost, there being no 'factory laws' to restrain the greed of the employer, but since capital is plentiful the surplus-value is shared among many capitalists, and the rate of interest is low.

Methods of Extortion

Q. What did you mean by saying that capital without labour is helpless? *A.* The most ingenious machinery can do nothing but rust or rot unless it is kept going by labourers.

Q. Why do not the labourers decline to work the machinery for the capitalist? *A.* Because they have no other means of making their livelihood.

Q. How could this be remedied? *A.* The State could compete with the capitalist by providing employment for the labourers, and paying them the full value of their productions.

Q. What would be the effect of this upon the private capitalist? *A.* His power would be gone at once, since no labourers would work for him, except on such terms as would leave him no surplus-value whatever.

Q. Is not the existence of capital in private hands an evil? *A.* Yes, certainly; but capital, as such, would cease to exist.

Q. Is not wealth in private hands an evil? *A.* Large accumulations of wealth by individuals are an evil, but the evil is different in kind, for they could no longer be used to carry out the capitalist system.

Q. Why not? *A.* Because the capitalist system presupposed the existence to two factors, and is unworkable and impossible without them.

Q. What are these two factors? *A.* First, private property in accumulated wealth; and, secondly, the presence of property-less labourers in the market who are forced to sell their services at cost price.

Q. What do you mean by cost price? *A.* The wages which will give them a bare subsistence and enable them to work on the morrow, this being the cost of the daily reproduction of the force or power to labour which constitutes their sole property.

Q. Could not the capitalists obtain labourers by offering them the full value of their productions? *A.* Possibly, but since the only object of the capitalist system is to produce for profit, they would cease to wish to employ them when the source of interest and profit was cut off.

Q. But supposing, in spite of their previous principles, they still wished to employ them, what would be the result? *A.* The labourers would have nothing to complain of in this case; but the result would be that private capital would gradually dwindle away since it would not be replaced by surplus-value, and the capitalist could not compete with the State on equal terms.

Q. What has hitherto prevented the workers from combining for the overthrow of the capitalist system? *A.* Ignorance and disorganisation.

Q. What has left them in ignorance? *A.* The system itself, by compelling them to spend all their lives upon monotonous toil, and leaving them no time for education.

Q. What account have they been given of the system which oppresses them? *A.* The priest has explained that the perpetual presence of the poor is necessitated by a law of God; the economist has proved its necessity by a law of Nature; and between them they have succeeded in convincing the labourers of the hopelessness of any opposition to the capitalist system.

Q. How is it that the labourers cannot see for themselves that they are legally robbed? *A.* Because the present method of extracting their surplus value is one of fraud rather than of force, and has grown up gradually.

Q. Has this not always been the case? *A.* Certainly not. Under the slave-owning system there was no fraud involved, but only force.

Q. What similarity is there between the slave-owning and the capitalist system? *A.* The parallel is complete, with the single exception that force was used in place of fraud.

Q. Explain this. *A.* The slave-owner received the produce of the slave's toil, and returned to him part of it in the shape of food, clothing, and shelter. The capitalist takes the whole produce of the labourer's toil, and returns to him such proportion of it as will provide him with necessaries.

Q. What constitutes the chief difference between capitalism and slave-owning? *A.* The fact that the capitalist goes through the form of bargaining with the labourer as to the amount of the portion of the produce that shall be returned to him.

Q. What is this farce called? *A.* Freedom of contract.

Q. In what sense is it free? *A.* In this sense – that the labourer is free to take what is offered or nothing.

Q. Has he anything to fall back upon? *A.* He has absolutely nothing in countries where the tyranny of capitalism is untempered by any form of Socialism.

Q. What is the case in England? *A.* Humanity has revolted against the reign of the capitalist, and provided the workhouse as a last resource for the labourer, taxing the capitalist for its support.

Q. How has the capitalist turned this piece of Socialism to his own ends? *A.* By rendering the workhouse so unpleasant to the poor that starvation is often thought preferable; and by insisting that no useful work done in the workhouse shall be brought into his market, where its presence would disturb his calculations, and impair his profits.

Q. Why does he allow it to exist at all? *A*. Because he knows that its existence may stave off for a time the Revolution which he dreads.

Q. What do you mean by the Revolution? *A*. The complete change in the conditions of society which will abolish all unjust privileges, distinctions of rank, or difference between wage-payers and wage-earners, and will render the workers their own employers.

Q. What other method of appropriating surplus-value has prevailed besides those of slavery and capitalism? *A*. In purely agricultural countries, as for instance in Ireland and South-Eastern Europe, different types of landlordism have been quite as effectual.

Q. Does landlordism represent the forcible or the fraudulent method? *A*. Force is its chief element, since it labels the surplus-value 'rents,' and uses all the resources of civilisation in the shape of police and soldiery to enforce their payment by the people, but the element of fraud is present, since the labourer is told that he is free to give up his holding if he does not wish to pay rent.

Q. Mention a special type of landlordism? *A*. The system called *corvée*.

Q. How does this work? *A*. The labourer is allowed to work on his own land for a certain number of days, and to keep for himself all the produce of his toil during that time, on the condition that he spends all his remaining time upon the land which belongs to the landlord, who appropriates its fruits.

Q. How does this differ from the capitalist method of appropriation? *A*. Chiefly in the fact that the labourer knows exactly when he is working for his own benefit, and when for that of the landlord; while under the capitalist system there is no line of distinction and neither he nor anyone else can tell precisely the exact length of time during which he gives away his labour gratis, although it is clear that his first two or three hours are for himself and the remaining seven or eight for some one else.

Q. Can you show this to be the case? *A*. As the producers only get from one-fourth to one-third of the total produce, the remainder of their work obviously goes to benefit the non-producers.

Machines and their Use

Q. What is the use of machinery? *A*. Labour-saving machinery is used, as its name indicates, to reduce the cost of production.

Q. What do you mean by the cost of production? *A*. The amount of human labour necessary to produce useful things.

Q. How ought this reduction of the necessary hours of labour to affect the labouring class? A. It ought to benefit them in every way, by increasing their wealth as well as their opportunities of leisure.

Q. Has it done so? A. Certainly not.

Q. Why not? A. Because the capitalist class has appropriated to itself nearly all the benefit.

Q. What, then, has been the result? A. The available surplus-value has largely increased, and the idle classes have become more numerous and more idle.

Q. Support your opinion by that of an economist? A. 'It is questionable,' says John Stuart Mill,[1] 'if all the improvements in machinery have lightened the day's toil of a single man.'

Q. In what aspect of the case is this correct? A. In respect of the whole labouring class as a body.

Q. What is the effect upon individuals of the introduction of a labour-saving machine? A. It lightens the day's toil to a certain number of labourers most effectually, by taking away their employment altogether, and throwing them helpless on the streets.

Q. Is such a lamentable event frequent? A. It is a matter of every-day occurrence.

Q. What is the result to their employer? A. He 'saves their labour' in the sense of getting the same work done by the machine without having to pay their wages.

Q. Is this a permanent advantage to him individually? A. As long as he has a monopoly of the machine, it is a great advantage to him, but other capitalists soon introduce it also, and compel him to share the spoil with them.

Q. In what way is this result obtained? A. By competition. The owners of the machines try to undersell each other with a view to keeping the production in their own hands.

Q. How far does competition beat down prices? A. Until the normal level of capitalist profits is reached, below which they all decline to go.

Q. What inference do the economists draw from the result of competition? A. That the whole nation shares equally in the advantage of the machine, since prices are everywhere reduced.

Q. What fallacy underlies this argument? A. The same fallacy which vitiates every argument of the economists, and that is the assumption that the labourers have no right to complain so long as the employers are content with taking only the normal rate of profits as their share of the surplus-value.

Q. What other consideration is omitted by the economists? A. The fact that society is divided into two classes of idlers and workers. They assume again that the workers have no right to complain, so long as they seem to obtain an equal share with the idlers in the advantage gained by the saving of their own toil.

Q. How do they seem to share this advantage? *A.* By the reduction in cost of articles which they buy.

Q. Is not cheapness of production a benefit to the workers? *A.* It is only an apparent, not a real benefit.

Q. How could it be rendered real? *A.* It would be real if all who consumed were also workers. As it is, the working-class get all the disadvantage of the low wages, and of the adulteration, which has been described as a form of competition.

Q. What makes the reduction of cost appear advantageous to the wage-earners? *A.* The fact that their wages are paid in money.

Q. How is this? *A.* The money-price of all articles has risen enormously during the last three centuries owing to the increased abundance of gold. The money wages have risen also, but not in anything like the same proportion.

Q. What has prevented them from rising in the same proportion? *A.* The cheapening of the labour-cost of the necessaries of life, which has thus been rendered an empty boon to the wage-earners.

Q. Give an instance of the misapprehension of these facts. *A.* The regular boast of the Free-Traders, recently reiterated by John Bright,[2] is that the Liberals have given the labourers two loaves whereas the Tories wished them to be content with only one.

Q. What is this boast based upon? *A.* The undeniable fact that bread is cheaper in England under Free Trade than under Protection.

Q. Then how can you tell that the labourer does not get twice as much bread as he would otherwise enjoy? *A.* Simply because it has been proved again and again on the highest authority that the labourers as a body at present obtain so bare a subsistence that it does not suffice to keep them in health; therefore they could not at any time have lived on half the amount.

Q. What would be the effect if bread became twice as dear? *A.* Wages would necessarily rise. A Wiltshire farm labourer could not maintain his family on half their present food; and though capital cares nothing about individuals, it takes good care that the labourers shall not starve in a body.

Q. What, then, is the general result of the cheapness which is caused by the introduction of labour-saving machinery? *A.* The advantage of the cheapening of luxuries is obviously reaped directly by the idlers, since the workers cannot afford to purchase them. In the case of necessaries the advantage seems at first sight to be shared between idlers and workers; but ultimately the idlers secure the whole advantage, because money-wages are proportioned to what money will buy, and the iron law keeps them down to the price of a bare subsistence.

Q. Do the labourers suffer any direct disadvantage from machinery?

A. Certainly they do. Numbers of them are thrown out of employment at each fresh invention; their position is rendered precarious in the extreme; and there is a constant tendency to replace skilled labour by unskilled, and men by women.

Q. If this is so, would not the workers be wise to destroy the machinery? *A.* To destroy what they have themselves produced, merely because it is at present stolen from them, would be absurd.

Q. What course should they pursue? *A.* Organise their ranks; demand restitution of their property; keep it under their control; and work it for their own benefit.

Distribution of Wealth

Q. Is it the case that the prices of articles would be raised if the community were organised on Socialist principles? *A.* Not necessarily, nor in most cases; but in some this would certainly be the result.

Q. On what principle? *A.* The principle governing the price of all ordinary things would be that the worker should receive the full value of his labour.

Q. Would not this always raise the price of his production? *A.* No, it would only ensure its being paid to him instead of to an idler.

Q. Explain this? *A.* In many cases the full labour-value of an article is paid by the consumer, although the producer gets only his bare subsistence, all the surplus-value being intercepted by the numerous unnecessary middlemen.

Q. Why is this not always the case? *A.* Because the employer of labour, instead of always dividing the surplus-value among middlemen, often competes with his neighbours by offering a share of it to the consumer.

Q. How can he do this? *A.* Simply by selling his goods below their full labour-value.

Q. Give an instance of this? *A.* A notorious example of this occurs in the match-box trade, for although several middlemen secure their share of the surplus-value of the match-box makers, they are still sold to the public at a lower price than their full labour-value, the buyer thus becoming a partner in the employer's theft by receiving a share of his stolen goods.

Q. Who are the middlemen who intercept and share the surplus-value produced by the labourer? *A.* The unnecessary agents and distributors, the holders of stocks, bonds, and shares of every description, and all those who are supported by the wealth-producers either in idleness or in useless labour, of which latter class of persons flunkeys are a conspicuous example.

Q. Do not the rich support their own flunkeys, and maintain in comfort those who produce luxuries for them? *A.* Certainly not. These people are maintained entirely by the workers, though the maintenance is passed through the hands of the rich, who therefore imagine that they produce it.

Q. Is not expenditure for luxuries 'good for trade,' and so beneficial to the workers? *A.* It is only good for the trade of the producers of luxuries by exactly the amount which it withdraws from the producers of useful things.

Q. Would not the money employed upon luxuries otherwise be idle? *A.* By no means. The rich are not in the habit of keeping their riches in a stocking, and the bankers are compelled to keep all the money lent them in full use, or they would themselves be ruined.

Q. What then is the result of spending money upon luxuries? *A.* The destruction of a certain amount of wealth and the absolute waste of the labour spent in reproducing it.

Q. Does not the expenditure of a wealthy man in keeping up a large household benefit the poor? *A.* Decidedly not.

Q. What then is the result of spending money in maintaining flunkeys? *A.* The utter waste of all the food and clothing they consume.

Q. Would not they in any case consume food and clothing? *A.* Certainly: but they would repay the waste by producing useful things themselves.

Q. How does all this work affect the labourers? *A.* It compels them to produce more food and clothing than would otherwise be necessary, or else to consume less of it themselves.

Q. How is this? *A.* Because the food which the flunkeys eat cannot be also eaten by the labourers; while the labourers are obliged to produce it, since somebody must do this, and it is perfectly evident that the flunkeys do not.

Q. Does not this apply to all the idle classes? *A.* Certainly. We have only to ask where the food which they eat and the clothes which they wear, come from, and we see that they are produced by somebody else without any return being made for them by the idlers. That is to say, they represent unpaid labour, or in other words surplus-value.

Q. Then if one man is living in idleness, what is the inevitable result? *A.* That another man is producing what he consumes; or that several are each doing more than their fair share of work to make up for his deficiency.

Q. How would Socialism deal with this question of work? *A.* It would compel every one to do his share of the necessary work of the world.

Q. Under what penalty? *A.* Under penalty of starvation, since those who refused to work would get nothing to eat.

Q. What would happen to the old and infirm and the children? *A.* They would be as they are in any society, a perfectly just charge upon the able-bodied workers, increasing the necessary work of the world by the amount which must be devoted to their maintenance and education.

Q. Would the workers then receive the full value of their toil?

A. Deductions from it for such purposes as those just mentioned are, of course, inevitable, and must be made under every form of society, as well as certain other deductions for other measures of public utility.

Q. What deductions can be prevented by Socialism? *A.* Nothing could be subtracted from the labourers' reward for the purpose of maintaining in idleness any persons whatever who are capable of work, nor for the aggrandisement of private individuals, or for the furthering of objects of no public utility merely to satisfy individual caprice.

Theories of Profit

Q. What is the use of money? *A.* It facilitates the exchange of articles, especially those of unequal value.

Q. How is this effected? *A.* If A produces wheat, and B cloth, money serves as a convenient measure of the labour-value of each. A exchanges his wheat for money, and buys cloth with that. B exchanges his cloth for money and buys wheat with that.

Q. Are they both enriched by the bargain? *A.* Not in the matter of exchange-value, since wheat which has cost a day's labour exchanges for cloth which has cost the same, but in the matter of use-value they are both enriched, since each gets what he wants, and gives what he does not want.

Q. Is this always the case? *A.* Always, in the ordinary exchange between producers who are working for their own benefit, and exchange goods for money, and that money for other goods.

Q. Can a profit be made out of money transactions altogether apart from the exchange of goods? *A.* Yes, by gambling either on the race-course or on the stock-exchange, but in this case one gambler's gain is another's loss.

Q. What other form of exchange now prevails? *A.* That of those who, not being workers, produce no goods, but yet have command of money.

Q. How do they use it? *A.* They exchange their money for goods, and those goods back again into money.

Q. Then what is the use of the process if they only get money at the end, when they had money at the beginning? *A.* Because at the second exchange they get more money than they gave at the first.

Q. How has this fact been explained by economists? *A.* By the mere statement that the money-monger either gave less money than the goods were worth at the first exchange, or got more than they were worth at the second.

Q. What consideration did they omit in this theory? *A.* The fact that these same money-mongers are in the market both as buyers and sellers, and that without a miracle they cannot all gain on both transactions, but must lose in selling precisely the amount they gain in buying.

Q. What other inadequate explanation has been put forward? *A.* The theory that in buying machinery they buy something which has the power of adding an extra exchange-value to the goods upon which it is employed.

Q. What made this theory seem plausible? *A.* The fact that with a machine the labourer can produce goods much faster than without it.

Q. Does not this add exchange-value to his productions? *A.* Not unless he has a monopoly of the machine, and can thus fear no competition except that of hand-labour; otherwise the exchange-value of his goods sinks in proportion to the increased rapidity of their production.

Q. Explain this. *A.* If he can make two yards of cloth in the time which he formerly devoted to one, and all other weavers can do the same, the price or exchange-value of two yards sinks to the former price of one; though, of course, the use-value of two is always greater than that of one.

Q. Are not monopolies frequent? *A.* No individual capitalist can keep a monopoly for any great length of time, as all inventions become common property at last, and, although it is true that the capitalists as a body have a monopoly of machinery as against the workers, which adds a fictitious value to machine-made goods, and will continue to do so until the workers take control of the machinery, yet this extra value is too small to account for a tithe of the profits of the money-mongers.

Q. What is the one thing needful, which they must be able to buy in the market, in order to make these profits? *A.* Something which shall itself have the power of creating exchange-value largely in excess of its own cost, in order that at the end of the transaction they may have secured more money than they have expended.

Q. What is to be bought in the market having this power? *A.* There is only one thing with this power, and that is the labourer himself, who offers his labour-force on the market.

Q. On what terms does he offer it? *A.* Competition compels him to be content with its cost price.

Q. What is this? *A.* Subsistence wages, that is, enough to keep himself and his family from starvation.

Q. What does this represent in labour? *A.* The value produced by his labour expended usefully for two or three hours every day.

Q. Is he, then, at leisure after two or three hours' work? *A.* By no means. The bargain between him and the capitalist requires him to give ten hours or more of work for the cost price of two or three.

Q. Why does he make such an unequal bargain? *A.* Because, in spite of all so-called freedom of contract, he has no other choice.

Q. Has the capitalist no conscience? *A.* Individuals cannot alter the system, even if they would; and the capitalist is now often represented by a company, which, if it had a conscience, could not pay its five per cent.

Q. After the labourer has produced the price of his own wages, what does he go on to do? *A.* To produce exchange-value, for which he is not paid at all, for the benefit of the capitalist.

Q. What is the value produced by this unpaid labour called? *A.* Surplus value, as we said before.

Q. What does the capitalist do with the surplus value? *A.* He keeps as much as he can for himself under the name of profits of his business.

Q. Why does he not keep it all? *A.* Because out of it he has to pay landlords, other capitalists from whom he has borrowed capital, bankers and brokers who have effected these loans for him, middlemen who sell his wares to the public, and finally the public, in order to induce them to buy from him instead of from rival manufacturers.

Q. How does he justify this appropriation of surplus-value by his class? *A.* He tries to persuade himself that capital has the power of breeding and producing interest by as natural a process as the reproduction of animals.

Q. Can he find any dupes to believe in so absurd a theory? *A.* He instils a genuine belief into himself and others that this is really the case.

Q. What is the inference from this? *A.* That the labourer ought to be grateful to the capitalist for furnishing him with employment.

Q. For what have the labourers really to thank the capitalist? *A.* For defrauding them of three-quarters of the fruits of their toil, and rendering leisure, education, and natural enjoyment almost impossible for them to attain.

Inadequate Objections

Q. What kind of objectors do Socialists mostly meet with? *A.* Those who from interested motives prefer the present anarchy to the proposed organisation of labour, and those who consider Socialists as a set of well-meaning persons busied about an impracticable scheme.

Q. What objection do they chiefly urge against Socialism? *A.* That Socialists, if poor, are interested schemers for the overthrow of an excellent society, in order that, being themselves idle and destitute, they may be able to seize upon the wealth accumulated by more industrious people.

Q. What have they to say against Socialists of wealth and industry? *A.* That they must obviously be insincere in their Socialism, or they would at once give away all their capital, instead of denouncing what they themselves possess.

Q. How should Socialist working men meet the charge? *A.* With contempt. The idea that people who are treated with injustice have no right to demand justice because they would be gainers by its enforcement, is too absurd to require refutation.

Q. How should wealthy Socialists reply? *A.* They should point out that, so long as the capitalist system remains, it is impossible to evade the responsibility of wealth by merely transferring it to other persons.

Q. Explain this by an instance? *A.* In a capitalist society the mere purchasing of an article in the market involves the exploitation of the labourers who produced it; and this is not in any way remedied or atoned for by giving away the article afterwards to somebody else.

Q. How does this illustrate the case? *A.* The owner of capital cannot prevent it from exploiting the labourers by giving it away. It cannot be used as Socialism enjoins except under an organised system of Socialism.

Q. Can the wealthy Socialist do nothing to frustrate the capitalist system? *A.* He can mitigate the severity of competition in all his personal relations. Beyond that he can do nothing except use his wealth in helping on the Socialist cause.

Q. How may Socialists reply to the taunt that their scheme is impracticable? *A.* By quoting the opinion of J.S. Mill that the difficulties of Socialism are greatly over-rated; and they should declare that, so far from being an impracticable Utopian scheme, it is the necessary and inevitable result of the historical evolution of society.

Q. How can they prove this? *A.* They can point to the fact that production is becoming more and more socialised every day.

Q. Explain this? *A.* Production, which was once carried on by individuals working separately for themselves is now organised by companies and joint-stock concerns, by massing large numbers of producers together and uniting their efforts for a common end.

Q. For what end? *A.* For the profits of the shareholders of the company.

Q. How could the State take advantage of this? *A.* By taking into its own hands the organisation which the capitalists have prepared for it, and using it for the benefit of the producers alone.

Q. Would not the capitalists start fresh companies in opposition to those managed by the State? *A.* They could no more compete with the State than they can now with the Post Office; and they would be equally helpless in the case of the Railways and all the great industries.

Q. Would it not be easier for the capitalists to compete with the State in the case of smaller concerns? *A.* It would in any case be impossible for them to get labourers, since the State would be paying the labourers the full value of their labour, and they would therefore decline to work for the capitalists.

Q. Would the expropriated capitalists be entitled to compensation? *A.* As a matter of principle it is unjust to compensate the holders of stolen goods out of the pockets of those who have suffered the theft; but it might be expedient to grant some compensation in the shape of annuities.

Q. What is the tendency of the evolution of society? *A.* It tends always towards more complex organisation, and to a greater interdependence of all men upon each other: each individual becoming more and more helpless by himself, but more and more powerful as part of a mightier society.

Q. Is it true that individuality would be crushed by Socialism? *A*. On the contrary, it is crushed by the present state of society, and would then alone be fairly developed.

Q. What does J. S. Mill say on this point? *A*. 'The restraints of Communism would be freedom in comparison with the present condition of the majority of the human race. The generality of labourers in this and most other countries have as little choice of occupation or freedom of locomotion, are practically as dependent on fixed rules and on the will of others, as they could be in any system short of actual slavery.'

Q. What does Mr. Fawcett[3] say on the same subject? *A*. That there is no choice of work or possibility of change for the factory hand; and that the boy who is brought up to the plough must remain at the plough-tail to the end of his days.

Q. What other objection has been urged against Socialism? *A*. That it will take away all the incentives to exertion, and induce universal idleness in consequence.

Q. Is this the case? *A*. On the contrary, it will apply the strongest incentive to all alike for all must work if they wish to eat, while at present large classes are exempted by the accident of birth from the necessity of working at all.

Q. Name another common objection. *A*. That Socialism will destroy culture and refinement by compelling the leisured classes who have a monopoly of them to do some honest work.

Q. Is this the case? *A*. On the contrary, it will bring the opportunity of culture and refinement to all by putting an end to the wearisome labour that continues all day long; while the leisured class will learn by experience that work is a necessity for perfect culture.

Q. What other objection is often urged? *A*. That State management would give rise to jobbery and corruption.

Q. How may this be answered? *A*. By pointing to the present State organisation either of the police or the Post Office, in neither of which are jobbery and corruption conspicuous features.

Q. Would not the State be in a different position as regards the people? *A*. At present it is the people's master, but under any democratic scheme of Socialism it would become their servant, and merely be charged with carrying out their will.

Q. Name another objection to the practicability of Socialism? *A*. The cuckoo cry that 'if you make all men equal to-day, they will all be unequal to-morrow, because of their different natural capabilities.'

Q. What equality do Socialists aim at? *A*. Equality of opportunities, not of natural powers.

Q. What is the Socialist view of the duties of those who are especially gifted by nature? *A*. That they owe a larger return to the community than those who are less naturally gifted.

Q. What is the capitalist view of their rights and duties? *A.* That they are independent of all duties, and have the right of taxing the community, which supports them, for luxuries and waste to the full extent of their individual caprice.

Q. In accordance with this view, what method do capitalists take in dealing with them? *A.* Capitalists arrange that persons of extra industry and talent shall have every opportunity of enslaving their less fortunate neighbours, thus adding an inequality of conditions to the natural inequality of talent.

Q. What is the Socialist method? *A.* Socialists insist that the talented as well as the cunning shall be restrained by the organisation of society from appropriating the surplus-value created by their less fortunate neighbours.

Gluts and their Results

Q. To what is the periodical depression of trade, with its accompanying distress among the labourers, due? *A.* To the fact that individual capitalists are striving to enrich themselves alone, instead of co-operating to supply the needs of the community.

Q. Explain this? *A.* During a period of activity, when prices are high and the markets for goods are not over-stocked, a great competition goes on among capitalists, who wish to take advantage of the high prices and produce more quickly the goods which can command them.

Q. What is the effect of this competition? *A.* All the available labourers are employed; all the machinery is set going; and no effort is spared by the manufacturers to produce the utmost quantity of the goods which are in demand on the market.

Q. What is the inevitable result? *A.* A glut is shortly created of these goods. Far more than were wanted have been made. All the store-houses are full, and no more purchasers are to be found.

Q. What is the next step in the process? *A.* The capitalists soon get tired of heaping up what they cannot sell, and wish to stop production.

Q. How can they manage this? *A.* They turn off all their extra hands, and propose such a reduction of wages that the rest agree to strike rather than accept it.

Q. With what result? *A.* Production is stopped for a time, and the capitalists are not obliged to pay wages, or else agree to pay only for half time until the glut has gradually disappeared, as the goods are absorbed by the public.

Q. What follows? *A.* A fresh demand arises. The workers are all employed again, and the glut recurs with the utmost regularity.

Q. Is there any necessity for this periodical distress? *A.* Not the smallest.

Q. What is it that vitiates the whole system of production at present? *A.* The prevailing idea that goods are not to be produced for the sake of their usefulness, but for the sake of making a profit for capitalists and giving employment to labourers.

Q. What definite evil is the result of this idea? *A.* Adulteration and fraud of every description; cheap and nasty wares driving expensive and sound goods out of the market.

Q. Who are the greatest sufferers from all this? *A.* The workers themselves.

Q. In what way? *A.* Being the least able to protect themselves against adulteration and fraud, they are cheated to a fearful extent in all that they buy; and are the first to suffer from a glut in the market.

Q. How is this? *A.* Because they are first compelled to produce more food and clothing than can possibly be sold at a profit, and then are deprived of the means of buying what they have themselves produced, although they are in urgent need both of food and clothing, because the capitalists throw them out of work as soon as their work ceases to pay its percentage.

Q. What advice is given to the labourer by well-meaning reformers who do not understand the labour question? *A.* To be sober and thrifty.

Q. Is this advice sound? *A.* As addressed to the individual struggling against his neighbours under the capitalist system, it is excellent.

Q. How can it benefit the individual? *A.* It may enable him to 'rise' into the capitalist class; that is, to exchange his position in the ranks of the oppressed for one in those of the oppressors.

Q. What is the Socialist criticism of this advice? *A.* That as a panacea for the wrongs of the system, or as a cure for the sufferings of the labourers *as a class,* it is inadequate, because a general improvement in intelligence, thrift, and sobriety, if shared by the whole class of labourers, merely supplies the capitalist class with a better instrument for the production of surplus-value.

Q. What is the result of improvement in the ability of the workers in the present system? *A.* The same result as an improvement in machinery, namely, that goods are more rapidly produced by the workers, and accumulated by the capitalists; so that the periodical glut, with its accompanying crisis, depression, and distress, is more quickly achieved than before.

Q. Is there any possibility of an incidental advantage to the labourers? *A.* Only in this respect: the labourer is a two-edged tool in the hands of the capitalist; and when it becomes sharper and more efficient for his work, it becomes also more likely to cut the hand that uses it.

Q. Explain what you mean by this? *A.* A general improvement among the labourers in intelligence and sobriety will probably be followed by improved organisation, with a view to expropriating the classes that confiscate the fruits of their labour.

Q. Is this the end at which so-called 'social reformers' aim? A. By no means; but they seem incapable of understanding either the inefficacy in one way, or the efficacy in another, of their well-meant advice to the labourers as a class.

Q. What advice do the Malthusians[4] give to the labourer? A. To limit his family, as they think that overpopulation is the cause of the distress:

Q. Is this the case? A. It has never been so in England.

Q. How can this be proved? A. By the fact that the amount of wealth produced which might be exchanged for food for the workers, if the capitalist system did not prevent it, has always increased faster than the number of producers.

Q. Why is this? A. Because the labour of those who are working in concert is far more efficient than that of isolated workers, and machinery vastly enhances this efficiency.

Q. What is the element of truth in the Malthusian theory? A. It is perfectly true that a limited space of land cannot support an unlimited number of people, but as even England, to say nothing of the world, has not reached that limit to population, it has at present no bearing on the case.

Q. What is the element of truth as regards families? A. It is perfectly true that in the present capitalist system the man who has no children at all is in a better pecuniary position than the man with a large family, since, just as in actual warfare, children in the modern competitive battle-field are an encumbrance, where every man has to fight for his living, and maintain his family as best he may.

Q. How does the standpoint of the Malthusians differ from that of the Socialists? A. The former accept the basis of the capitalist society, namely, the existence of two distinct classes of wage-payers and wage-earners, and merely advise the workers to attempt to secure a larger wage.

Q. How do Socialists regard this advice? A. They consider that the discussion as to whether the workers shall enjoy one-half or one-third of the wealth which they have produced is comparatively unimportant, and they continue to urge the rightful claim of the workers to the full value of their own productions.

Q. How soon is this claim likely to be attended to? A. As soon as ever the majority of the workers really understand their own position, and consequently become convinced of the advantages of Socialism.

Q. How can the capitalists be converted to the same view? A. Appeals to justice may make isolated conversions of individual capitalists, but nothing short of a display of organised force will enable the idlers as a body to perceive the advantage of taking their due share in the necessary work of society under a just system of Socialism.

Revolution

Q. On what ground do capitalists defend the principle of competition? *A.* On the ground that it brings into play a man's best qualities.

Q. Does it effect this? *A.* This is occasionally its result; but it also brings out his worst qualities, by stimulating him to struggle with his fellows for the relative improvement of his own position rather than for the absolute advancement of the interests of all.

Q. Why does this happen? *A.* Because in ordinary competition one man's gain is another's loss.

Q. What is the theory of the Survival of the Fittest? *A.* That the class of persons who are most fitted to live and propagate their race in the conditions with which it is surrounded, is certain to survive the rest.

Q. Are the existing social conditions favourable to the survival of those persons whose character renders them most valuable to society? *A.* On the contrary, they favour the survival of the most valueless.

Q. What is the final result of such conditions and surroundings as the filth, foul air and squalor of a town rookery? *A.* The crushing out of those who are least able to adapt themselves to these surroundings; and the consequent survival of those who are most fit for filth, but least for decent social life.

Q. Does the law of the Survival of the Fittest affect men in the same way as it affects the lower animals? *A.* No; because it is possible for men to alter their surroundings, while other animals must simply adapt themselves to them, whatever they may be.

Q. What is the Revolution for which Socialists strive? *A.* A Revolution in the methods of the distribution of wealth corresponding to that which has already taken place in the means of its production.

Q. What change has already taken place? *A.* Wealth is now almost entirely produced by the associated effort of great numbers of men working in concert, instead of by individual effort as in former times; while individuals still possess command of its distribution, and use their power in their own interests.

Q. How are forms of government changed so as to re-adjust them to the economical changes in the forms of production which have been silently evolving in the body of society? *A.* By means of Revolutions.

Q. Give an instance of this? *A.* The French Revolution of 1789.

Q. Did that Revolution fail to attain its objects? *A.* Certainly not; but its objects were not those at which Socialists aim.

Q. What were its objects? *A.* The political expression of the fact that feudalism was demolished, and the reign of capitalism established on its ruins.

Q. What do you mean by this? *A.* The overthrow of the political supremacy of the landed aristocracy, and the establishment of a bourgeois plutocracy; that is, putting the political power into the hands of the merchants and money-lords of the middle-class.

Q. What change in the forms of production had rendered this inevitable? *A.* The fact that the possession of agricultural land had ceased to be the chief means to the attainment of wealth.

Q. What, then, had taken its place? *A.* The possession of capital and the use of machinery.

Q. In what sense was that Revolution a selfish struggle? *A.* After the displacement of the upper by the middle-class in political and social supremacy, the latter established its own power irrespectively of the rights of any other class.

Q. Is not the struggle which precedes and heralds the Social Revolution one of selfish class interests in the same way? *A.* By no means; Socialists do not aim at the supremacy of a class or section of the community at the expense of other sections.

Q. Do they not wish the workers to control the State? *A.* Certainly they do.

Q. Is not this the supremacy of a class? *A.* No, for they insist that every able-bodied person of sound mind should do a fair share of necessary work. When all are workers, the workers will be no longer a class, but a nation.

Q. What, then will become of the class-selfishness of the workers? *A.* Selfishness will then become public spirit, when the motives which formerly led men to work for the interests and advancement of themselves alone, operate for the benefit of the whole human race with which their class has become identified.

Notes

1. John Stuart Mill (1806–73); economist and philosopher; exponent of Utilitarianism.
2. John Bright (1811–89); was an orator and statesman, son of a Rochdale miller. Member of Cabinet and Privy Council 1868–70. With Cobden advocated Free Trade and was representative of the emerging manufacturing class after the Reform Bill of 1832.
3. Rt Hon Henry Fawcett (1833–84). Started on a legal career but lost his sight in 1868 and turned to political economy. Entered Parliament as Liberal for Brighton in 1865 and Hackney in 1880. Was appointed Postmaster-General. Won esteem for his championship of the common people.
4. Thomas Robert Malthus (1766–1834); clergyman and economist. Author of *An Essay On The Principle of Population* which was used by reactionary people to justify a number of attacks on working people's standards of living. His adherents followed his ideas and called themselves Malthusians.

3
Why I am a Socialist

ANNIE BESANT

Introduction

Annie Besant was born in London into a middle-class family and given a careful education by Ellen Marryat, sister of the popular novelist Captain Frederick Marryat.

Her political education began in 1866 when she met the radical solicitor, W.P. Roberts, the miners' advocate. She married the Reverend Frank Besant in 1867, with whom she had two children, and separated from him in 1873. The marriage apparently resulted in her conversion to atheism. In 1874 she met Charles Bradlaugh, joined the National Secular Society and became staff writer on Bradlaugh's journal, the *National Reformer*.

The partnership between Annie Besant and Charles Bradlaugh continued throughout the 1870s and 1880s. It was a productive and influential association, and Annie soon became widely known as an excellent speaker and writer. By 1885 she had publicly embraced the Socialist cause and, probably influenced by George Bernard Shaw, joined the Fabian Society.

She had many men friends, among whom were Shaw, Edward Aveling, Herbert Burrows and W.T. Stead. She had a wide range of interests and made a name for herself as a free-thinker, feminist, author, editor, publisher, science teacher, social reformer, strike leader and trade unionist.

One of the best known campaigns that she and Bradlaugh were involved in was that for the provision of birth control. In 1877 the two of them were prosecuted for republishing Charles Knowlton's *Fruits of Philosophy* in which birth control was advocated. Giving evidence at their trial, Annie pointed out that knowledge of birth control was available to the wealthy, but that the poor remained ignorant – nor could they afford to buy what was available. Besant and Bradlaugh were found guilty but released on a technicality.

The trial caused quite a stir in London society. It resulted in Annie's losing the custody of her daughter to her husband, who already had custody of their son.

During the 12 or so years that Annie Besant was involved in political life in London, there was hardly a radical movement in which she did not play a part. As one of the few prominent women of the era, she was in constant demand as a speaker and writer. She also found time to qualify as a science teacher and to

32

publish a number of journals called *Corners*. These included such titles as *Science Corner*, *Art Corner* and *Young People's Corner*. The radical focus of these journals became more socialist as time went on.

Though Annie Besant joined the Social Democratic Federation in 1888, she never accepted the class struggle as a theory and felt more at home among the intellectual socialists in the Fabian Society. But in spite of this she gave every possible assistance to workers participating in the struggle. She gave leadership to the Match girls in their strike against Bryant & May in 1888, an episode which resulted a year later in the dockers' strike for the 'tanner'.

Ms Besant was elected to the London School Board in 1888, topping the list of eleven candidates.

Towards the end of the 1880s Annie Besant turned to theosophy, and joined the Theosophical Society in 1889. Her partnership with Charles Bradlaugh began to break up in 1887, and by 1991 she had forsaken the socialist movement altogether. After this she spent most of her time in India, becoming an important representative of the international movement. On her visits to England until 1914, she continued to take an active role in politics, and spoke on the subject of women's suffrage to large crowds. She continued to express her sympathy for women who were poor, badly housed and exploited. In 1924 a meeting was held in London, attended by 2,000 people, to commemorate her 50 years of public work. Many of the best known figures in the labour movement were among the speakers.

Why I am a Socialist was printed by Annie Besant and Charles Bradlaugh at 63 Fleet Street, London E.C. in 1886.

Sources

Bellamy and Saville, *Dictionary of Labour Biography*, vol. 4, p. 21 (article by David Rubenstein).

Arthur H. Nethercot, *The First Five Lives of Annie Besant*, Rupert Hart-Davis, 1961.

* * *

'A Socialist! You don't mean to say you are a Socialist!' Such is the exclamation with which anyone who adopts the much-hated name of Socialist is sure to be greeted in 'polite society'. A Socialist is supposed to go about with his pocket full of bombs and his mind full of assassinations; he is a kind of wild beast, to be hunted down with soldiers if he lives under Bismarck, with sneers, abuse, and petty persecutions if he lives under Victoria. The very wildness of the epithets launched at him, however, shows how much there is of fear in the hatred with which he is regarded; and his opponents, by confining themselves to mere abuse, confess that they find themselves unable to cope with him intellectually. Prejudice and passion, not reasoned arguments, are the weapons relied on for his destruction. Once let the working classes understand what Socialism really is, and the present system is doomed; it is therefore of vital necessity that they shall be prevented from calmly studying its proposals, and shall be so deafened with the clamour against it that they shall be unable to hear the 'still small voice' of reason. I do not challenge the effectiveness of the policy – for a time. It has been the policy of the governing classes against every movement that has been aimed against their privileges; Radicalism has been served in exactly similar fashion, and now that Radicalism has grown so strong that it can no longer be silenced by clamour, it is the turn of Socialism to pass through a like probation. There is always an ugly duckling in Society's brood; how else should be maintained the succession of swans?

With a not inconsiderable number of persons the prejudice against the name of Socialist is held to be a valid reason for not adopting it, and it is thought wiser to advocate the *thing* without affronting the antagonism aroused against the *name*. With such a policy I have ever had no sympathy. It seems to me the wiser, as well as the franker course, to boldly wear any name which expresses an opinion held, and live down the prejudice it may awaken. The name Socialist is in itself a fine name, connoting as it does the social union; it is the recognised label of the school which holds as its central doctrine that land and the means of production should be the property of the social union, and not of privileged individuals in it; it is the one name which is recognised all the world over as the name of those who are opposed to political, religious, and social tyranny in every land; of those who look with brotherly sympathy on the efforts of every nation which is struggling for its freedom; of those who are on the side of the poor and the toiling everywhere; of those who recognise no barriers of nationality, of class, or of creed, but who see a brother in every worker, a friend in every lover of the people. Every political name is of the country in which it is born; but the name Socialist, like the name Atheist, is of no one land; it is valid in every country; it is whispered on Russian steppe, in German field, in French city, in Italian vineyard; and wherever it is heard the chains of the captive for a moment seem lighter, for Hope has lifted them, and the careworn faces of the toilers brighten, as a gleam from a sunnier day gilds the tools over which they bow.

Pass we from the name to the thing, from 'the outer and visible sign to the inward and spiritual grace'. Within the compass of a brief paper it is not possible for me to give all the reasons which have made me a Socialist, but there are three main lines of thought along which I travelled towards Socialism, and along which I would fain persuade my readers to travel also, in the hope that they too may find that they lead to the same goal.

I. *I am a Socialist because I am a believer in Evolution.* The great truths that organisms are not isolated creations, but that they are all linked together as parts of one great tree of life; that the simple precedes the complex; that progress is a process of continued integrations, and ever-increasing differentiations; these truths applied to the physical animated world by Darwin,[1] Huxley,[2] Haeckel,[3] Büchner,[4] and their followers, have unravelled the tangles of existence, have illuminated the hidden recesses of Nature. But the service to be done to science by Evolution was not completed when natural history was made a coherent whole instead of a heterogeneous heap of irrelevant facts; its light next fell on the universe of mind, and traced the growth of mentality from the lowest organism that responds to a stimulus up to the creative brain of man. And still it had work to do, and next it reduced to order the jarring elements of the sphere of morals, and analysed duty and conscience, right and wrong, obligation and responsibility, until it rendered intelligible and consequent all that seemed supernatural and incoherent. And both in mind and in morals Spencer[5] was the great servant of Evolution, illuminating the previous darkness by lucid exposition and by pregnant suggestion. But having done so much in the ordering of thought in every realm of study save one, it was not possible that Evolution should leave Sociology untouched, a mere chaos of unrelated facts, of warring opinions. Hither also came the light, and out of the chaos slowly grew a cosmos. Society was seen evolving from lowliest savagery, from the embryonic state of barbarism, through nomad life to settled order, through tribes to nation, through feudalism to industrialism, through industrialism to – Nowhither? Evolution complete? Further progress barred? Not so. For science, which cannot prophesy details of the future, can grasp tendencies of the present, and recognising the conditions of the social growth of the past, can see how the present has been moulded, and along which lines its further development must inevitably pass. Now the progress of society has been from individualistic anarchy to associated order; from universal unrestricted competition to competition regulated and restrained by law, and even to partial co-operation in lieu thereof. Production from being individualistic has become co-operative; large bodies of workmen toiling together have replaced the small groups of masters and apprentices; factory production has pushed aside cottage production, and industrial armies are seen instead of industrial units. Laws for the regulation of industry – which failed when they were made by a few for their own advantage, and were used in the vain effort to keep down the majority – have been carried and applied successfully to some extent in defence of the liberty of the majority against the oppression of a privileged few. Since the partial admission of the workers to the exercise of political power, these laws for the regulation of industry have rapidly multiplied, and at the same time laws which hindered the free association of the workers have been repealed. The State has interfered with factories and workshops, to fix the hours of labour, to insist on sanitary arrangements, to control the employment of the young. Land Acts and Ground Game Acts, Education Acts and Shipping Acts, Employers' Liability Acts and Artisans' Dwellings Acts, crowd our Statute book. Everywhere the old ideas of free contract, of non-interference, are being outraged by modern legislation. And it is not only Socialists who point to these reiterated interferences as signs of the tendencies of society. John Morley, in his 'Life of Cobden', notes that England, where Socialism is supposed to have but small influence, has a body of Socialistic legislation greater than can be found in any other country in the world.

II. *I am a Socialist because of the failure of our present civilisation.* In an article which appeared in the July number of the *Westminster Review*, after alluding to Professor Huxley's declaration that he would rather have been born a savage in one of the Fiji islands than have been born in a London slum, I put the following question, which I will venture to quote here. 'Is it rational that the progress of society should be as lopsided as it is? Is it necessary that, while civilisation brings to some art, beauty, refinement – all that makes life fair and gracious – it should bring to others drudgery, misery, degradation, such as no uncivilised people know? And these emphasised and rendered the bitterer by the contrast of what life is to many, the dream of what it might be to all. For Professor Huxley is right. The savage has the forest and the open sea, the joy of physical strength, food easily won, leisure sweet after the excitement of the chase; the civilised toiler has the monotonous drudgery of the stuffy workshop, the hell of the gin-palace for his pleasure-ground, the pandemonium of reeking court and stifling alley for his lullaby; civilisation has robbed him of all natural beauty and physical joy, and has given him in exchange – the slum. It is little wonder that, under these circumstances, there are many who have but scant respect for our social fabric, and who are apt to think that any change cannot land them in a condition worse than that in which they already find themselves.'

Now if this view should spread widely among the inhabitants of the slums, it is obvious that the present civilisation would stand in very considerable peril, and it would be likely to sink, as feudalism sank in France, beneath the waves of a popular revolution. But such a revolution, sweeping from the slums over the happier parts of the towns, would not be a revolution set going by men of genius, directed by men of experience and of knowledge, as was the French Revolution of 1789. It would be a mad outburst of misery, of starvation, of recklessness, which would for a brief space sweep everything before it, and behind it would leave a desolate wilderness. Walk at midnight through the streets near the Tower, along Shadwell High Street, or about 'Tiger Bay', and imagine what would happen if those drunken men and women, singing, shouting, fighting, in the street, were to burst the barriers that hem them in, and were to surge westwards over London, wrecking the civilisation which had left them to putrefy in their misery, and had remained callous to their degradation. Is it not the part of a good citizen to try to change a social system which bears such products as these in every great city?

The slum population, however, is not wholly composed of such persons as I have spoken of. Large numbers of honest, temperate, industrious people are forced by poverty, and by the necessity of being near their work, into the dismal fate of living in the slums. And among them is spreading a discontent which is pregnant with change. Education is awakening in them desires and hopes which find no satisfaction in the slums. It is opening to them wider views of human life, and the penny newspaper tells them of enjoyments and luxuries of which they would have known nothing, pent in the dreary mill-round of their toiling lives, had ignorance kept them blind. Slowly is being formed that 'educated proletariat' which shall work out its own salvation, and which shall refuse any longer to act as the basis on which is reared the pyramid of civilisation. The present civilisation rests on the degradation of the workers; in order that they may accept their lot they must be kept poor, ignorant, submissive; the culture of their superiors is paid for with their ignorance; the graceful leisure of the aristocrat is purchased by the rough toil of the plebeian; his dainty fingers are kept soft and white by the hardening and reddening of the poor man's hands; the workers are daily sacrificed that the idlers may enjoy. Such is modern civilisation. Brilliant and beautiful where it rises into the sunlight, its foundation is of human lives made rotten with suffering. Whited sepulchre in very truth, with its outer coating of princes and lords, of bankers and squires, and within filled with dead men's bones, the bones of the poor who builded it.

Most hopeful sign, perhaps, for the future is the fact that discontent with the present system is not confined to those who are in a special sense its victims. In every class of society are found men and women who look and work for a complete revolution in the method of the production and distribution of wealth. Among those who profit most by the present system are found the most eager workers against it, and many whose lot is cast among the 'comfortable classes' are striving to undermine the very constitution which gives them the privileges they enjoy. In them sympathy has triumphed over selfishness, and their own rich wine of life tastes sour when they see the bitter water of poverty pressed to their brothers' lips. They are indignant that their own hands should be so full while others' hands are empty; and would fain lessen their own heap in order that the share of their neighbours may be made equal with their own. At present the Socialist movement in England is far more a middle-class than a working-class one; the creed of Socialism is held as an intellectual conviction by the thoughtful and the studious, and is preached by them to the workers, who have everything to gain by accepting it, and some of whom have already embraced and are teaching it. Instead of being a class movement, it is a movement of men and women of all classes for a common end, and the Socialist army is composed of persons of various social ranks, who have renounced for themselves the class distinctions they are banded together to destroy.

III. *I am a Socialist because the poverty of the workers is, and must continue to be, an integral part of the present method of wealth-production and wealth-distribution.* Under that method land, capital, and labour, the three factors in wealth-production, are divorced from each other, and landless, capital-less labour – which must sell itself to live – lies at the mercy of the privileged classes. The owner of the land demands a share of the produce raised on or from it, and this share is claimed by him not because he helps in gaining the produce, but because he owns the raw material of the soil, and can prevent anyone from utilising it, if he so pleases. The land is his; for him the rain softens and the sunshine warms the soil; for him sweet Mother Nature bares her fragrant bosom, and pours out the treasures with which her arms are laden; for him she has been working through the silent centuries, growing her forests, carbonising her buried vegetable treasures, storing her vast unseen realms with gem and ore of metal, building through myriads of ages by life and death, by creation and destruction, by swift birth and slow decay. And all this toil of ages, wrought out by the mighty unseen forces, finds its end in my Lord Emptyhead, who stretches out his useless hands over the noble product, and cries to his countless brothers, 'This is mine!' Then he bargains with them, and claims the right to tax their labour in exchange for permitting them to use what ought to be the common property, and to tax it, moreover, in proportion to its success. Thus Dukes of Westminster, of Bedford, and of Portland; Marquises of Londonderry, of Anglesey, and of Bute; Earls of Derby and of Dudley; with many another beside; all these grow ever and ever wealthier, not because they work, but because their ancestors by force or fraud got grip of the soil, and in days when the people were unrepresented made laws which secured to them and their descendants the monstrous monopoly of natural agents. As the people multiply and press ever more and more on the means of subsistence, they have to pay more and more to the owners thereof; and while private property in land is permitted to exist, so long will the landless lie at the landlord's mercy, and wealthy idler and poverty-stricken worker will form integral parts of our social, or rather anti-social, system.

Similarly is a share of the worker's product claimed by the class which holds as individual property the accumulated wealth made by generations of toilers, the present means of production; this wealth is obtained by forcing labour to accept as 'wage' less than the value it creates; unless it will accept these terms it is not permitted to create any value at all, so that it has the choice between starvation and exploitation. The share of its own produce which it receives as wage varies from time to time; sometimes it is less, sometimes more; but it is always less than the value made by it. Only when there is a 'profit' to be made – that is when the capitalist can get out of his 'hands' more value than he returns to them as wage – will he employ them. The machines which have been invented by human genius, and which ought to lessen human labour, are used to make fortunes for a few. A skilful workman sees a possible improvement; his master reaps the profit of the improved machine, patenting it for his own enrichment. Huge fortunes rapidly made date from the invention of machinery, because only by the possession of machinery can a man utilise the labour of many for such swift gain. Possessing this, he is in a position of advantage which enables him to say to his fellow-men: 'You shall use my machinery on condition that you are content with bare subsistence, and leave to me the wealth which flows from you and the machine.' Thus machinery, which is one of the advantages of civilisation, gives wealth to its individual owner, and bare subsistence to the toilers who work with it. And so long as the possession of all the mechanical advantages is in the hands of individuals, so long will they be able to enslave and exploit those who have only their natural tools, and the machine-owner may lie at his ease and watch the growing piles of his wealth, as his bondmen heap it together, and gratefully accept the fraction of it which his higher servants fling to them as wage. Poverty will last so long as one class depends on another for 'employment', so long as one man must sell another man his labour at whatever rate the condition of the market may fix. Free men may associate their labour for a common end, and divide the common product; slaves are obliged to let their labour be at the direction of their master, and to accept subsistence in exchange.

Class distinctions will endure while men stand in the position of employer and employed; the one who holds the means of subsistence feels himself superior to the one who craves them. And this is not all. The life-surroundings of the rich fashion an organism easily distinguishable from the organism produced by the life-surroundings of the poor. Take two healthy week-old babies, one the child of a ploughman and the other the child of a duke; place them side by side, and the keenest eye will not be able to separate the aristocrat and the plebeian. But give to one the best education and to the other none, and place them side by side when each is grown to manhood, and the easy polished manner and soft speech of the one will be contrasted with the clumsy roughness and stumbling articulation of the other. Education, training, culture, these make class distinctions, and nothing can efface them save common education and equally refined life-surroundings. Such education and life-surroundings cannot be shared so long as some enjoy wealth they do not earn, and others are deprived of the wealth they do earn. Land and capital must be made common property, and then no man will be in a position to enslave his brother by placing before him the alternative of starvation or servitude. And because no system save that of Socialism claims that there shall be no individual monopoly of that on which the whole nation must depend, of the soil on which it is born and must subsist, of the capital accumulated by the labour of its innumerable children, living and dead; because no system save that of Socialism claims for the whole community control of its land and its capital; because no system save that of Socialism declares that wealth created by associated workers should be shared among those workers, and that no idlers should have a lien upon it; because no system save that of Socialism makes industry really free and the worker really independent, by substituting co-operation among workers for employed and employing classes; because of all this I am a Socialist. My Socialism is based on the recognition of economic facts, on the study of the results which flow inevitably from the present economic system. The pauper and the millionaire are alike its legitimate children; the evil tree brings forth its evil fruits.

Notes

1. Charles Darwin (1809–82); grandson of Erasmus Darwin. Initially wanted to be ordained but was appointed naturalist to the Beagle, and whilst on a voyage to South America, began collecting evidence on evolution. His findings were published in 1859 in *The Origin of Species*.
2. Rt Hon Thomas Henry Huxley (1825–95); physiologist who supported Charles Darwin's *Origin Of Species*, which created considerable controversy when it was published. He led an active and influential public life over many years and was world renowned for his scientific work.
3. Professor Ernst Heinrich Haeckel (1834–1919); Professor of Zoology at Jena University, he eagerly accepted the findings of Charles Darwin on evolution. An outspoken Rationalist, his *Riddle Of The Universe* was translated into over 20 languages and sold over two million copies. He developed Darwin's work and was an excellent populariser of scientific work.
4. Friedrich Karl Christian Ludwig Büchner (1824–99); teacher of medicine at Tubingen University who was deprived of his position when he published a controversial work, *Force and Matter*.
5. Herbert Spencer (1820–1903); philosopher who was a lifelong friend of Huxley. He advocated and developed the ideas of evolution particularly in his two works, *First Principles* published in 1862 and *Principles of Biology* in 1864 and 1867. He was influential in America as well as in England.

4

What Socialism Means:
A Call to the Unconverted

SIDNEY JAMES WEBB

Introduction

Sidney Webb was born in 1859 in London and was the second son of a radical publican. After attending the City of London School and the Birkbeck Institute, he went to work as a clerk in the City office of a firm of colonial brokers. He then took evening classes in order to enter for the Civil Service open examination. On passing it he became a second division clerk in the War Office.

While rising rapidly through the ranks of the Civil Service Webb read for the Bar in Gray's Inn, to become, in 1885, an LL B of the University of London. His active interest in politics began when he joined the Zetetical Society to get practice in public speaking. It was here that he met George Bernard Shaw, who soon realised that Webb's remarkable memory and analytical ability was a potentially valuable asset for socialist propagandists.

Shaw introduced Webb to the newly formed Fabian Society. By 1885 both Webb and Shaw had become members of the Society's committee, and Webb produced his first unsigned pamphlet, *Facts for Socialists*. Webb's memory and organisational ability, combined with Shaw's wit and command of the English language made an important contribution to the influence of the Fabian Society in its early years. Shaw in fact once described Webb as the 'ablest man in England'.

Webb's potential was recognised by others, among them a certain Beatrice Potter, who asked for his assistance in her work on Charles Booth's *Survey*. Though she and Webb were very different in terms of temperament and background, they became firm friends. They were married in 1892, and their lifetime partnership became legendary.

Relieved of the need to earn a living because Beatrice had sufficient to keep them both in comfort, Sidney Webb was able to devote his life to politics and writing. He was elected to the London County Council as Progressive member for Deptford, a seat which he held until 1910.

His main interest was higher education, and he helped to develop the idea of technological education. He also played a part in the campaign to establish the University of London as a full educational institute. When in 1894 a wealthy Fabian, Henry Hutchinson, left his fortune to further the ends of the Society, the Trustees of the estate, including Webb, decided to establish an institute of

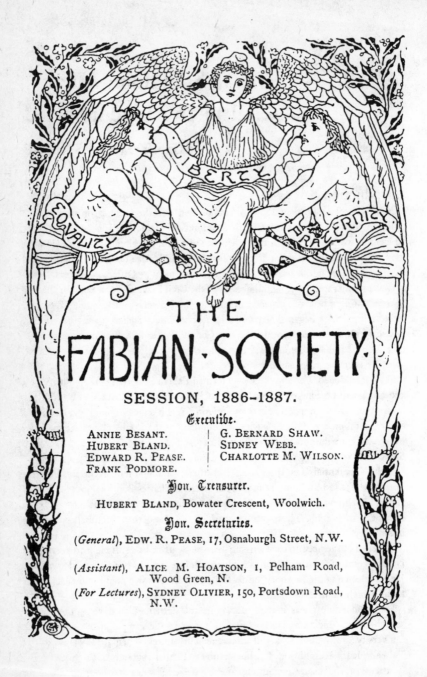

THE
FABIAN·SOCIETY·

SESSION, 1886-1887.

Executive.

ANNIE BESANT.   G. BERNARD SHAW.
HUBERT BLAND.   SIDNEY WEBB.
EDWARD R. PEASE.   CHARLOTTE M. WILSON.
FRANK PODMORE.

Hon. Treasurer.

HUBERT BLAND, Bowater Crescent, Woolwich.

Hon. Secretaries.

(*General*), EDW. R. PEASE, 17, Osnaburgh Street, N.W.

(*Assistant*), ALICE M. HOATSON, 1, Pelham Road,
Wood Green, N.

(*For Lectures*), SYDNEY OLIVIER, 150, Portsdown Road,
N.W.

university standard aimed at 'curing the economic ignorance of the capital'. The result was the London School of Economics and Political Science.

Beatrice and Sidney pursued their joint research and writing into the history of trade unionism and then progressed to an investigation into the history of local government in England from 1688.

During the First World War, Webb was involved in an advisory capacity on a number of important committees. He became closely involved with the Labour Party leaders. In 1918 he stood as parliamentary candidate for the University of London and just failed to be elected as a result of the Conservative Party's summoning every possible vote in order to defeat him. In the general election of 1922, he stood for and won the seat for Seaham Harbour in Durham which he retained in two subsequent elections. Beatrice and Sidney thoroughly enjoyed their association with the constituents and he wrote the *History of the Durham Miners* for them, while she ran classes for the miners' wives.

In 1923 their reputation was at its peak and Sidney was Chairman of the Labour Party. In his presidential address, he introduced the phrase 'the inevitability of gradualness' which has come to be used as the epitome of Fabianism. He was a conscientious but uninspired MP, though he did achieve ministerial rank as president of the Board of Trade in 1924.

After accepting Ramsey MacDonald's request that he go to the House of Lords and run the Colonial Office from there, Webb became Lord Passfield in 1927. He correctly assessed his work there as unsuccessful.

In 1932 Beatrice and Sidney went on a visit to the Soviet Union where, as Sidney noticed with surprise, they were received as 'a kind of minor royalty'. Three years later, after another visit, they wrote *Soviet Communism: A New Civilisation*. They were both over 70 by that time.

When Beatrice died in 1943 the Order of Merit was conferred on Lord Passfield in recognition of their joint achievements. Sidney died in 1947 and his ashes, together with Beatrice's, were placed beneath the flags of Westminster Abbey.

What Socialism Means is a typical example of Fabian socialism, with its reliance on the economic ideas of Mill, Cairnes and Walker. Together with the rest of the early Fabians Webb had studied Marx's *Capital* and undertaken a thorough course of study covering the Utopian socialists, the Chartists and the Positivists. Webb himself soon rejected Marx's ideas in favour of those of Jevons, who in his view, offered a better explanation of the cause of poverty in society. His research ultimately led to his disillusionment with Fabianism, and his declining years were devoted to advocating and promoting the achievements of Soviet Communism.

What Socialism Means was printed from the report of a lecture delivered for the Fabian Society on 7 May 1886, and revised in January 1888.

Sources

Margaret Cole, *Dictionary of Labour Biography*, Bellamy and Saville, vol. 11, p. 376. This gives a full list of their writing, and the sources from which their biographies can be obtained.

★   ★   ★

Nothing is more universal than the widespread illusion as to what Socialism really means, and as to how Socialists intend to obtain its adoption. It seems almost impossible to bring people to understand that the abstract word 'Socialism', denotes, like 'Radicalism', not an elaborate plan of Society, but a principle of social action. Socialists easily recognise that the adoption of the principle can only be extended by bringing about a slowly dawning conviction in the minds of men; it is certain that no merely forcible 'revolution' organised by a minority, can ever avail, either in England or elsewhere. We seek therefore to influence only convictions, so as thereby to bring about the great bugbear of our opponents, the 'Social Revolution' − a revolution in the opinions men form of the proper Society in which to live, and in the kind of action to which these opinions lead them.

There are many who desire to help in social reconstruction, but who are not quite decided to act; many who sympathise, but who are timid; many, indeed, who are Socialists, but are not conscious of their Socialism. It is to these especially that we must address ourselves asking them always to remember that Socialism is more than any Socialist, and its principles more than any detailed system or scheme of reform. The Fabian Society has no such plan or scheme; its members are led by their Socialist principles to work for social reform in a certain definite direction, but the future evolution of Society no man can exactly forecast, and to human evolution no final goal can be set. The moment will never come when we can say, 'Now Socialism is established, let us keep things as they are.' Constant evolution is the lesson of history: of endings, as of beginnings, we know nothing.

Socialism inevitably suffers if identified with any particular scheme, or even with the best vision we can yet form of Collectivism itself. In this, as in many other cases, the public are so much concerned with details, that they miss the principle: they 'cannot see the forest for the trees.' But it is no more fair to identify Socialism with any modern prophet's forecast of it, than it would be to identify Christianity with the 'New Jerusalem' of the Swedenborgians. Nevertheless, such misconceptions will inevitably persist, and those who may embrace Socialism, must be warned that they are not likely to receive 'honour among men' in consequence; they are certain to be misconstrued, misrepresented, and reviled, and to be regarded as advocates of dynamite outrages or childish absurdities, even by those who are gradually learning their very doctrines.

Socialism is emphatically a new thing, a thing of the present century −

and one of the unforeseen results of the great industrial revolution of the past 150 years. During this period man's power over the rest of nature has suddenly and largely increased: new means of accumulating wealth and also new means of utilising land and capital have come into being.

Many do not realise what a change has resulted from this industrial revolution. At the beginning of the last century, the whole value of the land and capital of this country is estimated to have amounted to less than 500 millions sterling; now it is supposed to be over £9,000 millions; an increase eighteenfold. Two hundred years ago, rent and interest cannot have amounted to 30 millions sterling annually – now they absorb over 450 millions. Socialism arose as soon as rent and interest became important factors; it began with our own century: in its birthplace in England it was, however, was beaten back for a time by the hasty misunderstandings of Malthus[1] followed by the 'acute outbreak of individualism' unchecked by the old restraints, and invested with almost a religious sanction by 'a certain soulless school of "writers",' from which even Professor Foxwell[2] asserts England to have suffered for the last century.

This hasty misinterpretation of economic science was set right by John Stuart Mill[3] (who describes in his 'Autobiography' (p. 231) his own conversion from mere extreme Democracy to a complete Socialism), and at the present moment Socialism, which had never ceased on the Continent, permeates the whole world of thought and politics here as elsewhere. Even the tide of 'Orthodox Political Economy' is now running strongly in its favour, and we have Cambridge professors publicly claiming to be Socialists, and turning out Socialists by scores as their pupils.

What is the cause of this new criticism of the existing order? It has arisen because the great increase in wealth has been allowed to flow mainly to individuals, so that the enormous increase per head of the wealth production has failed to exterminate or even to alleviate poverty. In this London, the wealthiest city of the world, there is also the greatest mass of poverty and misery. It has miles upon miles of palaces, serried ranks of costly carriages in Hyde Park, such signs of abundant wealth as no other land can show. Its mere rental value is nearly forty millions sterling annually. Yet in this city homeless little children beg for bread, strong men die of starvation and want every night, and there is an array of over 300,000 persons, as many as would make the whole city of Brussels or Birmingham, in frequent receipt of workhouse relief. We should dwell a little on this. So dazed are we by the perfection of the organisation, that we are only too unconscious of the misery around us. Think of this army of 300,000 strong men, brave women and little children, absolutely destitute in this city where we are so comfortable; an army of 300,000 unable to get bread, or to obtain shelter from the cutting blast, and obliged during any one year to resort to the cold mercy of official charity. One in every five of the population dies in the workhouse or hospital. This is not a picture of London alone: things are much the same throughout the Kingdom. We have a total of over 3,000,000 in the pauper class; one in ten of the population, or one in eight of the wage earning classes.

These men, our brothers, were not born paupers; they, too, had once hope, and some youthful aspirations, which the hard world has gradually quenched in the pitiless struggle from which we favoured ones have reaped so much of the benefit; the iron has entered into their souls during that dreadful losing fight down the hill of poverty, until our brother, once erect and toiling for our benefit, is borne down before us to a pauper's grave.

Not only do we exact life-long labour from the poor, for which, as we have seen, so many receive in return just sufficient to keep them alive: we take their lives also. In the worst parts of London the death rate is four times that of neighbouring 'respectable' districts, and any doctor who has practised among the poor knows that their most fatal disease is poverty.

'At present the average age at death among the nobility, gentry and professional classes in England and Wales was 55 years: but among the artisan classes of Lambeth it only amounted to 29; and while the infantile death-rate among the well-to-do classes was such that only 8 children died in the first year of life out of 100 born, as many as 30 per cent succumbed at that age among the children of the poor in some districts of our large cities. The only real cause of this enormous difference in the position of the rich and poor with respect to their chances of existence lay in the fact that at the bottom of society wages were so low that food and other requisites of health were obtained with too great difficulty' (Dr. C. R. Drysdale, 'Report of Industrial Remuneration Conference' 1886, p. 130).[4]

Our Society, it appears according to this non-Socialist, robs the wage workers of Lambeth of 26 years of life each; they die before their time, like worn-out draught horses, and their innocent children like flies. They die in their own slums of diseases, which we, in our wealth, know how to prevent; one or two will die tonight in London alone of actual starvation.

This is not all. Year by year our comforts and our pleasures increase, and year by year those iron-monsters, the never ceasing machines, grow in number and complexity. Do we realise that year by year the accidents to the workers also increase, the number of fatal accidents doubling every 20 years? Last year we raised more coal than 20 years ago, smelted more iron, made more journeys, and all at less money cost: but we also killed many thousand of the workers, unhonoured martyrs of our civilization. How many we merely maimed is not to be ascertained. The cheap fuel with which we warmed ourselves last winter was not coal but lives of men.

This is what we have come to after 150 years of the greatest wealth-production the world has known; not only a greater aggregate production, but also an increased production per head of population. There is a small rich class endowed with every comfort the mind can describe; a middle-class, well-off, educated, leisured, powerful, and all roads open to it. These two, taken together and including all above the manual labour class *make up less than one fifth of the population*. On the other hand, is the great mass of the people (of whom one-eighth are actually in the pauper class), earning on an average perhaps 25/- per family per week. These are with necessarily rare exceptions, condemned to a life of unremitting toil; without leisure or higher education, no opportunity for real improvement, and also no hope of better things.

'To me, at least, it would be enough to condemn modern society as hardly an advance on slavery or serfdom, if the permanent condition of industry were to be that which we behold, that 90 per cent of the actual producers of wealth have no home that they can call their own beyond the end of the week; have no bit of soil, or so much as a room that belongs to them, have nothing of any kind except as much old furniture as will go in a cart: save the precarious chance of weekly wages which barely suffice to keep them in health; are housed for the most part in places that no man thinks fit for his horse; are separated by so narrow a margin from destitution, that a month of bad trade, sickness or unexpected loss, brings them face to face with hunger and pauperism... *This is the normal state of the average workman in town or country*' (Mr Frederick Harrison,[5] p. 429 'Report of Industrial Remuneration Conference', 1886).

What is the remedy of Socialism! We search – and have not to search long – for the causes of this misery. Nature itself has not, it is true, been exceedingly kind to us and we Socialists, as strongly as the Economists, demand that no useless mouths grow up to consume the too scanty store we can produce. We too, insist that there is no place at nature's table for any one who cannot or does not produce his quota, and we too, assert that there is – especially just now – grave danger that the number of such mouths may increase. We claim, indeed, that only in a Socialist community can any general limitation of population really be brought about. But we also call for a proper administration of that which is produced, so that if we must go upon short rations, these may at any rate be fairly shared.

Political Economists show us the causes of the existing poverty, and explain clearly enough the nature and extent of the deductions that go for rent, interest and the monopoly wages of exceptional ability. Official statisticians themselves enumerate these – in England at present – at two thirds of the annual produce of the workers.

There is no mystery about these things, though it may suit those who benefit by them who pretend that there is. The operations of unrestrained competition, with private ownership of land and industrial capital, is fully explained by Karl Marx, but even better by such writers as Mill, Cairnes[6] and Walker.[7] Economic rent and interest, they say, consists in reality of a toll levied upon production by the monopolist, and in exchange the monopolist, as such, gives nothing but permission to use the land and already accumulated capital.

'That useful function, therefore, which some profound writers fancy they discover in abundant expenditure of the idle rich, turns out to be a sheer illusion. Political economy furnishes no such palliation of unmitigated selfishness. Not that I would breathe a word against the sacredness of contracts. But I think it is important, on moral no less than on economic grounds, to insist upon this, that no public benefit of any kind arises from the existence of an idle rich class. The wealth accumulated by their ancestors and others on their behalf, where it is employed as capital, no doubt helps to sustain industry; but what they consume in luxury and idleness is not capital, and helps to sustain nothing but their own unprofitable lives. By all means they must have their rents and interest, as it is written in the bond; but let them take their proper place as drones in the hive, gorging at a feast to which they have contributed nothing' ('Some Leading Principles of Political Economy', p. 32, by the late John Elliott Cairnes, M.A., Emeritus Professor of Political Economy at University College, London; 1874).

Yet it is clearly inevitable that, so long as land and capital are in individual ownership rent and interest must continue to exist, creating what Mill called 'the great social evil of a non-labouring class.' For them the great mass of the workers are deprived of at least half the product of labour.

This is the Socialist case. It is founded on no new system of political economy, upon no new statistics. It is mainly the emphatic assertion of two leading principles. We recognise first, as the central truth of modern society, the interdependence of all. No man now works alone; by division of labour and mutual exchange all are sharing in each one's toil. Each worker, by the marvellously complex exchange-system shares in the fruits of the labour of those in the most remote parts of the earth, and is in unconscious partnership with every other worker. No individual can now claim as his own the product to which he is in reality giving only certain final touches.

We claim, in the second place, to apply the doctrines of economic science to the art of Government in insisting on the ethical right of the joint workers, *and the workers alone* to the whole produce of their labour, without any deduction for rent and interest, or any other form of mere monopolist's toll. We contend for the full recognition of the admitted fact that the whole produce of labour is created by labour alone – whether labour of hand or labour of brain – and that any form of society which enables idle owners of certain social products to exact for personal consumption a toll from helpless fellow citizens, although perhaps useful in the earlier stage of social evolution, is now bad; guilty as Mill and Cairnes themselves have in effect said, of causing unnecessary deaths and misery to the poorer classes.

This is essentially the Socialistic platform. We do not expect to realise this ideal all at once. Society is evolving fast under our eyes, and it is in this direction that it is changing. We have but the option of helping or resisting the change.

It is obvious that the scope of unrestrained private ownership will be once more altered. The limits, which have already gradually excluded slaves, public offices, highway tolls, post offices, 'sound dues,' and other monopolist freaks, must now be drawn so as to leave in the hands, or at least under the full control, of the community, that without which no man can live – the great means of wealth production, land and industrial capital.

Individual Socialists, whilst agreeing in this necessity, entertain different views as to the form of the social organisation to which we are now tending. There are three main schools of Socialist thought.

1. *Collectivists* lay stress on the necessity for equality of opportunity lest some be otherwise compelled to lead lives unnecessarily cramped and fettered. They wish with this end to extend public administration and public control of the means of production, the tendency to which has marked off modern society from the extreme individualism of the earlier part of the century.

2. *Anarchists* lay more stress upon the moral objections to any government coercion, and contend for private administration in a state of free co-operation with no other than moral regulation. Consumption is to be eventually according to real social needs, and to be regulated by voluntary restriction. Most Anarchists admit, however, that a period of collectivism will precede the attainment of their ideal, during which humanity gradually learns to become fit for it.

3. *Positivists,* so far as they have thought out their economic system, come clearly under this definition of Socialism. They would leave administration ostensibly in private hands but under increased government regulations; equal personal consumption, and by workers only, being realised chiefly by an advance in personal morality, and by the influence on public opinion of a philosophic priesthood. It is fair to add that most Positivists repudiate the name of Socialists. On the other hand the extreme Radical party in England is now practically Socialist of this type, often without being conscious of the fact.

But all forms of Socialism agree in the two general principles stated above. All agree in repudiating any claim by particular workers to the competitive exchange value of their particular products, which could be set up only by ignoring the unconscious co-operation by their fellows all over the world or by reverting to the wild individualism which is a characteristic of barbarism. And all agree with the Economist, in repudiating any moral claim in the monopolist as such, to the toll which he can levy.

It may be said that these are mere ideals which we hope to realise one day – not perhaps in our own lives, but living again in lives to come. What has Socialism hitherto done for the workers? What is its remedy for the present distress? The Socialist is, in the meantime, the most practical of politicians, the truest opportunist. While repudiating as unscientific, the idea that any mere palliative of existing evils can effect a cure of them, he is constantly urging the adoption of every practical measure of immediate relief. It is in his principles rather than in his practical politics that the socialist differs from the mere 'social reformer.' But principles are the only lasting springs of action.

Socialism, therefore, does not mean any particular plan or scheme of social re-organisation, nor the vain dream of equality of wealth. It means no contempt for machinery, no dislike of education or culture, no enmity to brain work or invention. It is, in fact, because we want more of these things that we are Socialists.

It is easy to bring objections against Socialism. There are always a thousand reasons against every social change. Yet the change comes, and the objectors silently learn wisdom. We need hardly trouble to reason with the man who says merely that he means to keep what he has got. Dawning conscience and increased social intelligence will bring the sons of such men over to our ranks. But may not the clever artisan or the skilled brain worker who now earns huge wages because of the scarcity of his talent, be justly allowed to consume the whole wages of his labour? There need be nothing to prevent him from doing this, in a society organised on a Socialist basis, but he should remember that countless other workers are helping him, and that his brain or skill is not his alone; it is the result of past ages; a social and not an individual product; while his training and education are essentially the fruit of social capital expended upon him.

Loss of liberty and independence, what of these? This is perhaps felt by most of those who enjoy a fair share under existing arrangements to be the weightiest objection to any increase in the present tendency to collectivism. On questions of personal liberty, Mill may be allowed some weight, and Mill emphatically declared that 'the restraints of Communism would be freedom in comparison with the present condition of the majority of the human race.' As to the present liberty and independence of the comfortable classes, on what are they based? The king's house at Dahomey stands solid on its mighty corner piles in the African sand, but their solidity is secured – so the natives will tell you – by the blood of the slave girls, crushed in the holes in which the piles were driven. The smiling landlord or mill-owner leans back in his saloon-carriage, rejoicing in the freedom of travel given by his long holiday, but he heeds not the extra hours of toil which his very property thus adds to the task of his serfs all over the world. There is economic servitude for the ordinary worker as unrelenting in its impersonal grip as the harshest trammels of the slave-owner.

Yes, Socialism means a loss of such liberty. Freedom which can only be enjoyed by the oppression of the rest is but license of the tyrant, and

> 'True freedom is to share
> All the bonds our brothers wear.'[8]

Any loss of personal liberty which the few may suffer (in any case, the liberty only to control the labour of others) will be far outweighed by the greater safety, independence and leisure of the many. Socialism necessarily implies by its fairer distribution of social pressure, an aggregate gain in personal freedom.

But whatever the seeming objections, those who recognise the economic causes of social evolution, are constrained, of necessity, to join forces with the socialist movement.

It is not a comfortable gospel that we preach to the middle and upper classes – no glad tidings of great joy – but it is one of which you will not be able to escape the unpleasant conviction. Perhaps those are happier who do not know, who have never thought of the source of their income: coming to them like manna from heaven. But you who do know whence comes your rent and interest, will see discomforting visions. As you feed the fire, you will see the miner, bent double underground, in his toil, giving up his life that you may be warmed. As you look upon your daughters growing up around you in your sheltered and cultured home, you will see behind them the daughters of other mothers, slaving seamstresses, working sixteen hours for 'eleven pence ha'penny'; nay, selling themselves into a life of infamy, for want of the bread which you, by your position of social vantage, are forcing them to give up to you.

Then there will be no escape. Those of you who do know, those of you who are no longer in blissful ignorance; those of you who realise this economic toil levied on the scanty earnings of the poor – will be compelled to come over to us for very shame, and work with all your might to stop the sooner this fearful drain upon the insufficient average pittance, which is all that we can as yet extract from the rest of nature.

You have but one alternative. By steadily turning away your eyes, and caring only for your own comforts, by luxurious and selfish living, by making to yourself a false idol of art, or religion, or literature you may perhaps be able in time to stifle your conscience, and drown the despairing cries of the misery which you are taking your part in creating. But then do not be surprised if the long suffering masses, roused at last from their ignorant patience, and deserted by those who ought to have been their leaders, shake in their despair the whole social structure about your ears, crying of your class, of its good as of its evil, 'cut it down, why cumbereth it the ground?' It is to prevent matters coming to such indiscriminate ruin that we are, and you should be, Socialists.

Notes

1. T.R. Malthus; *see* J.L. Joynes, *The Socialist Catechism*, n. 4.
2. Herbert Somerton Foxwell (1849–1936); professor of Economics, University College, London. Lecturer and Fellow of St John's College, Cambridge.
3. John Stuart Mill; *see* J.L. Joynes, *The Socialist Catechism*, n. 1.
4. Industrial Remuneration Conference, 28–30 January, 1885. A full report of the proceedings was published in 1885.
5. Frederick Harrison (1831–1923); publicist and historian. A lawyer by profession. Was active in support of Trades Unionism and Radicalism. He was not a Socialist but advocated many progressive causes.
6. John Elliott Cairnes (1823–75); professor of Political Economy at University College, London. Author of *Some Leading Principles of Political Economy*.
7. Amasa Walker (1799–1875); American economist, professor at Harvard University, Congressman 1862–3. Supported prohibition and restriction of the sale of intoxicating liquor.
8. J.R. Lowell, *In The Right With Two of Three*, in Josiah C. Wedgwood & Allan Nevins, *Forever Freedom*, Pelican 1940, p. 126. The verse is misquoted and should read:

> 'True freedom is to share
> All the chains our brothers wear'

5

What Socialism Is

GEORGE BERNARD SHAW (1856–1950)

Introduction

Bernard Shaw was born in Dublin and educated at a private school before becoming a clerk in a land agent's office. In 1876 he left Dublin to seek his fortune in London.

Following a period of poverty and rejection, he became art critic on the *Pall Mall Gazette* in 1885, the first step in his long and distinguished career as an art, music and drama critic.

His plays, however, did not achieve immediate success. Though his first piece, *Widowers' Houses,* appeared in 1892, it was not until 1903 that he achieved his first winner with *Man and Superman.* From then on his dramatic output continued at a steady rate until his death.

Shaw started out as a rationalist, rejecting organised religion at the age of ten. He did not enter a church for the next 20 years. His political education began with the reading of Marxist texts, and he met Henry Mayers Hyndman and William Morris when speaking on Marxism at a street corner meeting.

Shaw was among the leading socialists around the turn of the century, joining the SDF and the Socialist League. He was among the first members of the Fabian Society, joining in 1884. The educated, intellectually tolerant and middle-class nature of the society appealed to Shaw, who advocated the transformation of society by those with what he considered to be superior brains and organisational skills, rather than by the working people.

Shaw brought a lively good humour to the Fabians and he formed a close friendship with Sidney Webb. Of the first 13 Fabian Tracts, published between 1884 and 1890, 10 were written by either Shaw or Webb. Shaw was particularly prolific in his political writing, which was published in contemporary radical journals such as *Justice, The Commonweal* and Annie Besant's *Our Corner.*

The magnitude of the historic changes that took place during Shaw's 90 years of life were such that Shaw could barely adapt to each new conjuncture. He was not convinced that the Labour Party was genuinely socialist in outlook, and his high idealism, caustic criticism and skill as a humorist and satirist made him appear to be outside the post-1918 socialist scene.

The difficulties contained in his political outlook are neatly summed up in his *Labour Monthly* obituary, written by R.P. Dutt: 'Shaw was an artist. He should not be judged primarily as a political thinker, despite the prodigious mental energy and vigour. All the contradiction in the world can be found jostling one another in the ocean of his output...he was a Marxist and an anti-Marxist, a revolutionary and a reformist, a Fabian and a despiser of Fabianism, a Communist and a crusader against super-tax.'

Shaw's greatest contribution was in transforming the ideas of politics into language readily understood by ordinary people. His plays came into their own with the advent of radio. Though the problems tackled in the plays have by and large now been solved, they still reach an audience through the brilliance of the dialogue and the dramatic construction. This ability was clearly expressed in his pamphlet *What Socialism Is*, published as early as 1890.

Sources
Labour Monthly obituary, R.P. Dutt, December 1950, p. 529.
Alick West, *A Good Man Fallen Among Fabians*, Lawrence & Wishart, 1950.

★   ★   ★

What 'Unsocialism' Is

We English have a habit of speaking of England as if it belonged to us. We are wrong: England is now private property; and if a labouring man out of employment makes so free with 'his country' as to lie down for a night's sleep on it without paying its owners for the accommodation, he is imprisoned as a rogue and a vagabond. The price we must pay for our living room rises as the population grows; for the more people there are, the higher they will bid against one another in hiring land in the market for houses and places of business. In London, for instance, the price paid annually to the ground landlords goes up by £304,634 every year, without counting the additional charge for new buildings or repairs and improvements to old ones. After payments of one sort or another to the owners of the whole country have been deducted from the produce of the workers' labour the balance left for wages is so small, that if every working-class family got an equal share, each share would only come to £75 a year, which (though it would seem a fortune to some poor people) is not enough for a comfortable living, much less for saving. Nevertheless the proprietary classes, without working at all for it, divide among them enough to give over two hundred thousand rich families more than £1,500 a year, and still leave more than £300 a year per family for over a million and a quarter families of moderately well-off people in addition to what they make by their professions and businesses.

The Extreme Cases

The above figures, bad as they are, only represent averages, and give no idea of the extreme cases of wealth and poverty. Some of our great landowners get upwards of £4,000 a week without ever doing a stroke of work for it; whilst the labourers on their estates, working early and late from the time they are lads until they go into the union as aged and worn-out paupers, get eleven shillings a week. As women get lower wages than men when they work, but receive just as large incomes from property when they are rich and idle, a comparison between the share of our yearly produce that goes to a poor working woman at the East end of London, working sixteen hours a day for a shilling, and the rich, idle lady at the West end, is still more startling. These are facts and figures which no one disputes.

What Comes of Inequality

If you are a person of common sense and natural feeling you must have often thought over these terrible inequalities and their cruel injustice. If you are rich, you perhaps think that inequality is a good thing – that it fosters a spirit of emulation, and prevents things from stagnating at a dead level. But if you are poor, you must know well that when inequality is so outrageous as the figures above shew, it fosters nothing but despair, recklessness and drunkenness among the very poor; arrogance and wastefulness among the very rich; meanness, envy and snobbery among the middle classes. Poverty means disease and crime, ugliness and brutality, drink and violence, stunted bodies and unenlightened minds. Riches heaped up in idle hands mean flunkeyism and folly, insolence and servility, bad example, false standards of worth, and the destruction of all incentive to useful work in those who are best able to educate themselves for it. Poverty and riches together mean the perversion of our capital and industry to the production of frippery and luxury whilst the nation is rotting for want of good food, thorough instruction, and wholesome clothes and dwellings for the masses. What we want in order to make true progress is more bakers, more schoolmasters, more wool-weavers and tailors, and more builders : what we get instead is more footmen, more gamekeepers, more jockeys, and more prostitutes. That is what our newspapers call 'sound political economy.' What do you think of it? Do you intend to do anything to get it remedied?

No Remedy without Political Change

As things now stand, the produce of industry can be increased in two ways only. The first is to increase the population in order to set more people working; but this of course increases the demand for land to work on, and thus raises rent; so that it is the property-holders and not the workers who are made richer. The second is to get hand work done by machinery, to introduce railways, and to organise labour in factories. But the first cost of machinery, railways and factories has to be paid for out of savings, and not out of the money that people are living on. Now the only people who can spare money to save are those who have more than enough to live on: that is to say the rich. Consequently the machinery is introduced, and the factories built at the expense of the rich; and as they pay for it, they expect to get all the advantage that comes by using it; so that here again the workers are left as badly off as ever. The worst of it is that when the rich find out how easy it is for them to get still richer by saving, they think it is as easy for everybody as for themselves; and when the worker complains, they say 'Why don't you save as we do?' or 'How can you expect to be well off if you are not thrifty?' They forget that though you can save plenty out of £18 a week without stinting your family, you cannot save anything out of eighteen shillings without starving them.

The Three Monopolies

Moreover the propertied classes, by giving their younger sons an expensive education, are able to put them into the learned professions and the higher managerial posts in business, over the heads of the wage-workers, who are too poor to get more than a very short schooling. So that out of the price paid to them for the use of the land, the propertied classes buy the machinery; and out of the profits of the machinery they buy the education which gives to their working members a monopoly of the highly paid employments; whilst the wage-workers are hopelessly cut out of it all. Here are the figures for the United Kingdom:

*Income of Propertied Classes (10,500,000 persons)	£850,000,000
Income left for Wage-workers (26,500,000 persons)	500,000,000
Total National Income	£1,350,000,000

This means that the rich are masters of the wage-workers. The rich alone can afford to go into the House of Commons, or to sit upon the County Councils and Municipal Corporations. Yet the whole country is governed by these bodies. The workman's vote enables him to choose between one rich man and another, but not to fill the Councils and Parliament with men of his own class. Thus the poor keep the rich up; and the rich keep the poor down; and it will always be so whilst the land and the machinery from

---

* This item is made up of four hundred and eighty-five millions (£485,000,000) which go as Rent and Interest absolutely for nothing, and of three hundred and sixty-five millions (£365,000,000) incomes of professional men and profits of business management. (Fabian Tract No. 5, 'Facts for Socialists.') *B.S.*

which the nation's subsistence is produced remains in the hands of a class instead of in the hands of the nation as a whole.

What Socialism Is

Socialism is a plan for securing equal rights and opportunities for all. The Socialists are trying to have the land and machinery 'socialised,' or made the property of the whole people, in order to do away with idle owners, and to keep the whole product for those whose labour produces it. The establishment of Socialism, when once the people are resolved upon it, is not so difficult as might be supposed. If a man wishes to work on his own account, the rent of his place of business, and the interest on the capital needed to start him, can be paid to the County Council of his district just as easily as to the private landlord and capitalist. Factories are already largely regulated by public inspectors, and can be conducted by the local authorities just as gas-works, water-works and tram-ways are now conducted by them in various towns. Railways and mines, instead of being left to private companies, can be carried on by a department under the central government, as the postal and telegraph services are carried on now. The Income Tax collector who today calls for a tax of a few pence in the pound on the income of the idle millionaire, can collect a tax of twenty shillings in the pound on every unearned income in the country if the State so orders. Remember that Parliament, with all its faults, has always governed the country in the interest of the class to which the majority of its members belonged. It governed in the interest of the country gentlemen in the old days when they were in a majority in the House of Commons; it has governed in the interest of the capitalists and employers since they won a majority by the Reform Bill of 1832; and it will govern in the interest of the majority of people when the members are selected from the wage-earning class. Inquirers will find that Socialism can be brought about in a perfectly constitutional manner through Democratic institutions, and that none of the practical difficulties which occur to everyone in his first five minutes' consideration of the subject have escaped the attention of those who have worked at it for years. Few now believe Socialism to be impracticable except those with whom the wish is father to the thought.

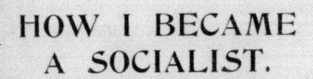

HOW I BECAME
A SOCIALIST.

By WILLIAM MORRIS.

Price One Penny.

6

How I Became a Socialist

WILLIAM MORRIS (1834–96)

Introduction

William Morris was born in London to a well-to-do family. He followed the accepted educational path of public school and Oxford University. Whilst at Oxford he met several young men who disparaged the artistic output of the mid-Victorian period. Morris associated the vulgarisation of art with the growth of capitalism and saw the answer at that time in a return to medieval relationships.

Recognising the ugliness of the art of the period as the result of the industrialisation of production in the interest of profits, Morris sought a solution in social terms. He found it in Marx's *Capital*. His reaction to basic Socialism was to assert that unless art became the people's art, it would cease to be; that workers must understand and appreciate art and that artists must consider themselves as workers. This conclusion led to the establishment of the Morris and Company firm, which transformed conceptions of Victorian middle-class living and became financially extremely successful.

Morris became a skilled artist. He made furniture, designed hangings, printed books and wove tapestries. He tried his hand at carpet making and upholstery and in both he excelled. He disliked the garishness of chemical dyes and pioneered a return to the use of vegetable dyes.

As a result of these efforts, Morris became increasingly conscious of the contradictions of capitalism, and he undertook to pass on this understanding in his writing, his speaking and through his political activity.

In 1883, he joined the Democratic Federation, but as a result of Hyndman's desire to dominate the organisation, Morris led a walkout at the end of 1884. The Socialist League was formed before the end of that year.

Within two months of its formation, the new party had brought out a paper, *The Commonweal*, and with the support of Aveling, Bax, Eleanor Marx and Frederick Engels, the paper began to flourish. But in 1890, when it fell into the hands of an Anarchist clique, Morris was driven out of the League and removed from the editorship of the paper.

Consequently, at the age of 57, Morris started to build up a new socialist organisation, the Hammersmith Socialist Society. By this time, however, his most active days were over.

Overall, Morris's contribution to the development of the revival of socialism was enormous. His penetration into the world of art and design opened new avenues away from narrow economic and political concerns. He saw the class struggle in all aspects of working-class life and his contribution stretched over many areas of activity. He had new ideas for artists, writers, poets and craftsmen. While expressing himself in revolutionary terms, his ideas were accessible: he succeeded in evoking a response from working people.

On his death at the age of 62, a branch of the Lancashire SDF made the following comment: 'Comrade Morris is not dead – there is not a socialist alive who would believe him dead, for he lives in the heart of all true men and women still, and will do so to the end of time.'

Sources

E.P. Thompson, *William Morris, Romantic to Revolutionary,* Lawrence & Wishart, 1955.
R. Page Arnot, *William Morris, A Vindication,* Martin Lawrence, 1934.

Introduction by H.M. Hyndman

When I returned this morning from following the hearse which carried William Morris's body from that old house on the Mall at Hammersmith, where so many Socialists have gathered to hear the charming conversation of our dead comrade and leader, it was with the feeling common to us all that we have lost one whose place can never be filled. The last time I had seen him there was on a bright Sunday morning, just before his sea-trip to the North. He seemed to me much better than he had been on my previous visit, and he talked almost as quickly and vigorously as of old on the various topics which interested him, working the while with pencil and brush on a design that lay before him. With that frank, open-hearted expression of his feelings about himself to his friends which was habitual with him, he in nowise disguised how irksome his illness, with its inevitable restriction of his activity, was to him. 'If it merely means that I am to be laid up for a little while, it doesn't so much matter, you know; but if I am to be caged up here for months, and then it is to be the end of all things, I shouldn't like it at all. This has been a jolly world to me, and I find plenty to do in it.' And then he went on to speak of the work before him, and the many things he had to complete. As, later, we took a turn or two round the garden together, and he still seemed to have gained strength, I hoped, in spite of his wasted frame and somewhat pinched face, that modern science might save for us for yet a few more years one of the greatest men of his time. But the end has come – too soon for the lovers of his work and himself; too soon, also, in view of what he was still in process of doing, for the world of art and letters; too soon certainly, for that newer world of Socialism for which he had worked so hard and had already accomplished so much.

It is not my purpose to speak here at any length of William Morris as a writer and an artist. I doubt whether anyone can judge adequately at present of the value of what he has done. That his poetry and his prose were both exquisite in their kind, even critics acknowledge who just now seem to be inclined to belittle him with faint praise. To those of us to whom 'The Life and Death of Jason' and the 'Earthly Paradise,' not to speak of 'The Defence of Guenevere,' were among the chief literary delights of early manhood, this sort of depreciatory comment appears altogether out of place. After the cold classicism of Tennyson, and the tumble and turmoil of Swinburne's vigorous early poetry, these charming volumes of Morris's came as a sweet and delicious music. If it all seems too easy and too musical, we can only wish that a few of the versifiers we have still with us could be too facile and too tuneful in the same way. The charm which steals over the reader of Morris's verses may well enthral the lovers of poetry of the next and succeeding generations more than it attracts the hasty critics of our own. It is true that neither in his prose nor in his verse do you find a trace of that genial and almost boisterous humour which frequently broke out in his familiar conversation. And that seems strange; for that he had much that was Chaucerian in his humour, as in his rhythm, is beyond all question. The verses which he wrote from time to time for the Socialists are in quite another style. Naturally enough their great merit is overlooked by men who think that his reputation would have been greater if he had died before he became active in the Socialist movement. To such people the 'Dream of John Ball' – *The Times* calls it the 'Dream of John *Bull*' – is doubtless a weak and ineffective piece of prose! We know better.

As an artist, however, Morris had a greater influence than as a man of letters. That love, appreciation, and accurate reflection of nature and beauty of form which comes out at every turn of his poetry – the twittering of birds, the sighing of the wind among trees, the splendour of the sunshine, the cool pleasantness of evening, was ever with him, and he couldn't keep still for desire to give expression to that which he felt. What was inartistic and untrue jarred upon him so acutely that he was driven to try and put it right all at once. This accounts for the complete revolution which he brought about – aided by others, it is true, but in great part of his own initiative – this accounts, I say, for the revolution which he wrought not in one but in many departments of art. Furniture, decoration, wall paper, coloured glass, block printing, book-printing, tapestry, ironwork, 'restoration' of ancient buildings – his influence was greatly felt in all of them, and in some he lived to see complete change in the taste of the educated classes, and even of the public at large. Of such a man as this, with his marvellous versatility and genius in all arts but one, it may be truly said that death is but an incident, and not the most important incident, in his career. His life as expressed in his work is as living to us today as when he himself sat chatting and smoking in that lofty room at Hammersmith with the glorious Eastern carpet hanging down on the one side and the equally splendid portraits by Rossetti standing out from the wall on the other.

It was many years after I had enjoyed Morris's poetry, and mocked a little, as ignorant young men will, at his aesthetic armchairs and wall-papers – did he not say himself, 'There are no greater fools than those who buy my papers – except those who don't'? – that I met the man himself. What a shock the first meeting was. It was in 1879. I had written some articles on India in the *Nineteenth Century* which had made a little stir, and Mr. Henry Broadhurst invited me to deliver an address on India to a committee of some sort of which Morris was a member, at 19, Buckingham Street, Strand. Morris had been more active than perhaps anybody else against the Turks. I, as it chanced, though having no love for the Turks, had worked hard on the other side against Russia. I imagined him as a refined and delicate gentleman easily overwrought by his sentiments. That was not his appearance in the flesh, as we all know. Refinement undoubtedly there was in the delicate lines of the nose and the beautiful moulding of the forehead. But his hearty voice, his jolly vigorous frame, his easy sailor-like dress – the whole figure gave me a better opinion of the atrocity-mongers, as I considered them, than anything I have seen before or since. Not until the end of 1882 or the beginning of 1883 did I see Morris again. Then the SDF (as the Democratic Federation) was holding a series of meetings on 'Practical Remedies for Pressing Needs' in the large hall at Westminster Palace Chambers. The subjects were the now familiar Eight Hours Law, Free Meals for Children, Nationalisation of Railways, and so on. Morris came to the first discussion, and forthwith joined the body. It is difficult, perhaps, for men who have come into the movement of late years to understand how we welcomed capable recruits in those days of very small things. True, we had with us, Helen Taylor, Joynes, Champion, Burrows, Quelch, Williams, James Murray, and other active people; but, even so, we were few and Socialism was new. Morris, with his great reputation and high character, doubled our strength at a stroke, by giving in his adhesion. And how he worked! He was as ready to do anything as the youngest and least known of us. In fact, he resented attempts being made to keep him back from doing things which he really ought not to have done. Writing, speaking in and out of doors, conferring, full of zeal and brimming over with good humour and suggestion – it all seems but yesterday. When *Justice* was started with Edward Carpenter's money – in January, 1884, he threw himself into it with vigour, and wrote frequently. We then thought and said that we should all work on together in harmony to the end. Alas! that was not to be. Happily, however, the differences which arose in the autumn of 1884 were composed, and for many years past the relations of the SDF and all its branches with William Morris were as cordial as they ever had been before. Again he wrote poems for *Justice,* again he lectured for our branches and kindly contributed to our funds. He spoke, also, most vigorously and generously in support of our Parliamentary candidates in Burnley and Walworth; and his last appearance on a public platform was at our New Year's meeting in the Holborn Town Hall in January last. He then met with a reception from the crowded audience so hearty and so enthusiastic that I know, from what he said afterwards, that he felt that his work for the cause was fully understood and appreciated by the men whom he was endeavouring to serve. He was ill at the time, and I fear that even coming to this meeting was an overtasking of his strength. None who were present will ever forget the touching appeal that he then made or the words of council and good cheer that he then spoke.

And now we have lost the man whom we all loved and respected – the great poet and artist who devoted his high faculties to the service of the race. William Morris we shall see no more; but the memory of what he was will ever remain with us – sweet as the music of his verse, and encouraging as the hearty welcome with which he never failed to greet his comrades in the cause.

H. M. Hyndman,
6 October 1896

*   *   *

I am asked by the Editor to give some sort of a history of the above conversion, and I feel that it may be of some use to do so, if my readers will look upon me as a type of a certain group of people, but not so easy to do clearly, briefly and truly. Let me, however, try. But first, I will say what I mean by being a Socialist, since I am told that the word no longer expresses definitely and with certainty what it did ten years ago. Well, what I mean by Socialism is a condition of society in which there should be neither rich nor poor, neither master nor master's man, neither idle nor overworked, neither brain-sick brain workers, nor heart-sick hand workers, in a word, in which all men would be living in equality of condition, and would manage their affairs unwastefully, and with the full consciousness that harm to one would mean harm to all – the realisation at last of the meaning of the word *commonwealth.*

Now this view of Socialism which I hold today, and hope to die holding, is what I began with; I had no transitional period, unless you may call such a brief period of political radicalism during which I saw my ideal clear enough, but had no hope of any realisation of it. That came to an end some months before I joined the (then) Democratic Federation, and the meaning of my joining that body was that I had conceived a hope of the realisation of my ideal. If you ask me how much of a hope, or what I thought we Socialists then living and working would accomplish towards it, or when there would be effected any change in the face of society, I must say, I do not know. I can only say that I did not measure my hope, nor the joy that it brought me at the time. For the rest, when I took that step I was blankly ignorant of economics; I had never so much as opened Adam Smith,[1] or heard of Ricardo,[2] or of Karl Marx. Oddly enough, I *had* read some of Mill, to wit, those posthumous papers of his (published, was it in the *Westminster Review* or the *Fortnightly?*) in which he attacks Socialism in its Fourierist[3] guise. In those papers he put the arguments, as far as they go, clearly and honestly, and the result, so far as I was concerned, was to convince me that Socialism was a necessary change, and that it was possible to bring it about in our own days. Those papers put the finishing touch to my conversion to Socialism. Well, having joined a Socialist body (for the Federation soon became definitely Socialist), I put some conscience into trying to learn the economical side of Socialism, and even tackled Marx, though I must confess that, whereas I thoroughly enjoyed the historical part of *Capital*, I suffered agonies of confusion of the brain over reading the pure economics of that great work. Anyhow, I read what I could, and will hope that some information stuck to me from my reading; but more, I must think, from continuous conversation with such friends as Bax[4] and Hyndman[5] and Scheu[6], and the brisk course of propaganda meetings which were going on at the time, and in which I took my share. Such finish to what of education in practical Socialism as I am capable of I received afterwards from some of my Anarchist friends, from whom I learned, quite against their intention, that Anarchism[7] was impossible, much as I learned from Mill against *his* intention that Socialism was necessary.

But in this telling how I fell into *practical* Socialism I have begun, as I perceive, in the middle, for in my position of a well-to-do man, not suffering from the disabilities which oppress a working man at every step, I feel that I might never have been drawn into the practical side of the question if an ideal had not forced me to seek towards it. For politics as politics, i.e., not regarded as a necessary if cumbersome and disgustful means to an end, would never have attracted me, nor when I had become conscious of the wrongs of society as it now is, and the oppression of poor people, could I have ever believed in the possibility of a *partial* setting right of those wrongs. In other words, I could never have been such a fool as to believe in the happy and 'respectable' poor.

If, therefore, my ideal forced me to look for practical Socialism, what was it that forced me to conceive of an ideal? Now, here comes in what I said of my being (in this paper) a type of a certain group of mind.

Before the uprising of *modern* Socialism almost all intelligent people either were, or professed themselves to be quite contented with the civilisation of this century. Again, almost all of these really were thus contented, and saw nothing to do but to perfect the said civilisation by getting rid of a few ridiculous survivals of the barbarous ages. To be short, this was the Whig[8] frame of mind, natural to the modern prosperous middle-class men, who, in fact, as far as mechanical progress is concerned, have nothing to ask for, if only Socialism would leave them alone to enjoy their plentiful style.

But besides these contented ones there were others who were not really contented, but had a vague sentiment of repulsion to the triumph of civilisation, but were coerced into silence by the measureless power of Whiggery. Lastly, there were a few who were in open rebellion against the said Whiggery – a few, say two, Carlyle[9] and Ruskin.[10] The latter, before my days of practical Socialism, was my master towards the ideal aforesaid, and, looking backward, I cannot help saying, by the way, how deadly dull the world would have been twenty years ago but for Ruskin! It was through him that I learned to give form to my discontent, which I must say was not by any means vague. Apart from the desire to produce beautiful things, the leading passion of my life has been and is hatred of modern civilisation. What shall I say of it now, when the words are put into my mouth, my hope of its destruction – what shall I say of its supplanting by Socialism?

What shall I say concerning its mastery of and its waste of mechanical power, its commonwealth so poor, its enemies of the commonwealth so rich, its stupendous organisation – for the misery of life! Its contempt of simple pleasures which everyone could enjoy but for its folly? Its eyeless vulgarity which has destroyed art, the one certain solace of labour? All this I felt then as now, but I did not know why it was so. The hope of the past times was gone, the struggles of mankind for many ages had produced nothing but its sordid, aimless, ugly confusion; the immediate future seemed to me likely to intensify all the present evils by sweeping away the last survivals of the days before the dull squalor of civilisation had settled down on the world. This was a bad look-out indeed, and, if I may mention myself as a personality and not as a mere type, especially so to a man of my disposition, careless of metaphysics and religion, as well as of scientific analysis, but with a deep love of the earth and the life on it, and a passion for the history of the past of mankind. Think of it! Was it all to end in a counting-house on the top of a cinder-heap with Podsnap's drawing-room in the offing, and a Whig committee dealing out champagne to the rich and margarine to the poor in such convenient proportions as would make all men contented together, though the pleasure of the eyes was gone from the world, and the place of Homer was to be taken by Huxley? Yet, believe me, in my heart, when I really forced myself to look towards the future, that is what I saw in it, and, as far as I could tell, scarce anyone seemed to think it worth while to struggle against such a consummation of civilisation. So there I was in for a fine pessimistic end of life, if it had not somehow dawned on me that amidst all this filth of civilisation the seeds of a great chance, what we others call Social-Revolution, were beginning to germinate. The whole face of things was changed to me by that discovery, and all I had to do then in order to become a Socialist was to hook myself on to the practical movement, which, as before said, I have tried to do as well as I could.

To sum up, then, the study of history and the love and practice of art forced me into a hatred of the civilisation which, if things were to stop as they are, would turn history into inconsequent nonsense, and make art a collection of the curiosities of the past, which would have no serious relation to the life of the present.

But the consciousness of revolution stirring amidst our hateful modern society prevented me, luckier than many others of artistic perceptions, from crystallising into a mere railer against 'progress' on the one hand, and on the other from wasting time and energy in any of the numerous schemes by which the quasi-artistic of the middle classes hope to make art grow when it has no longer any root, and thus I became a practical Socialist.

A last word or two. Perhaps some of our friends will say, what have we to do with these matters of history and art? We want by means of Social-Democracy to win a decent livelihood, we want in some sort to live, and that at once. Surely any one who professes to think that the question of art and cultivation must go before that of the knife and fork (and there are some who do propose that) does not understand what art means, or how that its roots must have a soil of a thriving and unanxious life. Yet it must be remembered that civilisation has reduced the workman to such a skinny and pitiful existence, that he scarcely knows how to frame a desire for any life much better than that which he now endures perforce. It is the province of art to set the true ideal of a full and reasonable life before him, a life to which the perception and creation of beauty, the enjoyment of real pleasure that is, shall be felt to be as necessary to man as his daily bread, and that no man, and no set of men, can be deprived of this except by mere opposition, which should be resisted to the utmost.

Reprinted from *Justice* [11]

Change of Position – not Change of Condition

To the Socialist, who is earnest in wishing to stimulate the genuine and practical desire of the workers towards freedom, and who knows well that no mere good nature of individuals can make a system tolerable which is designed for the benefit of the privileged classes only – to the Socialist the aim is not the improvement of condition but *the change in position* of the working classes. For he has full confidence that the change in position must have the immediate consequence of the bettering of condition. I am aware that to many or most of the readers of Justice these remarks will seem trite, yet I think some form of the thought in them is necessary to be put before people at present. For, to say the truth if I were a non-Socialist and were interested in the preservation of the society of privilege, I should conceive a hope from the present situation of the possibility of hoodwinking the working men into accepting what I should name (to them) a kind of semi or demi-semi-Socialism, which would do no sort of harm to the society of privilege. I should condescend to Socialism, and pat it on the back. I should say, as, indeed, I have heard such worthies say, 'Socialism, my friends, cannot give what it promises, but I am pleased to see you Socialists, because all this labour agitation will call people's attention to the "condition of the working classes," and will "improve it." You will find that you must work *with* the capitalists and not *against* them, so that you may extend markets, contend successfully with other nations and improve business. By that means, though this Socialist agitation is founded on principles which are wrong, and cannot be carried out in practice, yet it will have given you enhanced wages, reduction of the hours of labour, more permanency of employment, better housing, gas and water galore, and an extended franchise. And then (but I don't know when) you will be happy and contented, and, which is more to the point, so shall we.'

That, I say, will be the sort of line to take for those who wish to keep labour – i.e., usefulness – out of its heritage, and I think it will be taken, I fear not wholly unsuccessfully. For the present necessities of working people are so great that they must take what they can get, and it is so hard for them in their miserable condition to have any vivid conception of what a life of freedom and equality can give them that they can scarcely, the average of them, turn their hopes to a future which they may never see.

And yet if that future is not to be indefinitely postponed they must repudiate this demi-semi-Socialism. They must say: '£2 a week instead of £1; eight hours work instead of nine, ten, twelve; out-of-door relief galore to supplement the out-of-work periods; comfortable (Lord help us!) lodgings found by the municipality – all these are fine things indeed. But we will not even think of them unless we can use them for getting all the benefits which we *know* will follow on the abolition of privilege and the realisation of equality. That is, in short, what we mean to have. What those benefits may be we cannot imagine in detail; but we know that the sum of them will mean a decent self-respecting life for us all. We are Socialists and believe in Socialism, and the day will come when we shall partly be able to estimate our gains by looking back and wondering that we once thought it worth while to strive for such petty advantages as those you have been telling us of.'

And again and again it must be said that in this determination we shall be justified when the working classes make it their determination; and further, for last word, that the first step towards this consummation is the union in one party of all those in the movement who take that view of the movement, and not merely the gas and water and improved trade union view. The view not of improved condition for the workers, but of essentially changed position.

Justice, May Day, 1895

The Promise of May

Certainly May Day is above all days of the year fitting for the protest of the disinherited against the system of robbery that shut the door betwixt them and a decent life. The day when the promise of the year reproaches the waste inseparable from the society of inequality, the waste which produces our artificial poverty of civilisation, so much bitterer for those that suffer under it than the natural poverty of the rudest barbarism. For it is undoubtedly true that full-blown capitalism makes the richest country in the world as poor as, nay poorer than, the poorest, for the life of by far the greater part of its people.

Are we to sit down placidly under this, hoping that some blessing will drop down from heaven upon us which will bring content and self-respect and a due share of the beauties and joys of the earth to the classes that produce all that is produced, while it will bring no lessening of the dignity and ease and sweetness of life with which the possessing (and wasting) classes are now endowed?

Most of you will smile at that question, but remember that this opinion was not long ago universally held, and is still held by many.

They think that civilisation will grow so speedily and triumphantly, and production will become so easy and cheap, that the possessing classes will be able to spare more and more from the great heap of wealth to the producing classes, so that at least these latter will have nothing left to wish for, and all will be peace and prosperity. A futile hope, indeed, and one which a mere glance at past history will dispel. For we find, as a matter of fact, that we were scarcely emerging from semi-barbarism, when open violence was common, and privilege need put on no mask before the governed classes, the workers were not worse off than now, but better. In short, not all the discoveries of science, not all the tremendous organisation of the factory and the market, will produce true wealth, so long as the end and aim of it all is the production of profit for the privileged classes.

And I say this is an irresistible instinct on the part of the capitalists, an impulse like hunger, and I believe that it can only be met with another hunger, the hunger for freedom and fair play for all, both people and peoples. Anything less than that the capitalist power will brush aside but that they cannot; for what will it mean? The most important part of their machinery, the 'hands' becoming *men*, and saying, 'Now at last we will it; we will produce no more for profit but for *use*, for *happiness*, for *life*.'

Justice, May Day, 1896

Notes

1. Adam Smith (1723–90); Scottish political economist. The founder of classical economics as a science. His reputation was made with his work, *The Wealth of Nations*, the philosophy of which was individual interest.

2. David Ricardo (1772–1823); political economist considered by Marx to be the greatest master of classical economics, and Member of Parliament 1819–23.

3. Francois Marie Charles Fourier (1772–1837). French Utopian-Socialist critic of capitalist society, who expected to achieve his aims by peaceful propaganda of Socialist ideas among the Capitalists. He failed to understand the nature of class society.

4. E. Belfort Bax (1854–1926); socialist writer especially on history and philosophy. A barrister by profession, was a founder member of the Democratic Federation, and then in 1884 left the Federation with Morris to form the Socialist League. Helped form the British Socialist Party in 1911 but abandoned the party in 1916 because of his, pro-war position. Distinguished himself by being strongly opposed to women's suffrage.

5. H.M. Hyndman; *see* Chapter 11.

6. Andreas Scheu (1844–1927); prominent member of both the Austrian and British Socialist movements. Founder member and activist of the Social Democratic Federation. Emigrated to Britain in 1874.

7. Anarchism: a petty-bourgeois sociopolitical trend that is hostile to all authority or organisation. Extreme individualism.

8. Whigs made themselves special guardians of the liberties of the people. They hoped to gain from popular expansion and the development of individual freedom. As the opposition party to the Tories, Whigs represented the manufacturers against the landed gentry.

9. Thomas Carlyle: *see* Tom Mann *The Socialists' Program*, n. 1.

10. John Ruskin (1819–1900); romantic and critic. Studied and taught at Oxford. His ideal was patriarchal handicraft production which he sought to revive. Had considerable influence among working people.

11. *Justice*: organ of Social Democracy. Published 1884–1933; edited by H.M. Hyndman, Harry Quelch and W.H. Lee.

7
The Socialists' Program

TOM MANN

Introduction

Tom Mann was the son of a colliery clerk in Foleshill near Coventry. Tom started work on a colliery farm at nine years old and was sent down the pits at the age of ten. He crawled on his hands and knees in the darkness, with belt and chain dragging boxes full of dirt and coal through the tunnels.

When his family moved to Birmingham when he was 13, he started work as a printer's devil before serving an apprenticeship as a toolmaker in an engineering factory. When he was 16, the working day was reduced to nine hours, giving him an opportunity to expand on his very elementary education. He attended evening classes three days a week, finding time to attend political meetings where he was able to hear such speakers as Charles Bradlaugh, Annie Besant and George Jacob Holyoake.

He moved to London in search of work in 1876, and was employed in a number of engineering factories. He joined the Amalgamated Society of Engineers (ASE) in 1881. It was then that he read Henry George's *Progress and Poverty,* from which he gained an understanding of the nature of the economic system and an urge to participate in direct political action in order to change it.

He was soon to be found in the thick of any struggle by which workers hoped to better themselves and their condition. In 1885 he joined the Battersea Branch of the Social Democratic Federation, of which John Burns was also a member. The two of them set about campaigning for an eight-hour day for workers in industry, and Tom Mann's pamphlet, *What a Compulsory Eight-hour Working Day Means to the Workers,* spearheaded the attack.

Tom Mann's reputation as a propagandist and agitator increased and his leadership of the 1889 dock strike was accepted without question. His reputation so alarmed the establishment that he was in fact unable to get a job in London and had to move to Bolton in Lancashire. Here his powers of oratory grew.

Mann took part in a great many campaigns at home and abroad. From 1889 to the last 1930 hunger march, he was among the leaders in almost all the working people's struggles, of skilled and unskilled workers alike. There is hardly an industry in Britain that did not become better organised as a result of his efforts.

Mann did not confine his campaigning to trade unions. He was General Secretary of the Independent Labour Party (ILP) 1894–8, and an advocate of anti-militarism. In 1896 he contested Aberdeen North as ILP candidate in a straight fight against the Liberal candidate Captain Pirie. His selection as the ILP candidate took place at a meeting on 25 April 1896, during which he gave a speech reproduced here as *The Socialists' Program*, as it was published by the Labour Press Society, Manchester. Aberdeen North was a strong Liberal constituency and Mann was beaten by only 430 votes in a total poll of 4,500.

Tom Mann advocated the socialist objective of the 'common ownership of the means of production and distribution'. He supported shorter working hours, municipalisation, pensions and the nationalisation of selected industries and the land.

In 1912 Mann was imprisoned for publishing a 'Don't Shoot' leaflet appealing to soldiers not to intervene in strikes, and in 1920 he became a founder member of the British Communist Party.

Mann was a lifelong member of the engineering union that began as the ASE, and it was while he was Secretary of the union that the changes took place that led to the creation of the Amalgamated Engineering Union (AEU).

Sources
Tom Mann's Memoirs, Labour Publishing Company, 1923.
Dona Torr, *Tom Mann*, Lawrence & Wishart, 1936.

*   *   *

Friends, you are probably aware that I am here on the express invitation of a number of electors of North Aberdeen. I am not here to ask anyone to kindly invite me. I would be ashamed of any such behaviour, and hope I ever shall be ashamed of anything that savours of such behaviour. Having accepted the invitation which was duly forwarded, I am glad to know that I am here as the first of the candidates to address an open meeting of the electors of North Aberdeen; to state my principles and my policy fearlessly, fully, and frankly, not caring in the least whether you are pleased with it or whether you are displeased with it.

I have certain definite views which in past years I have advocated as effectively as I have known how. These views will be advocated by me during this campaign, and whether they are liked or lumped, they won't be modified to please the electorate. I shall ask you to remember in the first instance that we are citizens of a country that stands, in many senses, pre-eminent amongst the civilised nations of the world, and I am not insensible to the importance of our country industrially and commercially, neither am I insensible to the voice that our country is capable of exercising the influence she possesses and the commanding position she generally obtains and upholds in the Councils of the nations. Whilst that is so, I wish to make it perfectly clear at the outset, that I am not one who is able to subscribe to the general policy, that because we have what is termed the British empire, which, in area, is very vast, whose citizens are practically one-sixth of the inhabitants of the globe, and because our country, in particular, is very wealthy indeed, when compared with most civilised nations – I am not prepared on that account to bow down and worship all that is, as though everything were as it ought to be. On the contrary, I come before you as a workman, and in my capacity as a workman, with the responsibilities of a workman's life, having been brought into contact with the rough and tumble side of life, being myself what is termed a skilled artisan, and having been for many years a member of one of the recognised trade unions of our country, which indeed, covers not only our own country, but is international in a genuine sense, covering foreign countries and the colonies; having been also brought into direct contact with the labourer's side of life as distinct from the skilled artisan's, knowing, therefore, what a worker's position is by my own everyday experience, and having carefully studied the general industrial and social situation, I am not, as a result, prepared to worship institutions that exist as if they were even approximately perfect.

On the contrary, I am one of those who have declared my dissatisfaction with things as they are, who holds that the institutions that we have in our country require to be changed in a very important and serious sense, because I know, only too well – and many of you must know also – that there is a very large proportion of our fellow-men and women in the busy cities and towns, aye, and in villages, who are deprived of the means of an ordinary livelihood, not through any fault of their own, but because of an awkward industrial and social environment that they are powerless to control. Therefore are they in the slough of despond, bound down with the bonds of poverty, and as a consequence are suffering most acutely. As an ordinary citizen, an ordinary man of the world, I have recognised it to be my bounden duty during the past, and at this hour, to endeavour to understand what ought to be my individual relationship with other men and other women, not with one section of the community, but with the whole community. I have tried to understand how it comes about that one section of our country can, with very little effort on their part, obtain not only an abundance of that which is necessary for life and well-being, but much more than is sufficient for themselves and those dependent on them, whilst those working very hard and working relatively very long, can scarce get enough of the bare necessaries of life.

In face of the appalling fact known to every student of our industrial and social position, that there are not merely thousands, or tens of thousands, or hundreds of thousands, but actually millions of our fellow citizens who cannot at any time obtain sufficient of the bare necessaries of life – in face of such mental, physical, and moral degradation – I am not prepared to worship the grandeur, the so-called glory of the British Empire. No country can be looked upon as satisfactory that does not afford a proper livelihood for every decently-behaved citizen. Whilst I am not prepared to decry our own country as against other countries, I refuse to be associated with those who seem to find some satisfaction in declaring that a Britisher is a very superior person to any other countryman and I refuse to subscribe to any such policy because in the aggregate we may truthfully be described as a rich and wealthy nation, that, therefore, all is comparatively well. I know that all is not well, but very far from well, indeed; and therefore, I have been what many persons like to term 'An Agitator,' and I am at this time *An Agitator, and intend to remain one.*

If the respectabilities of North Aberdeen are not pleased with the general behaviour of such an agitator there will be no pleading on my part that you should try to. I only want to make a frank, full confession, being, as I have said, utterly indifferent as to what your judgment shall be after you have heard my statement. I do now interchange views with you by asking if you are aware of the standard of life that obtains throughout the length and breadth of our country. When I speak of our country, of course I am referring to the entire British Isles. Are you aware that 24s. per week represents the average wage received by the whole adult male workers of Britain, and that out of that there has to be paid in some districts no less than an average of 9s. per week as rent for reasonable accommodation for an ordinary-sized family; and further, that when I describe that as the average – I am using official figures, quoting, indeed, from Robert Giffen, the statistician to the Board of Trade, who, in his evidence recently before the Royal Commission on Labour (of which I happened to be a member) made the statement that £60 a year represented the earning capacity of the ordinary adult male in Britain; now, I venture to declare that £60 per year is not sufficient to secure those means of life and well-being that we may at this time in reason expect to be able to obtain as respectably-behaved and industrious citizens.

Program and Policy

I therefore ask you to recognise this, that the whole of my program and the whole of my policy will bear directly upon raising the standard of life for the entire working population of our nation. Holding, as I do, that Parliament should exist primarily for the purpose of contributing to the advancement of those who create the wealth of the nation, in order that there shall be an honest, and therefore equitable, apportionment of the wealth created amongst those who take part in creating it. The poverty, and as a consequence, the crime and misery, that exist are of so appalling a character that we have those who profess to have regard for their removal in almost every rank of life. It is perfectly true that there are such among politicians, that some statesmen can be mentioned, that philanthropists can be named outside the ranks of working men and women, and outside the ranks of those with whom I commonly associate, but whilst that is so, I am bound to ask you to recognise that good intention is not in itself sufficient to remove the serious evils we are burdened with. We must not only be possessed of good intentions, we must have the requisite knowledge to understand the exact why and wherefore of our relatively degraded position, and also must we be able to understand what principle it is necessary to apply in order to rectify the evil. Now, without any disparagement of any individual, or any section of Parliamentarians, I am bound to express my conviction that the average man that seeks to get returned to Parliament is not generally characterised as a student of sociological conditions. The average man, who has sought to get returned to Parliament, and has generally succeeded, has rather been a man of the capitalist or landlord class – classes raised entirely on the shoulders of the real workers – whilst the workers themselves, the actual wealth producers of our nation, have hitherto, for the most part, been content to return to Parliament, and to other places, those very plutocrats and aristocrats who have been living at their expense, and who intend, and have always admitted that they intend to uphold, to maintain, to buttress up the existing orthodox institutions that shall admit in future of a plutocracy and aristocracy living at the expense of a democracy.

Democracy and the Sovereign

I believe I am correct in stating that throughout the world there is now a general awakening to a consciousness that there is something vitally wrong in the constitutions of our various civilised nations: that the caste or class system has hitherto been permitted to dominate over the mass of the people. Some of them are kind enough to declare that the people, unless they are controlled, unless they are guided, unless they are manoeuvred, unless they are driven, cannot exist except as so many cattle. Such are the declarations in one form or another made by representative plutocrats and autocrats. And in one country we find a despotic Czar, without any semblance of representative government, who can, at his own sweet will, decree that certain citizens shall be banished for ever from their country, and the order is peremptorily carried out; who can decree that because a man dares to exercise his manhood and express dissatisfaction with the conditions that obtain, that that is to be a sufficient crime to warrant his expulsion from his fatherland, and to carry him to a penal settlement. In another country, we have a despotic Kaiser, who, although there is something in the nature of a representative government, has at present a sufficient backing on the part of the plutocracy that he can and does wield a power and an influence that is distasteful and nauseating to the nature of a really developed man or woman. In another country – our nearest neighbour – we have what purports to be a republican government. It is in a funny position, I am bound to admit, just now, but they are very rarely in other than a funny position. Over this people there is neither Czar nor Kaiser, nor Empress Queen. Nevertheless there is a dominating plutocracy exercising control over the mass of the people, and insisting on a plutocratic domination continuously.

In our own country we have a limited monarchy – a monarch that is respected, and perhaps deservedly so, for various reasons. But all the same I am bound to express my conviction that in proportion as men become men and women become women they will require neither Czar, Kaiser, nor Empress Queen. I am identified with those who hold that an intelligent community should be their own government, if they require a government at all; that to entrust sovereign power, even with various limitations, indicates the relative childhood of a nation, and if it should be the case – as I venture to suggest it is – that the British nation are developing mentally, why, then, the time is approaching when, with much respect – and with much grace, doubtless – we shall be able to dispense with sovereigns altogether. But let none suppose that I place very much value upon that. I have purposely referred to it for the sake of frankly indicating the trend of opinion which I am favouring; but at the same time I know full well that a mere Republican Government, as ordinarily understood, as witnessed in any civilised country that can be named today, would do us no good whatever – because none of them have recognised where the real burden comes in.

Why Poverty Exists

It is for me, therefore, to ask you to please recognise this, that the first essential of civilised life, perhaps also of savage life, are food, clothing, shelter, and some amount of recreation. We have not them in sufficient abundance. Why have we them not? Does not the productive capacity of our people in Britain admit of a much higher standard than that which obtains? The answer is: Yea, for an absolute certainty. If it does, then by what means can we make the requisite changes that shall drive poverty from the land, and establish foundations of peace and plenty? I argue that our prime use for parliament should be to enable the democracy to obtain such control of its own industrial and social destiny, as shall enable them to become triumphant over those conditions.

If it be true, as I allege, that nature has been sufficiently kind as to supply the children of men with all that is essential to real life and well-being; and if it be also true, that our own nation amongst others, has developed the requisite mental capacity to know how to control the raw material of nature, so that with a wise expenditure of power we possess, with comparative ease, we can produce enough and to spare for everybody, why, then, it becomes our bounden duty to endeavour to understand how it has come about that we have not as yet applied that power wisely, and why we should still require workhouses, jails, street-corner loafers, beggars by the hundred thousand, and ne'er-do-wells in increasing shoals. You require the ne'er-do-wells on the one side, with the jail birds and the slum dwellers, because on the other side you tolerate the system, acquiesce in the system, and have approved of the system that encourages and upholds and maintains, and affords scope and opportunities for company promoters and all that pertains thereto, who live by fleecing, by scheming, by dodging, by trickery, by rascality, and by developing all the qualities that enable them to prosper. And it has generally been that the more successful the exploiter, the greater readiness has been exhibited on the part of the electorate to return such a one (because he has been successful, forsooth!) to the Legislative Assembly in order that there he can continue to exercise a dominant influence, socially, industrially, and politically. But apparently the eyes of a portion of the electorate are being opened, and now there is less satisfaction in fighting for a man simply because he occupies an important position in the social scale; there is less satisfaction now in returning anyone unless they have previously been subjected, as it were, to a cross-examination, and their desires understood and their principles examined and approved of. I do not for one moment pretend that the electorate of Great Britain is remarkably wise; but I think we are warranted in saying that we are getting a little wiser than we were; and if anyone should be disposed to apply this and say, 'Well, we shall show our wisdom by rejecting you,' I shall still acquiesce with the greatest grace and thankfulness. All the same, I ask you now, is it not the case that you and I as citizens of this country, responsible like other citizens for families, being desirous of discharging our duties in a becoming and honourable fashion, unwilling to live at other peoples expense, but not being specially desirous that other able-bodied people should live at our expense – is it not admissible or desirable that we should seek now to apply very definite principles for the rectification of these defects? Are there any here whose social condition is such, or may have been such, that they have never hungered for a meal, who have never known, except by hearsay, what it is to be in want, and who sometimes wonder whether there are any unemployed apart from those who are really indifferent to work? If there are, then I ask you to please put yourself to the trouble to understand the facts of the case, and if you are willing to go, even to the governmental sources – which are not always distinctly favourable to those who are unemployed – and you will find even from such a report as that issued monthly, 'The Labour Gazette,' through the agency of the Labour Department of the Board of Trade, that the proportion of unemployed, as registered by the various unions, is positively appalling compared with what you have probably thought has been the case. I need not trouble to dwell upon this, but I will quote Carlyle:[1] 'Do you notice the horses in the street, and see how relatively well-fed and sleek-coated they are, and are you disposed to urge that it is impossible for British citizens to be equally well fed with British horses?' Such was Carlyle's question, such is mine; and I declare to you, and you know it to be true, that there are hundreds of thousands of British men, women and children whose actual condition is much inferior to the ordinary cart-horse. Carlyle said: 'Do you ask whether it is impossible to obtain as good conditions for British men and women? If so, then clear out of the way and make room for better men and women.' I reiterate Carlyle's statement, and declare that those with whom I am associated – and I hope they will not consider it egotistical – have vowed as men and women may be permitted to vow, and, like Carlyle declare, that for ourselves and our children who are following us, we will spend ourselves in the endeavour to secure to the men, women, and children of our country at least as good conditions as we now give to the ordinary cart-horse.

The Way to Peace and Plenty

The cautious will be disposed to say: 'Of course we can endorse so elementary a statement, but we are not all sure where you would lead if you had the chance.' Then I will tell you by quoting one simple sentence from the autobiography of John Stuart Mill, who ought to be known, and, I presume, is pretty well-known in this district. Speaking, I believe, for himself and his wife, he said: 'The social problem of the future we consider to be how to secure the greatest individual liberty of action, with the common ownership of the raw material of the globe, and the equal participation by all in the benefits of combined labour.' That is the basis upon which I am here tonight. That is the economic basis upon which I am running this election campaign; and if any of you – press included – desire to argue against my Collectivist principles, do not forget that, at the same time, you must argue down the Collectivist principles, clearly expressed, of John Stuart Mill. If you will say that John Stuart Mill was not identified with our particular school of thought, I am prepared to admit the fact, seeing that John Stuart Mill died some years before it was possible for him to be closely identified with it. But if anyone is prepared to fairly face the question, and try to understand the attitude taken up by

Mill in his early years, his middle life, and towards the close of his life, than I think that you will be disposed to declare, that in quoting this sentence, I am quoting Mill's state of mind when he wrote that autobiography, and when doubtless he was in the fullest possession of a developed intellect. And what he saw was forthcoming has come. The social problem he spoke of as being likely to arise in the future, we are living right in the front of; we are in that particular stage when we must face the social problem. I am therefore proposing to deal with the methods whereby we will attack this social problem and try to solve it. The desire is to place within the reach of every properly behaved citizen all that is essential to real life and well-being, therefore we must not have excessive work, and we ought to have enough work.

The Eight Hours Question!

Today the unemployed do not get enough, and the over-worked, of course, get too much, and that lands us right off into the very simple statement and contention, that surely it is desirable that there should be an adjustment with regard to the working hours of men and women of our country. The very just and simplest statement that can be made is that as we find there are men working no less than 16 hours out of 24, and that other men who would be equally capable of work, and who would be glad to have the opportunity of working, are without work, and are suffering in consequence, surely good sense says let us ease up on the one side, and give a little work to the other side. Therefore, it is that the various Trade Unions of our country, as well as other labour sections, have for years been discussing the desirability until they have now reached the position that they say it is absolutely necessary that there should be regulation of working hours, and they have declared in favour of an eight hours working day as being one of the simplest and most practicable steps that can be taken to rectify some of the industrial and social evils of our time. If anybody should be disposed to say that this cannot cure the unemployed problem, I can accompany you in that, but I say it could do a good deal towards rectifying the evils we are now deploring. And it is right and proper and becoming from an economic, industrial, and from a social standpoint, that we should so regulate the working hours. In the first instance, surely it is desirable that not more than eight hours should be spent in obtaining a sufficiency of the bread that perisheth, if we can produce enough in that time. Surely, it is desirable in the interests of men and women who are already actually at work, and even more desirable is it for those men and women who have not the chance to work at all, and who should be afforded an opportunity by those who are working excessively! I know, of course, that it has been said – and probably with a considerable amount of truth – that in certain departments of industry men can soon learn to produce as much in eight hours as they were formerly producing in nine and ten, and good luck to them for being able to do so. But there are many departments of industry where that would be impossible for a very considerable time, and all that there is to be said is that, as soon as we reach a period when as much work can be done in eight hours as can be done in nine or ten, then let us come down to seven, or even six. And if it should appear rather stupid to any of you, then I ask; how do you propose to distribute the advantages of our nation's material progress? If it be true that year by year we are gaining a little over nature, and are capable of producing in five hours, and at a little later stage in four hours, that we formerly produced in six; how would you distribute, but by easing the daily burden all round, and generally equalising the reward of labour? Surely, of all measures, the one that ought to commend itself to the average man and the average woman is that for the regulation of working hours. I am, therefore, in favour of an eight hours' working day for the whole of the trades and industries of our nation. And if any should be disposed to ask: 'Would I refuse to accept any measure that was not really national,' I say 'No, I would not refuse.' If for instance, as happens to be the case, the miners made a special effort, as they have done, to demand an eight hours' day, and having, as I consider they have very special claims for attention in this direction without waiting for the general volume of the nation. If I were in the House I should continue, as I have done out of it, to advocate the reasonableness, wisdom, and the good sense on the part of the miners in insisting on the application of eight hours as the maximum working day in their industry, and if a little later other industries should be disposed to make advances, out of proportion to the general body, I should, of course be prepared to back up their demands, and to do all in my power to see that it was applied to them at the earliest possible moment; but I declare fearlessly and frankly in favour of a maximum eight hours working day for all.

Treatment for Physical Wrecks

That would do something towards solving the unemployed problems, but it could not really solve it. I know that something else would be necessary, and I know there are many classed as unemployed who are at the present hour physically unfit for labour for various reasons. They have been out of work too long a time, they have had insufficient food, and live in unhealthy conditions generally, and they cannot compete in accordance with the demands of the competitive system, nor are they likely ever to be able to, unless some special steps are taken, I therefore declare in favour of the State, that is the executive of the State, in conjunction with the various local governing bodies, taking such action as shall afford a reasonable outlet for the energy possessed by persons like unto whom I am referring. By this I mean that just as I, the father of a family, am bound to have regard for every child for which I am responsible, whether the child be capable or not, as compared with some others, is not the child's concern, it is my concern, and so with regard to the State. If we believe in Constitutional Government, if we believe in the community's Executive, if we are disposed to use it in the interest of the democracy, why, then, who will say it is not the duty of such an Executive to have regard for those who have been the victims of an awkward environment? Surely that is quite fair as a matter of common humanity. I ask that it should be recognised that those who have been victimised, from whatever cause, should have special attention paid to them, and I believe it would become quite an easy matter for the Executive Government along with the local administrative bodies, to obtain control of the land in the right districts, and place those persons either upon it, or in industrial undertakings in connection with such a colony, and thus make it possible for them first to receive the requisite training, and then to become actual producers of what they require to consume, and probably, at no distant date, of a margin over and above that. And if there are any disposed to say, 'Ah, but it would be a tax upon the community,' remember that, from the fact that they are living, they are a tax upon the community now. There is no jail-bird or street-corner loafer not living at the community's expense, and what I am proposing is simply a scientific method of providing for their requirements, and doing it in a becoming and dignified way that shall not disgrace our common humanity.

Production in Great Britain

In conjunction with this, I would ask you to recognise that the British nation is not producing a large proportion of food stuffs it consumes, and it is held by many, and by many whose opinions I think are worth noting, that it is desirable, aye, and becoming very necessary, that we should produce in Britain a larger proportion of food stuffs than we now do. The fact is we produce only one-third of the food stuffs we require to consume. It is not because the land will not yield, it is not because the requisite good sense does not exist, but it is because there has been a general rush to produce wealth by the capitalistic section in the easiest possible fashion, irrespective of the well-being of the community.

Without trying to put the blame on any particular shoulder, I simply ask that it be recognised that the day is rapidly approaching when British commercial supremacy will be seriously questioned and threatened. Nay, not approaching; it has approached, it is right here – I would remind you that the Right Hon. John Morley[2] quite recently referred to the fact – I think on the occasion of his last speech at Newcastle-on-Tyne, that every year brought us intensified competition from every Continental country, and that now we were to be confronted with the competition of Eastern nations. That means, of course, that Japan and China and India are all entering to cater for the world's markets, and therefore British supremacy, industrially speaking, is very seriously questioned. What the orthodox man has propounded is that the British worker shall buckle to, and by one means or another overcome the foreigner, and beat him and drive him to destruction. I tell you I despise and hate such a doctrine. Tell me that the only way for my salvation is, as it were, to drive somebody else to starvation and desperation, and I refuse to have salvation on those terms. I for one do not regret that the Continental nations are learning to produce commodities which were formerly produced by Britain, but, of course, that carries with it the absolute necessity of understanding in what direction we can develop our energy, so as to balance the requisite production of food stuffs with the production of manufactured commodities. Therefore, I anticipate that Britain must learn to produce more food-stuffs than she has done, because other countries will produce more manufactured commodities than they have done. And there is no earthly reason worth consideration why they should not do so, as, of course, there is no real, sound reason why we should not be more a food-producer and perhaps a little less a producer of coal and iron and other hardware. I ask you, therefore, if you endorse the ordinary commercial principle that what you have endorsed as part of this principle is increased and intensified competition with every European nation, with America, and now with the Japs and the Chinamen. If you can look forward to that, I cannot, and I do not want the support of those who can. I tell you plainly that I would be ashamed to subscribe to a policy that tells me I can only get food for myself and family, and other men like me, by fighting down and driving to despair other men equally courageous, equally lovable, and equally unobjectionable in every way. I therefore call for such attention being given to agriculture as shall enable us scientifically to divert the surplus energy from industrial pursuits to food-producing channels. This will bear rigid investigation, it will bear the investigation of scientific experts, and it will bear the investigation and receive the approval of the sound economists of the country.

Child Labour and Pensions for All

Now, a friend on my left shouted, 'The women first.' I admire his gallantry. I ask that it should be recognised, that all who are in a relatively helpless position should receive prime attention, therefore, I call for scientific attention being given to children. Their labour does not obtain in Aberdeen to the extent that it does in some other towns in Britain, but I believe it does obtain to a far greater extent than we would look upon with approval. Now, I know that the income of the ordinary parents are not sufficient to enable them to live in comfort, unless they get all that is possible through the agency indicated. But remember, I have subscribed, and do now subscribe, and ask you to try and do the same, to that definite kind of organisation that lands you into the Trades Union movement, to fight for and obtain – as men responsible for your families – a sufficient income to enable you to behave with requisite dignity, so that you can maintain your home without having to resort to the labour of mere infants. Therefore, I am opposed to infants going to work at twelve years of age even, and I should be glad to see, and should work for a raising of the age, at the earliest possible moment, to something considerably higher than that I have indicated, before children should be called upon to labour in the mills, the factories, or the workshops. Another important question that I am bound to work for, and that I think would commend itself to you, is adequate provision in the form of pensions for all industrial soldiers, for all genuine citizens who have laboured and have reached that period of life when assistance is absolutely required, because they are not in a fit condition to provide for themselves under the old conditions. Then they ought, as a matter of right, having worked in their day and contributed to the community's well-being, to receive from the community what is requisite for their adequate maintenance. Therefore, I am in favour of pensions for all, irrespective of the positions they occupy, and always making, of course, for that position when there shall be equality of opportunity for all, and when we shall approximate to equal conditions. Remember, I include here the infirm and the sick as well as the elderly. Every infirm person, every sick person, irrespective of the causes, should be cared for by the community, in the interests of the community; as well as in the interest of the child.

Nationalisation

With a view of bringing about that state of genuine co-operation, I look forward to, instead of this capitalistic system, we call for the nationalisation of the railways and waterways of our country. It is a sin and a shame that the railways should be primarily controlled in the interests of shareholders rather than in the interests of the industry of the country and of the travelling public. Ere long I shall expect to see developed that volume of opinion that will call for the control of the railways and waterways of our country by the community's executive in the interests of all, affording every reasonable facility for the opening up of the country to agriculture and to industry generally. I call for the nationalisation of the mines and minerals of the country. The minerals are the gift of nature, and are not by moral right the property of anyone handful of the community. I am identified with those who would at the earliest possible moment undertake to control them and regulate their output through the agency of state regulation, and not leave it to the caprice of the individuals who today control them for their own selfish interests. We must declare that the surface land must be common property. Land was not made by man or woman. It is the gift of Nature to the common children of men, and it is not for you nor for me nor for anybody above us or below us to exercise a monopoly-power over it. That we should have tolerated it so far is not very complimentary either to our intelligence or to our courage. I know the day is some distance off when land nationalisation is likely to be successfully carried through the British House of Commons. I, therefore, expect to see changes made in the direction of common or collective ownership by adding to the power of the local governing bodies. We have further South, Parish Councils, of a somewhat different character from yours. It is an administrative body, exercising functions other than those of the Parochial Board; but you, as well as we, have County Councils and District Councils, and we call, and I am now calling for the requisite power being invested in these bodies, so that through the agency of the State they may be enabled to obtain from the present owners, such land as the residents in the respective districts may be willing to cultivate collectively, paying rent (for rent will always have to be paid) to the recognised communal authority, and therefore securing to community all the advantages of the unearned increment which hitherto has gone to the mere landlord, who has done nothing whatever to produce it. In the seven points I have now enumerated, I have given:

Seven Definite Practical Proposals

If you should be disposed to say, 'Oh, but the country is not equal to it yet.' Why, what is Parliament for, and what are we for, and what are you for? To wait until somebody else can lead, and then you are to follow? I am not going to do that. I tell you in the plainest language that I will refuse to be a drag weight upon political opinion, and I refuse to be an observant of Mrs Grundy,[3] that I will not dare to speak the faith I have learned and understand, and I will not subscribe, if I know it, to any spasmodic or erratic policy; and I hope to be able ever to retain sufficient mental vigor and love of genuine progress as to dare to step out of the ordinary orthodox rut and to say: 'This is the way: Walk ye in it.' If you cannot, I will, anyway, or perish in the attempt. If you are disposed to say: 'Where is the money to come from to enable these changes to be made?' then I must remind you of certain facts – that the workers who produce the wealth of the nation do not receive more than one-half of that which they produce; that about one-fourth of the total community, as Chamberlain[4] once said, and he himself is included – toil not, neither do they spin, yet are they arrayed in much magnificence at the expense of those who do. I ask you to recognise that, through the agency of a graduated income tax, we would gladly rectify the anomalies that today exist, and provide adequately for all the changes I have suggested. If any of you are disposed to say: 'Is it idealism, after all?' I am not prepared to go back on my idealism, and I will not give one inch to any man amongst you for definite, practical, detailed, solid work, calculated to build up a newer and better country than we have yet known. I ask you to understand that if you and I know each other more closely, I will refuse to be a nonentity. I will refuse to be kicked and cajoled, but I will always be willing and glad to be consulted and to consult you. I will try to understand exactly your particular requirements, as the North Division of Aberdeen, but I will never pretend that Aberdeen is heaven and everywhere else is hell. I am, and intend to remain, cosmopolitan, but it does not debar me, or in any way prevent me, from giving every reasonable attention to local requirements.

I am prepared for any kind of opposition. Fearing no one's power, courting no one's favour, I state my case as a workman, who, if returned, would have some satisfaction in trying to fight on the floor of the House of Commons as I have endeavoured to fight outside, for those principles of truth and justice and equity, as I understand them, hoping thereby to contribute to the day when poverty shall be banished and peace and plenty shall prevail, when swords shall be beaten into ploughshares, and spears into pruning hooks, when nation shall not lift itself up against nation, shall learn war no more, and when brotherhood and sisterhood shall really be an established fact, with all the blessings that follow in its train.

Notes

1. Thomas Carlyle (1795–1881); historian and writer; author of *French Revolution* published in 1836 by which he made his name. Was known as a Rationalist and Humanitarian.

2. Rt Hon John Morley (1838–1923); statesman and author. Entered Parliament in 1883 where he occupied a number of high positions, eventually becoming Lord President of The Council between 1910 and 1914, when he retired from politics in protest against the war. His humanitarian conscience earned him the name of 'honest John Morley'.

3. Mrs Grundy: the surname of an imaginary person proverbially referred to as the personification of a tyranny of social opinion in matters of conventional propriety.

4. Joseph Chamberlain used the phrase 'the class who toil not neither do they spin' in a speech he made in Birmingham on 30 March 1883. He was involved in a dispute with Lord Salisbury and his phrase met with enthusiasm among the majority of workers.

8

Real Socialism

ROBERT BLATCHFORD (1851–1943)

Introduction

Robert Blatchford was born into a family of theatrical performers, so much of his childhood was spent travelling. His formal education was minimal. When he was 11, after the death of his father, the family settled in Halifax, where he started work in a lithographic printing works.

From this point Robert set about educating himself through reading. His mother apprenticed him to a brushmaker, but he left home before completing the apprenticeship.

He enlisted for the army, where he remained for seven years, attaining the rank of sergeant. This enabled him to undertake some formal education, and he obtained the army's second-class certificate of education. On being transferred to the Reserves he took a job as a clerk in the Weaver Navigation Company in Northwich, Cheshire, where he earned a guinea a week.

His writing career began in 1882 when a sketch of his was published in a local paper the *Yorkshireman*. A year later, with the help of his friend, A. M. Thompson, a writer on the Manchester *Sporting Chronicle*, he obtained a full-time journalistic post on *Bell's Life* as a news reporter and columnist.

When *Bell's Life* closed down, Blatchford and the family returned to the north-west where he started work on the *Sunday Chronicle*. It was in this period that his socialist education began. The responsibility for his conversion to the socialist cause was claimed by two men: Joseph Waddington, a member of the South Salford Social Democratic Federation, who took him on a tour of Manchester's slums in 1889 that resulted in a series of articles by Blatchford in the *Sunday Chronicle* that bitterly denounced housing conditions in the city; and Henry M. Reade, later a member of the Manchester Independent Labour Party.

Blatchford himself attributed his conversion to his hatred of social waste and to a pamphlet written by Hyndman and Morris, *A Summary of the Principles of Socialism*, first published in 1884.

During his period in Manchester, Blatchford became involved in the Labour Movement and helped form the city's Fabian Society. He had close connections with the local SDF, and with the Bradford Labour Union. He also maintained contacts with leaders of the new Unionism movement such as Leonard Hall, James

Bartley and John Burns.

Blatchford's increasing commitment to socialism was reflected in his writing for the *Sunday Chronicle*. He was eventually dismissed from his job on the paper when he accepted an invitation *to* stand as Independent Labour candidate for the Bradford Labour Union. Four other *Sunday Chronicle* employees left the paper with him, and they went on to start a socialist paper of their own *The Clarion*. This first issue sold 40,000 copies. A circulation of 34,000 was maintained for some years.

The Clarion was one of the liveliest socialist papers ever produced. Its writers gathered around themselves groups of likeminded people who set up clubs and cafés. Blatchford's personal involvement with the Clarion movement was mainly in the Cinderella clubs, which were social and education groups for slum children.

The Clarion movement spread rapidly and reached its peak around the turn of the century.

Blatchford wrote a number of books and pamphlets, one of which was Clarion pamphlet no. 23, *Real Socialism*, reproduced here, which was the tenth in the series that Blatchford had written.

Blatchford's main objective was to convert people to socialism at a time when these ideas were little known. He once wrote: 'I am an idealist by nature and conviction, and I believe that the socialist ideal is as precious to socialists as virtue is to a woman, or honour to a man.'

To Blatchford, the ethical correctness of socialism was so obvious that once grasped it would be accepted by all. In place of competition there would be co-operation. He claimed that he had never read Marx and was inclined to throw cold water on those who had, and therefore his concept of the class struggle was a personal one.

He was a prolific writer. His book *Merrie England* first serialised in the *The Clarion* sold over a million copies. It was arguably the most effective piece of socialist propaganda produced by the British labour movement.

Blatchford moved away from the ILP when the ILP Conference in 1893 refused to ratify Clause 4, which advocated socialism. He attacked organised religion in two books, *God and my Neighbour* and *Not Guilty; a Defence of the Bottom Dog,* in which he held that religion was a barrier to social progress.

But it was Blatchford's call for support for the British government at the beginning of the First World War that brought about the demise of the Clarion movement. By the end of 1914 Robert Blatchford had abandoned his socialist ideas, and in the 1924 general election he voted Conservative.

Sources

Dictionary of Labour Biography, eds John Saville and Joyce Bellamy, vol. 4, 1977, p. 34.
L. Thompson, *Portrait of an Englishman*, 1951.

*   *   *

CLARION PAMPHLET, No. 23.

Real Socialism:

What Socialism Is,

... AND ...

What Socialism Is Not.

BY

Robert Blatchford,

(NUNQUAM,)

EDITOR OF THE "CLARION."

PRICE ONE PENNY.

Published by the "Clarion" Newspaper Company, Limited,
72, Fleet Street, London, E.C.

1898.

What Socialism is Not

It is no use telling you what Socialism is until I have told you what it is not. Those who do not wish you to be Socialists have given you very false notions about Socialism, in the hope of setting you against it. They have brought many false charges against Socialists in the hope of setting you against them. So you have come to think of Socialism as a thing foolish, or vile, and when it is spoken of you turn up your noses (instead of trying to see beyond them) and turn your backs on it.

A friend offers to give you a good house-dog; but some one tells you it is mad. Your friend will be wise to satisfy you that the dog is *not* mad before he begins to tell you how well it can guard a house. Because, as long as you think the dog will bite you, you are not in the frame of mind to hear about its usefulness.

A sailor is offering to sell an African chief a telescope; but the chief has been told that the thing is a gun. Then before the sailor shows the chief what the glass is good for, he will be wise to prove to him that it will not go off at half-cock and blow his eye out.

So with *Socialism:* before I try to show you what it really is, I must try to clear your mind of the prejudice which has been sown there by those who wish to make you hate Socialism because they fear it.

As a rule, my friends, it will be wise for you to look very carefully and hopefully at anything which Parliament men, or employers, or Pressmen call bad or foolish, because what helps you hinders them, and the stronger you grow the weaker they become.

Well, my friends, the men who have tried to smash your unions, who have written against you, and spoken against you and acted against you in all great strikes and lock-outs, are the same· men who speak and write against Socialism.

And what have they told you? Let us take their commonest statements, and see what they are made of.

They say that Socialists want to get up a revolution, to turn the country upside down by force, to seize all property, and to divide it equally amongst the whole people.

We will take these charges one at a time.

As to *Revolution*, I think I shall be right if I say that not one Socialist in fifty, at this day, expects or wishes to get Socialism by force of arms.

In the early days of Socialism, when there were very few Socialists, and some of those rash, or angry, or unthinking men, it may have been true that Socialism implied revolution and violence.

But, today, there are very few Socialists who believe in brute force, or who think a revolution possible or desirable.

The bulk of our Socialists are for peaceful and lawful means. Some of them hope to bring Socialism to pass by means of a reformed Parliament; others hope to bring it to pass by means of a newer, wiser, and juster public opinion.

I have always been dead against the idea of revolution for many reasons. I do not think a revolution is *possible* in England. Firstly because the people have too much sense; secondly, because the people are by nature patient and kindly; thirdly, because the people are too *free* to make force needful.

I do not think a revolution is *advisable*. Because, firstly, it would be almost sure to fail; secondly, if it did not fail it would put the worst kind of men into power, and would destroy order and method before it was ready to replace them; thirdly, because a State built up on force is very likely to succumb to fraud; so that after great bloodshed, trouble, labour, and loss the people would almost surely slip down into worse evils than those against which they had fought, and find that they had suffered and sinned in vain.

I do not believe in force, and I do not believe in haste. What we want is *reason* and *right*; and we can only hope to get reason and right by right and reasonable means.

The men who would come to the top in a civil war would be fighters and strivers; they would not be the kind of men to wisely model and patiently and justly rule or lead a new State. Your barricade man may be very useful – at the barricades; but when the fighting is over, and his work is done, he may be a great danger, for he is not the man, usually, to stand aside and make way for the builders to replace by right laws the wrong laws which his arms have destroyed.

Revolution by force of arms is not desirable, nor feasible; but there is another kind of revolution from which we hope great things. This is a revolution of *thought*. Let us once get the people, or a big majority of the people, to understand Socialism, to believe in Socialism, and to work for Socialism, and the *real* revolution is accomplished.

In a free country, such as ours, the almighty voice is the voice of public opinion. What the public *believe in* and *demand* has got to be given. Who is to refuse? Neither King, nor Pope, nor Parliament can stand against a united and resolute British people.

And do not suppose, either, that brute force, which is powerless to get good or to keep it, has power to resist it or destroy it. Neither truncheons nor bayonets can kill a truth. The sword and the cannon are impotent against the pen and the tongue.

Believe me, we can overcome the constable, the soldier, the Parliament man, the landlord, and the man of wealth without shedding one drop of blood, or breaking one pane of glass, or losing one day's work.

Our real task is to win the trust and help of *the people* (I don't mean the workers only, but the British people), and the first thing to be done is to educate them — to teach them and tell them what we mean: to make quite clear to them what Socialism is, and what it is not.

One of the things it is not is an English imitation of the French revolution. Our method is persuasion; our cause is justice, our weapons are the tongue and the pen.

Next: As to seizing the wealth of the country and sharing it out amongst the people. First, we do not propose to *seize* anything. We do propose to get some things — the land, for instance — and to make them the property of the whole nation; but we mean that to be done by Act of Parliament, or by purchase. Second, we have no idea of 'sharing out' the land, nor the railways, nor the money, nor any other kind of wealth or property equally amongst the people. To share these things out — if they *could* be shared, which they could not be — would be to make them *private* property, whereas we want them to be *public* property, the property of the British *nation*.

Yet, how often have you been told that Socialists want to have the wealth equally divided amongst all? And how often have you been told that if you divided the wealth in that way it would soon cease to be equally divided, because some would waste and some would save?

'Make all men equal in possessions,' cry your friends the 'Impossibles,' 'and in a very short time there would be rich and poor, as before.'

This is no argument against Socialism, for Socialists do not seek any such division. But I want to point out to you that though it *looks* true, it is *not* true.

It is quite true that, did we divide all wealth equally tomorrow, there would in a short time be many penniless, and a few in a way of getting rich; but it is only true if we suppose that after the sharing we allowed private ownership of land and the old system of trade and competition to go on as before. Change those things: do away with the bad system which leads to poverty and to wealth, and we should have no more rich and poor.

Destroy all the wealth of England tomorrow — we will not talk of 'sharing' it out, but *destroy* it — and establish Socialism on the ruins and the bareness, and in a few years we should have a prosperous, a powerful, and a contented nation. There would be no rich, and there would be no poor. But the nation would be richer and happier than it ever has been.

Another charge against Socialists is that they are *Atheists*, whose aim is to destroy all religion, and all morality.

This is not true. It is true that many Socialists are Agnostics, and some are Atheists. But Atheism is no more a part of Socialism than it is a part of Toryism, or of Radicalism, or of Liberalism. Many prominent Socialists are Christians, not a few are clergymen. Many Liberal and Tory leaders are Agnostics or Atheists. I, for instance, am an Agnostic; but so, I believe, are Mr. Balfour[1] and Mr. John Morley.[2] Mr. Bradlaugh[3] was a Radical, and an Atheist; Prof. Huxley[4] was an opponent of Socialism, and an Agnostic. Socialism does not touch religion at any point. It deals with laws, and with *industrial* and *political* government.

It is not sense to say, because some Atheists are Socialists, that all Socialists are Atheists.

Christ's teaching is often said to be Socialistic. It is not Socialistic; but is is Communistic, and Communism is the most advanced form of the policy generally known as Socialism. I will explain the difference between Socialism and Communism presently.

The charge of *immorality* is absurd. Socialists demand a higher morality than any now to be found. They demand perfect *honesty*. Indeed, it is just the stern morality of Socialism which causes ambitious and greedy men – the rich men and the Parliament men – to hate Socialism and resist it.

Another charge against Socialists is the charge of desiring *Free Love*.

Socialists, it has been said, want to destroy home life, to abolish marriage, to take the children from their parents, and to establish '*Free Love*'.

'Free Love,' I may say, means that all men and women shall be free to love as they please, and to live with whom they please. Therefore, that they shall be free to live as 'man and wife' without marriage, to part when they please without divorce, and to take other partners as they please without shame or penalty.

Now, I say of this charge, as I have said of the others, that there are some Socialists in favour of free love, just as there are some Socialists in favour of revolution, and some who are not Christians; but I say also that a big majority of Socialists are not in favour of free love, and that in any case free love is no more a part of Socialism than it is a part of Toryism or of Liberalism.

It is not sense to say, because some Free-Lovers are Socialists, that all Socialists are Free-Lovers.

I believe there is not one English Socialist in a hundred who would vote for doing away with marriage, or for handing over the children to the State. I for one would see the State further before I would part with a child of mine. And I think you will generally find that those who are really eager to have all children given up to the State are men and women who have no children of their own.

Now, I submit that a childless man is not the right man to make laws about children.

As for the questions of free love and legal marriage, they are very hard to deal with, and this is not the time to deal with them.

But I shall say here that many of those who talk the loudest against free love do not even know what love *is*, or have not sense enough to see that just as love and lust are two very different things, so are free love and free lust very different things.

Again, you are not to fall into the error of supposing that the relations of the sexes are all they should be at present. Free *love*, it is true, is not countenanced; but free *lust* is very common.

And although some Socialists would be in favour of free *love*, I never heard of a Socialist who had a word to say in favour of prostitution. It may be a very wicked thing to enable a free woman to *give* her love freely; but it is a much worse thing to allow, and even at times compel (for it amounts to that, by force of hunger) a free woman to *sell* her love – no, not her *love*, poor creature, the vilest never sold that – but to sell her honour, her body, and her soul.

I tell you men, I would do a great deal for Socialism if it were only to do that one good act of wiping out for ever the shameful sin of prostitution. This thing, indeed, is so horrible that I never think of it without feeling tempted to apologise for calling myself a man in a country where it is so common as it is in moral England.

There are several other common charges against Socialists; as that they are poor and envious – what we may call Have-nots-on-the-Have; that they are ignorant and incapable men, who know nothing, and cannot think; that, in short, they are failures and wasters, fools and knaves.

These charges are as true and as false as the others. There *are* some Socialists who are ignorant and stupid; there are *some* who are poor *and* envious; there are some who are Socialists because they like cakes and ale better than work; and there are some who are clever, but not too good – men who will feather their nests if they can find any geese for the plucking.

But I don't think that *all* Tories and Liberals are wise, learned, pure, unselfish, and clever men, eager to devote their talents to the good of their fellows, and unwilling to be paid, or thanked, or praised, for what they do.

I think there are fools and knaves – even in Parliament – and that some of the 'Bounders-on-the-Bounce' find it pays a great deal better to toady to the 'Haves' than to sacrifice themselves to the 'Have-nots'.

And I think I may claim that Socialists are in the main honest and sensible men, who work for Socialism because they believe in it, and not because it pays, for it seldom pays at all, and it never pays well; and I am sure that Socialism makes quicker progress amongst the educated than amongst the ignorant, and amongst the intelligent than amongst the dull.

As for brains: I hope such men as William Morris,[5] Karl Marx, and Liebknecht[6] are as well endowed with brains as – well, let us be modest, and say as Lord Salisbury[7] or Sir William Harcourt.[8]

But most of the charges and arguments I have quoted are not aimed at

Socialism at all; but at Socialists.

Now, to prove that many of the men who espouse a cause are unworthy is not the same thing as proving that the *cause* is bad.

Some parsons are foolish, some are insincere; but we do not therefore say that Christianity is unwise or untrue. Even if *most* parsons were really bad men we should only despise and condemn the clergy, and not the religion they dishonoured and misrepresented.

The question is not whether all Socialists are as wise as Mr. Samuel Woods,[9] M.P., as honest as Jabez Balfour, or as moral as the Rev. George Brooks;[10] *the* question is whether *Socialism* is a thing in itself just, and wise, and *possible*.

If you find a Socialist who is foolish, laugh at him; if you find one who is a rogue, don't trust him; if you find one 'on the make,' stop his making. But as for Socialism, if it be good, accept it; if it be bad, reject it.

Here allow me to quote a few lines from 'Merrie England':

Half our time as champions of Socialism is wasted in denials of false descriptions of Socialism; and to a large extent the anger, the ridicule and the argument of the opponents of Socialism are hurled against a Socialism which has no existence except in their own heated minds.

Socialism does not consist in violently seizing upon the property of the rich and sharing it out amongst the poor.

Socialism is not a wild dream of a happy land where the apples will drop off the trees into our open mouths, the fish come out of the rivers and fry themselves for dinner, and the looms turn out ready-made suits of velvet with golden buttons without the trouble of coaling the engine. Neither is it a dream of a nation of stained-glass angels, who never say damn, who always love their neighbours better than themselves, and who never need to work unless they wish to.

And now, having told you what Socialism is *not*, it remains for me to tell you what Socialism *is*.

What Socialism Is

To those who are writing about such things as Socialism, or Political Economy, one of the stumbling-blocks is the hard or uncommon words, and another the tediousness – the 'dryness' – of the arguments and explanations.

It is not easy to say what has to be said so that anybody may see quite clearly what is meant, and it is still harder to say it so as to hold the attention and arouse the interest of men and women who are not used to reading or thinking about matters outside the daily round of their work and their play. As I want these Letters to be both plain and pleasant to all kinds of workers, even to those who have no 'book-learning', and to whom a 'hard word' is a 'boggart,' and a 'dry' description, or a long argument, a weariness of the flesh, I must beg those of you who are more used to bookish talk and scientific terms (or names), to bear with me when I stop to show the meaning of things that to you are quite clear.

If I can make my meaning plain to Members of Parliament, Bishops, Editors and other half-educated persons, and to labouring men and women who have had but little schooling, and have never been used to think or care about Socialism, or Economics, or Politics, or 'any such dry rot' – as they would call them – if I can catch the ear of the heedless and the untaught, the rest of you cannot fail to follow.

The terms, or names, used in speaking of Socialism – that is to say, the names given to ideas, or 'thoughts,' or to kinds of ideas, or 'schools' of thought, are not easy to put into the plain words of common speech.

To an untaught labourer 'Socialism' is a hard word, so is 'Co-operation'; and such a phrase, or name, as 'Political Economy' is enough to clear a taproom, or break up a meeting, or close a book.

So I want to steer clear of 'hard words,' and 'dry talk', and long-windedness, and I want to tell my tale, if I can, in 'tinker's English'.

These Letters are the words of a self-taught common soldier to the untaught common labourers and their tired, worried, unread wives.

What is Socialism?

There is more than one kind of Socialism, for we hear of State Socialism, of Practical Socialism, of Communal Socialism; and these kinds differ from each other, though they are all *Socialism*.

So you have different kinds of Liberals. There are old-school Whigs, and advanced Whigs, and Liberals, and Radicals, and advanced Radicals; but they are all *Liberals*.

So you have horse soldiers, foot soldiers, riflemen, artillery, and engineers; but they are all *soldiers*.

Amongst the Liberals are men of many minds: there are Churchmen, Nonconformists, Atheists; there are teetotalers, and there are drinkers; there are Trade-union leaders and there are leaders of the Masters' Federation. These men differ on many points; but they all agree upon *one* point.

Amongst the Socialists are many men of many minds. There are parsons, atheists, labourers, employers, men of peace, and men of force. These men differ on many points; but they all agree upon *one* point.

Now, this point on which men of different views agree, is called a *principle*.

A principle is a main idea, or main thought. It is like the kelson of a ship, or the back-bone of a fish – it is the foundation on which the thing is built.

Thus, the *principle* of Trade Unionism is 'combination', the combining, that is the joining together, of a number of workers for the general good of all.

The *principle* of Democratic (or Popular) Government is the law that the will of the majority shall rule.

Do away with the 'right of combination', and Trade Unionism is destroyed.

Do away with majority rule, and Popular Government is destroyed.

So if we can find the *principle* of Socialism; if we can find the one point on which all kinds of Socialists agree, we shall be able to see what Socialism really is.

Now, here in plain words is the *principle*, or root idea, on which *all* Socialists agree:

That the country, and everything in the country, shall belong to the whole people (the nation), and shall be used *by* the people and *for* the people.

That 'principle', the root idea of Socialism, means two things:

1. That the land and all the machines, tools and buildings used in making needful things, together with all the canals, rivers, roads, railways, ships, and trains used in moving, sharing (distributing) needful things, and all the shops, markets, scales, weights, and money used in selling or dividing needful things shall be the property of (belong to) the whole people (the nation).

2. That the land, tools, machines, trains, rivers, shops, scales, money, and all the other things belonging to the people shall be worked, managed, divided, and used by the whole people in such way as the greater number of the whole people shall deem best.

This is the principle of collective, or national ownership, and co-operative, or national, use and control.

Socialism may, you see, be summed up in one line, in four words, as really meaning

England for the English

I will make all this as plain as the nose on your face directly. Let us now look at the *other* side.

Today England does *not* belong to the English. It belongs to a few of the English. There are bits of it which belong to the whole people, as Wimbledon Common, Portland Gaol, the high roads; but most of it is 'private property'.

Now, as there are Liberals and Tories, Catholics and Protestants, Dockers' Unions and Shipping Federations in England, so there are

Socialists and Non-Socialists.

And as there are different kinds of Socialists, so there are different kinds of Non-Socialists.

As there is one point, or *principle*, on which all kinds of Socialists agree, so there is one point, or *principle*, on which all kinds of Non-Socialists agree.

Amongst the Non-Socialists there are Liberals and Tories; Catholics and Protestants; Masters and Workmen; Rich and Poor; Lords and Labourers; Publicans and Teetotalers; and these folks, as you know, differ in their ideas, and quarrel with and go against each other; but they are all Non-Socialists, they are all against Socialism, and they all agree upon *one point*.

So, if we can find the one point on which all kinds of Non-Socialists agree, we shall find the *principle*, or root idea, of Non-Socialism.

Well, the 'principle' of Non-Socialism is just the opposite of the 'principle' of Socialism.

As the 'principle' of Socialism is national ownership, so the 'principle' of Non-Socialism is *private* ownership. As the principle of Socialism is *England for the English*, so the principle of Non-Socialism is *Every Englishman for Himself*.

Again, as the principle of Socialism means two things, so does the principle of Non-Socialism mean two things.

As the principle of Socialism means national ownership and co-operative national management, so the principle of Non-Socialism means *private ownership* and *private management*.

Socialism says that England shall be owned and managed *by* the people *for* the people.

Non-Socialism says England shall be owned and managed *by* some persons *for* some persons.

Under Socialism you would have *all* the people working *together* for the good of *all*.

Under Non-Socialism you have all the *persons* working *separately* (and mostly *against* each other), each for the good of *himself*.

So we find Socialism means *Co-operation*, and Non-Socialism means *Competition*.

Co-operation, as here used, means operating or working together for a common end or purpose.

Competition means competing or vying with each other for personal ends or gain.

I'm afraid that is all as 'dry' as bran, and as sad as a half-boiled dumpling; but I want to make it quite plain.

And now we will run over it all again in a more homely and lively way.

You know that today most of the land in England belongs to landlords, who let it to farmers, or builders, and charge *rent* for it.

Socialists (*all* Socialists) say that *all* the land should belong to the English people, to the nation.

Some Socialists say the people should *take* the land, by force, or by new laws; and some Socialists say that the people should *buy* the land.

You know that the railways belong to railway companies, who carry goods and passengers, and charge fares and rates, to make *profit*.

Socialists *all* say that the railways should be taken, or bought, by the people. Some say that fares should be charged, some that the railways should be free – just as the roads, rivers, and bridges now are; but all agree that any profit made by the railways should belong to the whole nation. Just as do the profits now made by the Post-office and the Telegraphs.

You know that cotton mills, coal mines, and breweries now belong to rich men, or to companies, who sell the coal, the calico, or the beer, for profit.

Socialists say that all mines, mills, breweries, shops, works, ships, and farms should belong to the whole people, and should be managed by persons chosen by the people, or by officials elected by the people, and that all the bread, beer, calico, coal, and other goods should be either *sold* to the people, or *given* to the people, or sold to foreign buyers for the benefit of the British nation.

Some Socialists would *give* the goods to the people, some would *sell* them; but *all* agree that any profit on such sales should belong to the whole people – just as any profit made on the sale of gas by the Manchester Corporation goes to the credit of the city.

Now you will begin to see what is meant by Socialism.

Today the nation owns *some* things; under Socialism the nation would own *all* things.

Today the nation owns the ships of the navy, the forts, arsenals, public buildings, Government factories, and some other things.

Today the Government, *for the nation*, manages the Post-office and Telegraphs, makes some of the clothes and food and arms for the Army and Navy, builds some of the war ships, and oversees the church, the prisons, and the schools.

Socialists want the nation to own *all* the buildings, factories, lands, rivers, ships, schools, machines, and goods, and to manage *all* their business and work; and to buy and sell and make and use *all* goods for themselves.

Today some cities (as Manchester and Glasgow) make gas, and supply water to the citizens. Some cities (as London) let their citizens buy their gas and water from gas and water companies.

Socialists want *all* the gas and water to be supplied to the people by their own officials, as in Glasgow and Manchester.

Under Socialism all the work of the nation would be *organised* – that is to say, it would be 'ordered', or 'arranged', so that no one need be out of work, and so that no useless work need be done, and so that no work need be done twice where once would serve.

At present the work is *not* organised except in the Post-office, and in the gas and water works of the Corporations.

Let us take a look at the state of things in England today.

Today the industries of England are not ordered nor arranged, but are left to be disordered by chance and by the ups and downs of trade.

So, we have at one and the same time, and in one and the same trade, and, often enough, in one and the same town, some men working overtime and other men out of work.

We have at one time the cotton mills making more goods than they can sell, and at another time we have them unable to fulfil their orders.

We have in one street a dozen small shops all selling the same kinds of goods, and so spending in rent, in fittings, in wages of servants, and other ways about four times as much as would be spent if all the work were done in one big shop.

We have three great railway lines running from London to Scotland, and costing a great deal more for roads, and stations, and wages of men than need be if we would have only one main line.

We have one contractor sending men and tools and bricks and wood from North London to build a house in South London, and another contractor in South London going to the same trouble and expense to build a house in North London.

We have in Essex and other parts of England, thousands of acres of good land lying idle because it does not *pay* to till it, and at the same time we have thousands of labourers out of work who would be only too glad to till it.

So in one part of a city you may see hundreds of houses standing empty, and in another part of the same city you may see hard-working people living three and four families in a small cottage.

Then, under competition, where there are many firms in the same trade, and where each firm wants to get as much trade as it can, a great deal of money is spent by these firms in trying to get the trade from each other.

Thus all the cost of advertisements, of travellers' wages, and a lot of the cost of book-keeping arise from the fact there are many firms all trying to snatch the trade from each other.

In London, there are several gas and water companies. In Manchester there is only one – the Corporation.

In London gas and water are bad and dear. In Manchester they are good and cheap.

If the London County Council provided the gas and water, there would be no more water famines, and I should be able to see to write these lines without trouble, which I cannot do now, although my gas rate is over four shillings a thousand feet.

Non-Socialists claim that this clumsy and costly way of going to work is really the best way there is. They say that competition gets the work done by the best men, and at the lowest rate.

Perhaps some of them believe this; but it is not true. The mistake is caused by the fact that *competition* is better than *monopoly*.

That is to say, if there is only one tram company in a town the fares will be higher than if there are two; because when there are two one tries to undersell the other.

But take a town where there are two tram companies undercutting and working against each other, and hand the trams over to the Corporation, and you will find that the work is done better, is done cheaper, and the men are better paid than under competition.

This is because the Corporation is at less cost, has less waste, and does not want such big *profits*.

Well, under Socialism all the work of the nation would be managed by the nation – or perhaps I had better say by 'the people', for some of the work would be *local*, and some would be *national*. I will show you what I mean.

It might be better for each town to manage its own gas and water, to bake its own bread, and brew its own beer. But it would be better for the Post-office to be managed by the nation, because that has to do with all the towns.

So we should find that some kinds of work were best done locally, that is by each town or county, and that some were best done nationally, that is by a body of officials acting for the nation.

For instance, tramways would be local, and railways national; gas and water would be local, and collieries national; police would be local, and the army and navy national.

Let me now say a few words as to the different ideas of Socialists.

Socialists all go together in the wish to give England to the English, and in the wish to order the work, and to do it on co-operative lines. Where they differ is as to the best means of getting what they want, and as to the best ways of managing the work, and as to the proper way of sharing the earnings.

Some Socialists still believe that Socialism will have to be got by *force*. I think these are not many.

Some are in favour of *buying* the land, the railways, the machinery, and other things; and some are in favour of *taking* them, by force, or by new laws.

Then some say that there should be *no* wages paid at all, but that every one should do an equal share of work, and take whatever he needed from the nation's goods. Others say that all men should do an equal share of work, and have an equal share of the goods, or of the earnings.

Others say it would be better to pay wages, as now, but to let the wages be fixed by the Government, or by Corporations, or other officials, and that all wages should be equal.

Others, again, say that wages should be paid, that the wages should be fixed as above stated, and that different kinds of work should be paid for at different rates.

In one kind of Socialism the civil engineer, the actor, the general, the artist, the tram-guard, the dustman, the milliner, and the collier would all be paid the same wages.

In another kind of Socialism there would be no wages, but all would be called upon to work, and all who worked would 'take according to their needs'.

In another kind of Socialism the civil engineer would be paid more than the navvy, the opera singer more than the milliner, the general more than the sergeant, and the editor more than the scavenger.

For my part, I am a Communist, and Communists believe that everything should be in common, and that wages and prices should be unknown. But Communism is so far off that I do not mean to say more about it in this pamphlet.

No, I go for the *nearest* kind of Socialism. I call it Collectivism, and I describe it thus: –

Collectivism, or Practical Socialism

Motto: *England for the English.* The land and all the instruments of making, dividing, carrying, and exchanging goods to be the property of the nation, and to be managed *by* the nation *for* the nation.

The land and railways, collieries, etc., to be *bought* from the present owners, but not at fancy prices.

Wages to be paid, and goods to be sold. But the wages to be fixed by officials of the nation, or the towns, and the goods to be sold by the agents of the nation or the towns.

Different rates of wages to be paid for different kinds of work.

Here let me say that a collier or a sailor would get a good deal more, and a manager or inventor or clever artist *less* than now.

Thus, you see, Collectivism is really an extension of the *principles*, or ideas, of local government, and of the various corporation and civil services.

And now I tell you *that* is Socialism, and I ask you, what is there in it to prevent any man from being a Christian, or from attending a place of worship, or from marrying or being faithful to his wife, or from keeping and bringing up his children at home?

There is nothing in it to destroy religion, and there is nothing in it to destroy the home, and there is nothing in it to foster vice.

But there *is* something in it to kill ignorance and to destroy vice. There is something in it to shut up the gaols, to do away with prostitution, to reduce crime and drunkenness, and wipe out for ever the sweater and the slums, the beggars and the idle fops, the useless fine ladies and lords, and to make it possible for sober and willing workers to live healthy and happy and honourable lives.

For Socialism would teach and train all children wisely; it would foster genius and devotion to the common good; it would kill scamping and loafing and jerrymandering; it would give us better health, better homes, better work, better food, better lives, and better men and women.

And now I have told you what Socialism is, and what it is not, I hope you will be good enough to think about it, for *yourselves*.

Notes

1. Arthur James Balfour (1848–1930); 1st Earl of Balfour; statesman, author, Tory politician. Prime Minister (1902–5) and Foreign Secretary in Lloyd George's Coalition Government. Author of the Balfour Declaration supporting the establishment of a Jewish national home in Palestine.
2. John Morley: *see* Tom Mann, *The Socialists' Program*, n. 2.
3. Charles Bradlaugh (1833–91); used the pseudonym 'Iconoclast'. Secularist lecturer and editor of *Investigator* and *National Reformer*. Founder of National Secular Society. MP for Northampton; was prevented from taking his seat in Parliament for six years because he wanted to affirm instead of swearing on oath. Finally allowed to take his seat in 1866, and in 1888 he managed to get an Act through Parliament giving the right to affirm.
4. Huxley: *see* Annie Besant, *Why I Am A Socialist*, n. 2.
5. Morris: *see* Chapter 6.
6. Wilhelm Leibknecht (1826–1900); prominent figure in the German and international working-class movement. Friend and associate of Karl Marx and Frederick Engels.
7. Lord Salisbury, Fourth Marquis (1861–1947); President of the Board of Trade 1905 and Lord President of the Council, 1923.
8. Sir William Harcourt (1827–1904); Liberal politician famous for the phrase 'We are all socialists now.'
9. Samuel Woods (1846–1915); Secretary to the Trades Union Congress Parliamentary Committee 1894–1904.
10. George Brooks; minister of Robert Street Church, Grosvenor Square, London. Liberal candidate for Durham 1886. Author of *Industry and Property* in which he expresses extreme anti-socialist opinions.

9

Monopoly
or, How Labour is Robbed

WILLIAM MORRIS

Introduction

Monopoly was first published at the office of *The Commonweal* as Number 7 of the Socialist Platform series.

In it, Morris explains the labour theory of value as the root cause of exploitation in capitalist society. He urged the working class to reject any programme which did not advocate the abolition of private property in industry.

Morris was also clear that it would require a revolution to abolish capitalism and inaugurate socialism.

At least nine editions of the pamphlet were published by the Hammersmith Socialist Society, William Reeves, the Socialist League, the Glasgow Labour Literature Society and in the Freedom Library.

* * *

I want you to consider the position of the working-classes generally at the present day: not to dwell on the progress that they may (or may not) have made within the last five hundred or the last fifty years, but to consider what their position is, relatively to the other classes of which our society is composed: and in doing so I wish to guard against any exaggeration as to the advantages of the position of the upper and middle classes on the one side, and the disadvantages of the working-classes on the other; for in truth there is no need for exaggeration; the contrast between the two positions is sufficiently startling when all admissions have been made that can be made. After all, one need not go further than the simple statement of these few words: *The workers are in an inferior position to that of the non-workers.*

When we come to consider that everyone admits nowadays that labour is the source of wealth – or, to put it in another way, that it is a law of nature for man generally, that he must labour in order to live – we must all of us come to the conclusion that this fact, that the workers' standard of livelihood is lower than that of the non-workers, is a startling fact. But startling as it is, it may perhaps help out the imaginations of some of us – at all events, of the well-to-do – if I dwell a little on the details of this disgrace and say plainly what it means.

To begin, then, with the foundation; the workers eat inferior food and are clad in inferior clothes to those of the non-workers. This is true of the whole class, but a great portion of it are so ill-fed that they not only live on coarser or nastier victuals than the non-producers, but have not enough, even of these, to duly keep up their vitality; so that they suffer from the diseases and the early death which come of semi-starvation: or why say *semi*-starvation? Let us say plainly that most of the workers are starved to death. As to their clothing, they are so ill-clad that the dirt and foulness of their clothes forms an integral part of their substance, and is useful in making them a defence against the weather; according to the ancient proverb, 'Dirt and grease are the poor man's apparel.'

Again, the housing of the workers is proportionately much worse, so far as the better-off of them go, than their food or clothing. The best of their houses or apartments are not fit for human beings to live in, so crowded as they are. They would not be, even if one could step out of their doors into gardens or pleasant country, or handsome squares; but when one thinks of the wretched sordidness and closeness of the streets and alleys that they actually do form, one is almost forced to try to blunt one's sense of fitness and propriety, so miserable are they. As to the lodgings of the worse-off of our town workers, I must confess that I only know of them by rumour, and that I dare not face them personally; though I think my imagination will carry me a good way in picturing them to me. One thing, again, has always struck me much in passing through poor quarters of the town, and that is the noise and unrest of them, so confusing to all one's ideas and thoughts, and such a contrast to the dignified calm of the quarters of those who can afford such blessings.

Well! food, clothes, and housing – those are the three important items in the material condition of men, and I say flatly that the contrast between those of the non-producers and those of the producers is *horrible*, and that the word is no exaggeration. But is there a contrast in nothing else – education, now? Some of us are in the habit of boasting about our elementary education: perhaps it is good so far as it goes (and perhaps it isn't), but why doesn't it go further? Why is it elementary? In ordinary parlance, *elementary* is contrasted with *liberal* education. You know that in the class to which I belong, the professional or parasitical class, if a man cannot make some pretence to read a Latin book, and doesn't know a little French or German, he is very apt to keep it dark as something to be ashamed of, unless he has some real turn towards mathematics or the physical sciences to cover his historical or classical ignorance; whereas if a working-man were to know a little Latin and a little French, he would be looked on as a very superior person, a kind of genius – which, considering the difficulties that surround him, he would be: inferiority again, you see, clear and plain.

But after all, it is not such scraps of ill-digested knowledge as this that give us the real test of the contrast; this lies rather in the taste for reading and the habit of it, and the capacity for the enjoyment of refined thought and the expression of it, which the more expensive class really has (in spite of the disgraceful sloppiness of *its* education), and which unhappily the working or un-expensive class lacks. The immediate reason for that lack, I know well enough, and that forms another item of contrast: it is the combined leisure and elbow-room which the expensive class considers its birthright, and without which education, as I have often had to say, is a mere mockery; and which leisure and elbow-room the working class lacks, and even 'social reformers' expect them to be contented with that lack. Of course, you understand that in speaking of this item I am thinking of the well-to-do artisan, and not the squalid, hustled-about, misery-blinded and hopeless wretch of the fringe of labour – i.e., the greater part of labour.

Just consider the contrast in the mere matter of holidays. Leisure again! If a professional man (like myself, for instance) does a little more than his due daily grind – dear me, the fuss his friends make of him! How they are always urging him not to overdo it, and to consider his precious health, and the necessity of rest and so forth! And you know the very same persons, if they found some artisan in their employment looking towards a holiday, how sourly they would treat his longings for *rest*, how they would call him (perhaps not to his face) sot and sluggard and the like; and if he has it, he has got to take it against both his purse and his conscience; whereas in the professional class the yearly holiday is part of the payment for services. Once more look at the different standard for the worker and the non-worker!

What can I say about popular amusements that would not so offend you that you would refuse to listen to me? Well, I must say something at any cost – viz., that few things sadden me so much as the amusements which are thought good enough for the workers; such a miserable killing – yea, murder – of the little scraps of their scanty leisure time as they are. Though, indeed, if you say that there is not so much contrast here between the workers' public amusements and those provided for the middle classes, I must admit it, with this explanation, that owing to the nature of the case, the necessarily social or co-operative method of the getting up and acceptation of such amusements, the lower standard has pulled down the whole of our public amusements; has made, for instance, our theatrical entertainments the very lowest expression of the art of acting which the world has yet seen.

Or again, a cognate subject, the condition of the English language at present. How often I have it said to me: you must not write in a literary style if you wish the working classes to understand you. Now at first sight that seems as if the worker were in rather the better position in this matter; because the English of our drawing-rooms and leading articles is a wretched mongrel jargon that can scarcely be called English, or indeed language; and one would have expected, *a priori*, that what the workers needed from a man speaking to them was plain English: but alas! 'tis just the contrary. I am told on all hands that my language is too simple to be understood by working-men; that if I wish them to understand me I must use an inferior quality of the newspaper jargon, the language (so called) of critics and 'superior persons'; and I am almost driven to believe this when I notice the kind of English used by candidates at election time, and by political men generally – though of course this is complicated by the fact that these gentlemen by no means want to make the meaning of their words too clear.

Well, I want to keep as sternly as possible to the point that I started from – viz., that there is a contrast between the position of the working classes and that of the easily-living classes, and that the former are in an inferior position in all ways. And here, at least, we find the so-called friends of the working classes telling us that the producers are in such a miserable condition that, if they are to understand our agitation, we must talk *down* to their slavish condition, not straightforwardly to them as friends and neighbours – as *men*, in short. Such advice I neither can nor will take; but that this should be thought necessary shows that, in spite of all hypocrisy, the master-class know well enough that those whom they 'employ' are their slaves.

To be short, then, the working-classes are, relatively to the upper and middle classes, in a degraded condition, and if their condition could be much raised from what it is now, even if their wages were doubled and their work-time halved, they would still be in a degraded condition, so long as they were in a position of inferiority to another class – so long as they were dependent on them – unless it turned out to be a law of nature that the making of useful things necessarily brought with it such inferiority!

Now, once again, I ask you very seriously to consider what that means, and you will, after consideration, see clearly that it must have to do with the way in which industry is organised amongst us, and the brute force which supports that organisation. It is clearly no matter of race; the highest noble in the land is of the same blood, for all he can tell, as the clerk in his estate office, or his gardener's boy. The grandson or even the son of the 'self-made man' may be just as refined – and also quite as unenergetic and stupid – as the man with twenty generations of titled fools at his back. Neither will it do to say, as some do, that it is a matter of individual talent or energy. He who says this, practically asserts that the whole of the working-classes are composed of men who individually do not rise above a lowish average and that all of the middle-class men rise above it; and I don't think any one will be found who will support such a proposition, who is himself not manifestly below even that lowish average. No! You will, when you think of this contrast between the position of the producing and the non-producing classes, be forced to admit first that it is an evil, and secondly that it is caused by artificial regulations; by customs that can be turned into more reasonable paths; by laws of man that can be abolished, leaving us free to work and live as the laws of nature would have us. And when you have come to those two conclusions, you will then have either to accept Socialism as the basis for a new order of things, or to find some better basis than that, but you will not be able to accept the present basis of society unless you are prepared to say that you will not seek a remedy for an evil which you know can be remedied. Let me put the position once more as clearly as I can, and then let us see what the remedy is.

Society today is divided into classes, those who render services to the public and those who do not. Those who render services to the community are in an inferior position to those who do not, though there are various degrees of inferiority amongst them, from a position worse than that of a savage in a good climate to one not much below that of the lower degree of the unserviceable class; but the general rule is, that the more undeniably useful a man's services are, the worse his position is; as, for example, the agricultural labourers who raise our most absolute necessaries are the most poverty-stricken of all our slaves.

The individuals of this inferior or serviceable class, however, are not deprived of a hope. That hope is, that if they are successful they may become unserviceable; in which case they will be rewarded by a position of ease, comfort, and respect, and may leave this position as an inheritance to their children. The preachers of the unserviceable class (which rules all society) are very eloquent in urging the realisation of this hope, as a pious duty, on the members of the serviceable class. They say, amidst various degrees of rigmarole: 'My friends, thrift and industry are the greatest of the virtues; exercise them to the uttermost, and you will be rewarded by a position which will enable you to throw thrift and industry to the winds.'

However, it is clear that this doctrine would not be preached by the unserviceable if it could be widely practised because the result would then be that the serviceable class would tend to grow less and less and the world be undone; there would be nobody to make things. In short, I must say of this hope, 'What is that among so many?' Still it is a phantom which has its uses – to the unserviceable.

Now this arrangement of society appears to me to be a mistake (since I don't want to use strong language) – so much a mistake, that even if it could be shown to be irremediable, I should still say that every honest man must needs be a rebel against it; that those only could be contented with it who were, on the one hand, dishonest tyrants interested in its continuance; or, on the other hand, the cowardly and helpless slaves of tyrants – and both contemptible. Such a world, if it cannot be mended, needs no hell to supplement it.

But, you see, all people really admit that it can be remedied; only some don't want it to be, because they live easily and thoughtlessly in it and by means of it; and others are so hard-worked and miserable that they have no time to think and no heart to hope, and yet I tell you that if there were nothing between these two sets of people it would be remedied: even then should we have a new world. But judge you with what wreck and ruin, what fire and blood, its birth would be accompanied!

Argument, and appeals to think about these matters, and consciously help to bring a better world to birth, must be addressed to those who lie between these two dreadful products of our system, the blind tyrant and his blind slave. I appeal, therefore, to those of the unserviceable class who are ashamed of their position, who are learning to understand the crime of living without producing, and would be serviceable if they could; and, on the other hand, to those of the serviceable class who by luck maybe, or rather maybe by determination, by sacrifice of what small leisure or pleasure our system has left them, are able to think about their position and are intelligently discontented with it.

To all these I say: you well know that there must be a remedy to the present state of things. For nature bids all men to work in order to live, and that command can only be evaded by a man or a class forcing others to work for it in its stead; and, as a matter of fact, it is the few that compel and the many that are compelled; as indeed the most must work, or the work of the world couldn't go on. Here, then, is your remedy within sight surely; for why should the many allow the few to compel them to do what nature does herself compel them to do? It is only by means of superstition and ignorance that they can do so; for observe that the existence of a superior class living on an inferior implies that there is a constant struggle going on between them; whatever the inferior class can do to better itself at the expense of the superior it both can and must do, just as a plant must needs grow towards the light; but its aim must be proportionate to its freedom from prejudice and its knowledge. If it is ignorant and prejudiced it will aim at some mere amelioration of its slavery; when it ceases to be ignorant, it will strive to throw off its slavery once for all.

Now, I may assume that the divine appointment of misery and degradation as accompaniments of labour is an exploded superstition among the workers; and, furthermore, that the recognition of the duty of the working man to raise his class, apart from his own individual advancement, is spreading wider and wider amongst the workers. I assume that most workmen are conscious of the inferior position of their class, although they are not and cannot be fully conscious of the extent of the loss which they and the whole world suffer as a consequence, since they cannot see and feel the better life they have not lived. But before they set out to seek a remedy they must add to this knowledge of their position and discontent with it, a knowledge of the means whereby they are kept in that position in their own despite; and that knowledge it is for us Socialists to give them, and when they have learned it then the change will come.

One can surely imagine the workman saying to himself, 'Here am I, a useful person in the community, a carpenter, a smith, a compositor, a weaver, a miner, a ploughman, or what not, and yet, as long as I work thus and am useful, I belong to the lower class, and am not respected like yonder squire or lord's son who does nothing, yonder gentleman who receives his quarterly dividends, yonder lawyer or soldier who does worse than nothing, or yonder manufacturer, as he calls himself, who pays his managers and foremen to do the work he pretends to do; and in all ways I live worse than he does, and yet I *do* and he lives on my *doings*. And furthermore, I know that if I were to combine with my fellow-workmen, we between us could carry on our business and earn a good livelihood by it without the help(?) of the squire's partridge-shooting, the gentleman's dividend-drawing, the lawyer's chicanery, the soldier's stupidity, or the manufacturer's quarrel with his brother manufacturer. Why, then, am I in an inferior position to the man who does nothing useful, and whom, therefore, it is clear that I *keep*? He says he *is* useful to me, but I know I am useful to him or he would not 'employ' me, and I don't perceive his utility. How would it be if I were to leave him severely alone, to try the experiment of living on his usefulness while I lived on mine, and worked *with* those that are useful *for* those that are useful? Why can't I do this?'

My friend, because since you live by your labour, you are not free. And if you ask me, Who is my master? Who owns me? I answer *Monopoly*. Get rid of Monopoly, and you will have overthrown your present tyrant, and will be able to live as you please, within the limits which nature prescribed to you while she was your master, but which limits you, as man, have enlarged so enormously by almost making her your servant.

And now, what are we to understand by the word Monopoly? I have seen it defined as the selling of wares at an enhanced price without the seller having added any additional value to them; which may be put again in this way, the habit of receiving reward for services never performed or intended to be performed; for imaginary services, in short.

This definition would come to this, that Monopolist is *cheat* writ large; but there is an element lacking in this definition which we must presently supply. We can defend ourselves against this cheat by using our wits to find out that his services are imaginary, and then refusing to deal with him; his instrument is fraud only. I should extend the definition of the Monopolist by saying that he was one who was *privileged* to *compel* us to pay for imaginary services. He is, therefore, a more injurious person than a mere cheat, against whom we can take precautions, because his instrument for depriving us of what we have earned is no longer mere fraud, but fraud with *violence* to fall back on. So long as his privilege lasts we have no defence against him; if we want to do business in his line of things, we must pay him the toll which his privilege allows him to claim of us, or else abstain from the article we want to buy. If, for example, there were a Monopoly of champagne, silk, velvet, kid gloves, or doll's eyes, when you wanted any of those articles you would have to pay the toll of the Monopolist, which would certainly be as much as he could get, besides their cost of production and distribution; and I imagine that if any such Monopoly were to come to light in these days, there would be a tremendous to-do about it, both in and out of Parliament. Nevertheless, there is little to-do about the fact that all society today is in the grasp of *Monopoly*. Monopoly is our master, and we do not know it.

For the privilege of our Monopolists does not enable them merely to lay a toll on a few matters of luxury or curiosity which people can do without. I have stated, and you must admit, that everyone must labour who would live, unless he is able to get somebody to do his share of labour for him – to be somebody's pensioner in fact. But most people cannot be the pensioners of others; therefore, they have to labour to supply their wants; but in order to labour usefully two matters are required: first, the bodily and mental powers of a human being, developed by training, habit and tradition; and second, raw material on which to exercise those powers, and tools wherewith to aid them. The second matters are absolutely necessary to the first; unless the two come together, no commodity can be produced. Those, therefore, that must labour in order to live, and who have to ask leave of others for the use of the instruments of labour, are not free men but the dependents of others, i.e., their slaves; for, the commodity which they have to buy of the monopolists is no less than life itself.

Now, I ask you to conceive of a society in which all sound and sane persons can produce by their labour on raw materials, aided by fitting tools, a due and comfortable livelihood, and which possesses a sufficiency of raw material and tools. Would you think it unreasonable or unjust, that such community should insist on every sane and sound person working to produce wealth, in order that he might not burden the community; or, on the other hand, that it should insure a comfortable livelihood to every person who worked honestly for that livelihood, a livelihood in which nothing was lacking that was necessary to his development as a healthy human animal, with all its strange complexity of intellectual and moral habits and aspirations?

Now, further, as to the raw material and tools of the community, which, mind you, are necessary to its existence: would you think it unreasonable, if the community should insist that these precious necessaries, things without which it could not live, should be *used* and not *abused*? Now, raw material and tools can only be *used* for the production of useful things; a piece of tillage, for instance, is not used by sowing it with thistles and dock and dodder, nor a bale of wool by burning it under your neighbour's window to annoy him; this is abuse, not use, of all these things, and I say that our community will be right in forbidding such abuse.

Again, would it be unreasonable for the community to say that these means of production, if they are to be used and not abused, must be used by those who *can* use them, that is, by all the sane and sound persons engaged in earning their livelihood in concert; that they are to be so used according to fair and natural regulations agreed upon by the whole community in its sane mind; and that, furthermore, since they are to be used by all, they must not be exclusively possessed, i.e., *owned* by any; because, if any private persons, or groups of such, held the exclusive possession of ownership of them, they could withhold the use of them from those who could use them, except on terms which would place the useful persons in a position of inferiority to the useless; in other words they would be their masters, and would impose such a life on them as they chose. Therefore, I say, those raw materials and tools would be the property of the whole community, and would be used by every one in it, on the terms that they should repair the waste in them and not engross undue shares of them.

Here, then, is our reasonable community, in which all can produce, all do produce, no one has to pay poll-tax to be allowed to work, that is to live; in which no man need be badly off, unless by his own will; a society whose aim it is to make the most of its natural conditions and surroundings for the benefit of each and all of its members. These people I call reasonable men; but they have been called by other names, as breakers of the eighth commandment (or of all the commandments in the lump), brigands, assassins, greedy pillagers, enemies of society – in a word, Socialists.

Look at another society, and see if we like it better. In it, as in our first one, all sane and sound persons can produce wealth by their labour on raw material aided by tools; nor is there any lack of raw materials and tools in *this* society; yet there the resemblance ceases; for, one part of those who could do useful work will not, and consequently another part cannot; some of this second part can get no work to do, and are starved outright; others can get nothing but useless work to do, and thereby help to starve their brethren; and all those who produce anything, as we have seen before, are in an inferior position to those who do not.

The law of nature, that livelihood follows labour, is thus reversed, since those who work hardest get least, and those who work least fare best. Is this reasonable? Yet it is the direct and necessary result of those rights of property which the whole of our army, navy, police, judges, lawyers, parsons, etc., are banded together to sustain, by whatever amount of fraud and violence may be necessary for its safeguarding. It is the result of monopoly; for now the field is no longer used only for its primary use, the growing of corn, the feeding of beasts, the building of a house upon it; it is also *abused* by being employed as a rent-squeezing machine for the supposed benefit of an individual; and the like is the case with the tools of labour; the stored up labour of past generations, the machinery, the means of transit, all these things are no longer used merely as means of production; that has now become their secondary use, which the law does not trouble itself with at all, since it has all its attention turned to its enforcing their abuse (now become their primary use) for the benefit of the owners; their abuse as instruments for squeezing rent, interest, and profit out of the producers.

Those that thus, according to the (middle-class) ten commandments, are so anxious to prevent what they call theft, are thus the masters – nay, the owners – of all society under our present system; outside them there is nothing whatever but machinery, metal, brutal, and human, for enabling them to produce, not the greatest amount of wealth, but the greatest amount of profit; and when the masters fall short in getting what they consider the due amount of profit produced by this said machinery, they say times are bad; even though the warehouses and granaries are full, and the power of producing wealth with decreasing labour is every day growing. High prices to them and also, unluckily to their human machines, mean prosperity, because these latter are not in the least in the world rewarded for producing wealth for themselves, but for producing profits for their masters. The destruction of wealth by war and other calamities is good for their profit-grinding, therefore we have war. The waste of labour in all kinds of stupidities and fatuities is good for trade, therefore we have sham literature, sham art, sham enjoyment, newspapers, advertisements, jubilees, and all kinds of disgraces, to help our failing system to totter on a little longer, so that our sons instead of ourselves may have to face the inevitable ruin which, on these terms, must bring about the peace to come.

What help is there out of it all? I have spoken of the workers as the helpless machinery of commerce; and helpless they are so long as they are apathetically accepting their position *as* mere machinery in the hands of the masters of society; and yet it is they who have to bring about the change, and sweep away monopoly. The capitalists for any radical change are far more helpless than they are; because, as capitalists, as a class, they cannot even conceive of any other means of living except as pensioners on others, and it is their accepted duty, nay, their religion, to resist all change in this direction; nor as individuals have they any means of earning their livelihood, if you take away their pensions before you have begun to reconstruct a new world in which they would find a place like other people; it is, therefore, impossible that the change can be made from above to below. No, it is the classes which are necessary to what of real society still hangs together behind the monstrous machinery of monopoly, it is the workers themselves that must bring about the change. And it is at least an incidental purpose of Socialist propaganda that the change should be, if possible, brought about or at least guided by the conscious intelligence of the workers, that it may not be left altogether to the blind forces of hunger, misery, and despair, which the capitalist system is so steadily piling up for its own overthrow. Apart from all the conscious politics, all the pushing this way and that, of semi-extinct Toryism and vague crude democracy, which is undoubtedly paving the way for revolution, the time is coming when the monopoly of the means of production will lose its value, when the employers will begin to cease to employ. Cut-throat competition, ever cheapening means of production, and exhausting markets on one hand; on the other, the unceasing struggle of the workers to improve their condition at the expense of the capitalists, will make employment for profit more difficult both to get and to give; will, in fact, bring about deadlock and ruin in spite of occasional improvements in trade. But if the workers have learned to understand their position, which means if they have become determined to make the best of the nature which they have so far conquered, in despite of artificial restrictions on labour for the benefit of a class, they need not fear the coming crisis. That very increase in the productivity of labour, which will ruin capitalism, will make Socialism possible, and it cannot be doubted that the progress of the cheapening of production will be quickened prodigiously in the very first days of the new social order, and we shall all find it easy enough to live a very few years after the time when we found it so difficult to make profits.

Nevertheless, it would be disingenuous if I seemed to try to create the impression that the abolition of monopoly − of the artificial restrictions on production − would be plain sailing, that it would come quite peacefully and without strenuous effort of various kinds. Things now going on do not encourage one to think that; hypocrisy where the movement seems weak in power or limited in aim, unscrupulous and relentless repression where it seems threatening and well instructed; no real signs of privilege yielding a jot without compulsion. And you must remember that all our law and government, from Parliament to a County Court, has now got to be just an elaborate defence of that very monopoly which it is our business to clear away, though they by no means began with that. True it is, that if the whole class of workers could be convinced on one day or in one year of the necessity of abolishing monopoly, it would pass away like the clouds of night. But the necessities of the miserable, and the aspirations of the intelligent, will outrun the slower process of gradual conversion, and the anti-monopolists will find themselves in a position in which they will be forced to try to get hold of the executive, in order to destroy it and thus metamorphose society, not in order to govern by it and as they are now governed; in other words, they will have to sweep away all the artificial restrictions that stand in the way of free labour, and they will have to *compel* this step by some means or other. Those who set before them this necessity will doubtless differ at present as to the means whereby this will be done; but they should at least agree, and will agree when the time comes for action, that any means that are means, and are not unhuman, are good to use.

I have, then, tried to point out to you that the producing or useful class are in an inferior position to the non-producing or useless class; that this is a reversal of the law of nature which bids all to labour in order to live. That this monstrosity is the necessary result of private persons being allowed to treat the matters that are necessary to the fructification of labour as their *property*, and to abuse them by employing them as mere means of compulsion on the worker to pay tribute for leave to live. I have asked you to learn to agree with us Socialists in thinking it necessary to abolish this monopoly, and to combine together for its abolition and the reconstruction of society on the basis of the freedom of labour and the abolition of all privilege. I must add further, that no programme is worthy of the acceptance of the working-classes that stops short of the abolition of private property in the means of production. Any other programme is misleading and dishonest; it has two faces to it, one of which says to the working man, 'This is socialism or the beginning of it' (which it is not), and the other says to the capitalist, 'This is sham Socialism, if you can get the workers, or part of them, to accept this, it will create a new lower middle-class, a buffer, to push in between Privilege and Socialism, and save you, if only for a while.

But this true programme, which means the abolition of privilege, is enough, for it must and will lead directly to full socialism. It will draw the teeth of the dragon of capitalism, and make a society of equality possible; a society in which, instead of living among enemies in a state of things where there is nothing but a kind of armed truce between all men, we shall live among friends and neighbours, with whom, indeed, our passions or folly may sometimes make us quarrel, but whose interests cannot really be dissociated from our own.

10

Socialism and Trade Unionism

THE SOCIALIST GROUP OF THE LONDON SOCIETY OF COMPOSITORS

Introduction

The London Society of Compositors was an association of highly skilled craftsmen who had attained a tight control over entry to their trade. In 1902 the Society held a ballot to decide whether members should pay a compulsory levy to secure the return of a Member of Parliament. The proposal was adopted by 4,772 votes to 2,948.

Political action was therefore endorsed by the majority, and the activities of the socialist members led to the Society playing an important part in the affairs of both the Trades Union Congress and the Labour Party. Two of its secretaries won seats in the House of Commons.

The highly privileged position enjoyed by the members of the Society accounts for their views. They both opposed strikes and contended that trade unions were often responsible for strike situations through their 'ill-considered demands'. Such positions show how divorced such aristocrats of labour were from the problems and struggles of unskilled workers.

The following pamphlet was issued by the Society in 1902.

* * *

It is unfortunate that after some dozen years or more of Socialist propaganda there should still be considerable bitterness existing between Trade Unionists and Socialists. The cause of the unpopularity of the Socialists was not due to any desire on their part to irritate Trade Unionists, but arose out of the stupid prejudices of the spokesmen and leaders of the Trade Unionists themselves.

When one of the first Socialist organisations, the Social Democratic Federation, started its propaganda work to point out to the workers that the poverty and social ills which afflicted working men were due to economic causes which Trade Unionists did not recognise, it was met with rebuff and contumely. The official element of the Unions set themselves out to excite the political prejudices of their members against them. The Socialists, from the fact that they were formulating a new ideal, had to appear as critics of Trade Unionism, and were consequently put down as being both censorious and truculent. 'Socialists were paid agitators in disguise!' 'Socialist organisations were run by Tory money!' 'Their leaders were knaves, and the rank and file were either fools or fanatics!'

The outcome of such reprisals was that the sympathy which all Socialists had with Trade Unionism was for a time estranged, and the controversy went on the lines of Trades Unionism *versus* Socialism. The antagonism then engendered still survives in a more or less degree. But, though bitterness still exists, there are, happily, signs of a better feeling in a great section of the two parties since the dawn of the New Trade Unionism.

Now that the Socialist movement is recognised in the Labour world, the question can well be asked whether a more conciliatory attitude cannot be taken up between Socialists and Trade Unionists; whether the provinces of the two schools cannot be so defined that bitterness of feeling can be avoided on both sides? Surely it is better to work together on points of agreement than to wrangle on points of difference.

Socialists are staunch Trade Unionists. The new Trade Unionism[1] is evidence of this, for Socialists are responsible for calling it into existence. The Gasworks and General Labourers' Union is one of the New School of whom honourable mention can be made. It contains over 40,000 members, and its secretary is a prominent member of a Socialist body, numbering among its members numerous socialist adherents. The influence of the Gasworkers' Union at West Ham is enormous. The Socialist unionists there have elected members on all the local bodies, and have succeeded in raising the wages of the Town Council employees. It will also be remembered that when Mr. Cook, of the London Society of Compositors, raised the issue of the Trade Union wage-clause on the London School Board[2] he was prompted to put forward his proposal by a prominent lady Socialist member of that body. On the programme of every Socialist there is a special heading given to 'Labour', and Trade Union principles of such a character are insisted upon as were never dreamed of before, though Trade Union representatives both in Parliament and in local bodies have had opportunities of forcing the various proposals to the front. It is also well known that leaders of deputations to masters for better terms and conditions of labour are, in the majority of instances, Socialists, besides a large number of trade union organisers.

The movement which is now gaining ground in favour of Federation among Trade Unionists generally is one of Socialist origin. When yesterday the Socialists preached it, Trade Unionists disregarded it. Today, when the storm-cloud of Masters' Federations has appeared, the principle is accepted without demur. If Socialists, then, are ever playing the part of the staunch friend, the warm advocate and sound adviser to Trade Unionists, surely their acquaintance is worth cultivating, and their principles which guide them in Trade Union and social matters are worthy of the consideration of Trade Unionists generally. Why should not the latter come to some common understanding with friends, who, whatever their faults in grace and style when criticising the conservative methods of Trade Unionism may be, are always on the right side when the Trade Unionist is attacked by the common enemy – the capitalist?

At what point do the Trade Unionist and Socialist diverge?

Unfortunately the Trade Unionist never clearly defines his position nor gives full expression to his ideal.

It will be doing Trade Unionists no injustice if we assume that their object is to maintain wages and such usages of the trade which they recognise as conducive to their interests. It would be too much to say that they do not aspire to an increase of wages; but an increase of wages, as a rule, is only demanded because they have to meet social demands which are forced upon them – such, for instance, as a rise in rent, rates, and taxes, water and gas, railway fares, etc.

All the above advantages and demands may be summed up in the phrase which has lately come into vogue, namely, 'A Fair Wage.'

What is a 'Fair Wage?'

A fair wage may be said to be that sum of money for which the worker sells his labour to the capitalist. It represents that standard of comfort which the worker by custom, and convention and by combination, can obtain from the capitalist master.

The Socialists' conception of standard of comfort is social equality. The Trade Unionists' conception of standard of comfort is a restricted one, depending on the social position in which they happen to move. It may be said to be represented by their wages, or the sums of 30s., 35s., 40s., to 60s. per week, mostly by the lower figures of 30s. and 35s.

To remove any doubt as to the interpretation of the Trade Unionists' ideal you have only to get a book of rules of some society and examine its declared object. We give a couple of unions as an example. The object of the London Society of Compositors, as set out in its rules, is as follows: 'This Society is established to uphold and protect the wages of labour agreeably to the provisions contained in the London Scale of Prices, and such other prices, customs, and usages as belong to the profession not directly mentioned in the said Scale, to regulate the number of apprentices, turnovers,' etc.

The Operative Bricklayers' Society, one of the most powerful of the trade unions, states that its object 'is to provide funds to be applied to the following purposes, viz., the protection of the trade rights and privileges of its members; providing assistance to its members in search of work; the support of its members in case of sickness, accident, and superannuation; the burial of its members and their wives; and the promotion of their general welfare.'

Such ideals of comforts as set out in the above objects practically implies total acceptance of the jerry-built house with its attendant typhoid fevers and other maladies so fatal to adults and children; also food of an adulterated character, and clothing of a shoddy description.

If this be the ideal of Trade Unionists, then they must admit it is far behind that of the Socialists, who demand the highest education and culture which society can bestow in return for their labour.

Trade Unionists look solely to Unionism to maintain their miserable standard of living, ignorant of the economic laws working against them. Socialists accept Unionism as only one method to maintain their present standard of comfort, being economically conscious that their labour, like any ordinary commodity, is subject to competitive laws which compel them to sell at the market price.

It might at first sight appear that persons viewing things from such extreme points of view might have some difficulty in finding a common ground of agreement. As it happens, however, both Socialists and Trade Unionists have a common enemy, a common want, and a common economic force which continually and relentlessly drives them in one direction. Both are driven to defend attacks against their standard of living by the capitalist, and the one point of agreement between Socialists and Trade Unionists, therefore, is that they both desire to maintain and increase their present standard of living.

Let Trade Unionists accept this point of agreement as a working basis between themselves and Social-Democrats. Let them judge Socialist proposals by the test of their efficiency to raise their standard of comfort.

Trade Unionists enter a Union to resist the exactions of the capitalists, and to baulk attempts on their part to reduce wages. Socialists enter a Union for precisely the same reason. Given agreement on the object or ideal, there is really no obstacle but prejudice why Trade Unionists should limit their efforts to their present narrow bases. Why should not they, like the Socialists, avail themselves of political action and municipal effort?

Trade Unionists in the past have, at the ballot box, voted power to exploiting capitalists, masquerading in the guise of Tories and Liberals. Now, the two political parties represent the landlords and the commercial classes – both of whom, as Adam Smith says in his 'Wealth of Nations,' 'are in a constant conspiracy to keep down wages,' which, in plain language, means that they both aim at reducing the standard of living of the workers, and are, therefore, equally the natural enemy of the worker.

Liberal and Tory employers both consciously support the capitalist system of exploitation of labour, and, consequently, both are equally the enemy of Trade Unionists and Socialists. Trade Unionists, to be consistent, should, therefore, be independent in politics, and steer clear of both Liberals and Tories. They must select candidates to represent their interest outside the influence of the two political parties. The capitalists at present hold the laws of the State in the hollow of their hands, for they are the Liberals and the Tories. The Trade Unionists, in combination with the Socialists, should endeavour to take away this political power possessed by the capitalists by returning their own representative to the House of Commons, and modify the laws in their favour.

Trade Unionists of the past have stultified themselves as unionists by refusing to take political action. Their position has been a most ridiculous one. When Trade Unionists have wanted the intercession of Parliament they have had humbly to send deputations to meet members, who owe them no allegiance, in the lobby, instead of having representatives of their own to fight their battles on the floor of the House of Commons itself. Ignorant of the economic forces working against them, Trade Unionists have taken such a narrow view of social questions that they have not seen how independent working-class representatives in the House of Commons could help them. Viewing everything through the spectacles of individualism, like their employers, they have been too prejudiced to see how a contribution from their societies to a Parliamentary fund could individually help them. If they would view parliamentary action from the standpoint of the collective welfare of the people, they would soon realise its far-reaching effects.

A legal forty-eight hour working week, for instance, would bring benefit to all, and raise the standard of all by giving more leisure; thereby affording workers an opportunity of obtaining fresh air, and following artistic and intellectual pursuits. The temporary demand for extra labour would prevent wages falling, and the shorter working day once secured, the workers would be short-witted indeed if they could not devise a counterstroke to meet the attempts of the capitalist to reduce their wages in the future.

One of the strongest agents which work in favour of the capitalists is the necessity of the workers to find food and clothing for their families. This evil can be met by the State proposal which is now making such headway in England, namely, free Maintenance for Children. The old-fashioned prejudices fostered by the capitalists and their hangers-on, that it is degrading to accept anything from the State is fast dying out in the face of free Education, Free Libraries, Free Maintenance for all sickened with infectious fevers, putting aside the fact that the well-to-do have no sense of being pauperised when they enjoy the educational endowments left for the education and succour of the poor, and that the rich have no hesitation in quartering themselves on the public purse.

Free Maintenance for Children should be accepted by trade Unionists as tending to raise the standard of comfort. All should demand it with the object of personally benefitting themselves. If, according to capitalist statistics, the workers create fifteen hundred millions per year and receive short of five hundred millions a year, then they should avail themselves of any proposal which would fall on the one thousand millions of which capitalists deprive them. Free Maintenance for Children would be a tax on that surplus wealth which the capitalists and the aristocracy share between them. To the worker, free maintenance for his children would be equivalent to an additional income. His standard of living would rise. No doubt the capitalist would reduce his wages as much as possible, but the worker would then be able to fight him on more equal terms. His children being well cared for, he would be able to hold out against the capitalist for an indefinite period.

Trade Unionists, again, are confronted with a very conservative element in their union, which adds to the difficulty of maintaining their trade union rate of pay, namely, by men becoming aged at the comparatively early age of forty-five and fifty. At this age men do not care to throw up their situation for fear of not getting another. Such men, by their necessities and their family responsibilities, act as a conservative force and wet blanket to the union. Now, a State pension at fifty, coupled with free maintenance for children, would encourage these men to take up a bolder attitude, and would relieve the members of a union of much anxiety at the time of struggle and the fear of breaking down their superannuation fund. Trade unionists, then, should demand State pensions at the age of fifty. Surely, a State pension is better than the prison workhouse.

As to the tax from which the funds would be provided for these proposals, the expense can be met by a cumulative income tax on all incomes over £500 a year. Under this tax the richer the person the more he would pay; the bigger the exploiter the more he would have to disgorge. Such proposals as the foregoing seem bold, but the workers, as soon as they politically recognise their collective power, can secure the whole of them. They have the vote in sufficient numbers even now to secure them if they so desire. The expense of carrying them into execution would form but a fraction of the one thousand millions of which they are exploited every year.

The Housing Question is also worthy of attention. Trade Unionists should require the State to erect buildings to be let at a sum which would cover cost of construction and maintenance alone. This would give them a stationary rent, and when locked out by their employers they, as unemployed workers, would not be so liable to be turned into the street. Public opinion and their own voting strength would secure them in their holding. Healthy homes for the people would reduce mortality among the workers' children, and would materially help to increase the comfort of the worker.

There are many other palliatives which the workers might avail themselves of by political means to better their conditions, but space will not allow dealing with them.

The difficulty which Socialists experience with Trade Unionists is the feeling of exclusiveness which has grown up around them. They have formed themselves into groups to restrict the ever-growing exactions of the employers, but they have paid but little attention to the economic forces which are playing equally upon the masters as upon themselves. As a consequence workers have attached too much importance to old customs and fashions which stand in the way of improved methods of production. Very often the Unions have been led to support some old-fashioned privilege of slight relative importance to the main issue of maintaining a wage which will ensure them better living conditions.

Happily Trade Unionists now recognise that they can neither prevent the introduction of machinery nor improved methods of production. It is better for employees to recognise the inevitable, and, when threatened by machinery, like the compositors, make the best terms possible, while aiming always to maintain and increase their wages.

The workers, unconscious of economic development, unfortunately side with one political party or the other, not seeing that the one must inevitably be as antagonistic to their interests as the other. Tory and Liberal politically represent two classes, who divide the spoils between them. One is connected by tradition with the soil, the other with commerce. When they have a quarrel it is as between kites and crows for the possession of prey. To assert that a Tory is better than a Liberal, or a Liberal better than a Tory, is like affirming that one exploiter is less a thief than another. Employers live by exploitation, and each employer is desirous of getting a monopoly of trade that he may amass riches. To beat his opponent in the market he has to sell cheaper than he, and to sell cheaper he must reduce the cost of production of his goods, and to do this he must resort to labour-saving machinery and improved methods of production. For an employer to be benevolent and considerate, or allow the continuance of worn-out privileges under the plea of custom, is to place himself at a disadvantage with his competitors. Sooner or later he must come to grief, and his type cannot develop into a class.

The defeat of the engineers' attempt to break down the masters' lock-out has considerably modified the conservative policy of Unionists, and has created a distinct feeling in favour of Federation. The printing trade, the furnishing, the cotton and mining, and other industries, have it now under their consideration. This is a step in the right direction; but it has come rather late in the day to have much effect. The workers, if they had looked ahead, would have adopted it a quarter of a century back, when it might have been of great use to them. Unfortunately, they seem ready to repeat a similar blunder in not realising the power of political action.

If the employees federate they will now have to face a federation of the employers. Concentration of capital precedes combination of wage-slaves. Employers have this advantage – that they can federate and get into line, cash in bank, before the worker can get half way through discussing whether they shall enter upon a strike or resist attacks on the part of employers!

Employers from experience see the necessity of paying into a common fund, and soon come to a mutual understanding as to its distribution. The same acumen, unfortunately, cannot be attributed to the workers, who appear hopelessly divided in opinion as to the amount of contribution and benefit to be received. Federation at best will be but a game of see-saw, and it may be assumed that the present system gives the advantage to the capitalist. But Federation, though not an all-powerful weapon, is a necessity of the hour. It is a weapon of defence which Trade Unionists must avail themselves to restrain the ruthlessness of capitalism. When its incapacity to emancipate the worker from the aggression of capital has been demonstrated, then, let us hope, it will be the means of giving a further impetus to political action for palliative measures.

Until Trade Unionists form themselves into an independent party there can politically be no common agreement between them and Socialists, because while they support the capitalist class they are placing power in the hands of the exploiter, who is the common enemy. In the meantime, the policy of Socialists and Trade Unionists should be one of friendliness towards each other. Socialists must make it their first object to get some common basis of agreement with Trade Unionists, and endeavour to get the latter to admit that the object of Trade Unionism is to raise the standard of living and prevent exploitation. Such an admission would form a most reasonable basis, and one which all Trade Unionists would see their way to adopt. Political action would then follow as a natural sequence, and would help to still further place strikes in the background.

Now, a few words as to strikes. Strikes are the official outcome of Trade Unionism, just as wages are the logical outcome of capitalism. What is a strike? Nothing more than the collective refusal by a number of men to renew a contract. As sellers of labour Trade Unionists enter into a contract to exchange it for a sum of money representing their wages. The capitalist determines one day to purchase, if possible, labour at a lower price. The workers refuse to sell. Like other sellers, they hold their commodity back. This act constitutes a strike. It is a perfectly legitimate proceeding, and a position thoroughly logical to take up. To accept at command any offer from the capitalist would be to place themselves at his mercy, and Trade Unionists might start at once reducing their subsistence level to that of a Chinaman, and accept their fate at once. Strikes undoubtedly should be the last resort in a Labour dispute.

If Trade Unionists adopted the tactics of Socialists few strikes would take place. Opposed to strikes almost to unreasonableness, it is certainly odd that Socialists should be regarded as the chief instigators of them. Trade Unionists are responsible for a great number of strikes through their ill-considered demands, and also for their failure, by insisting upon them at an inopportune moment. Much more can generally be done by constant gentle pressure than by spasmodic attempts to storm the position. Strikes, to be successful, must be carefully planned. Money to carry it on should be collected before the struggle and not after. Everything should be in readiness so that the most favourable opportunity can be seized to assume the offensive, instead of allowing the employers to choose their time for a lock-out.

Trade Unionists, unfortunately, do not appreciate the economic forces at work in society, and the consequence is that instead of giving way voluntarily on certain points which evolution in production and distribution render inevitable, they turn obstinate, and false issues are raised which bring defeat.

Co-operation between Socialists and Trade Unionists should be adopted whenever possible, and when occasion offers an alliance should be entered into for common purposes, but the basis of the alliance should be carefully defined so that no ill will or rancour of feeling can survive should the compact have to be broken by the falling back of the less forward party through the influence of some personality that often unfortunately interposes itself in the political field.

In America a large section of Trade Unionists have already recognised that the class-war is inevitable under the present system of exploitation, and they have entered into an active alliance with the Socialist Party. It is to be hoped that the Trade Unions of Great Britain will ere long see their way to follow the example set by their American brethren in the United States.

Trade Unionists desire to improve their standard of living. Let them, then work as has been suggested in this pamphlet for their common object, adopting political action as a support to their Trade Union. They will soon find that they have a weapon in their hands by which they can not only benefit themselves but the whole people, and untold generations who will follow after them.

Notes

1. New Trade Unionism was the organisation of women workers, the unskilled and labourers. It was led by the socialists, Tom Mann, Annie Besant, John Burns and Ben Tillet in the 1880s.
2. Education had always been seen as an essential plank in socialist programmes.

When the Education Act establishing school boards of directly elected representatives was passed in 1870, the socialist movement saw opportunities for electing working men and women on to these boards. The major challenge was made in London, where as early as 1873 a tradition of working class representation on school boards was established. This spread over the whole country, and steadily increased until the boards were dissolved in 1903.

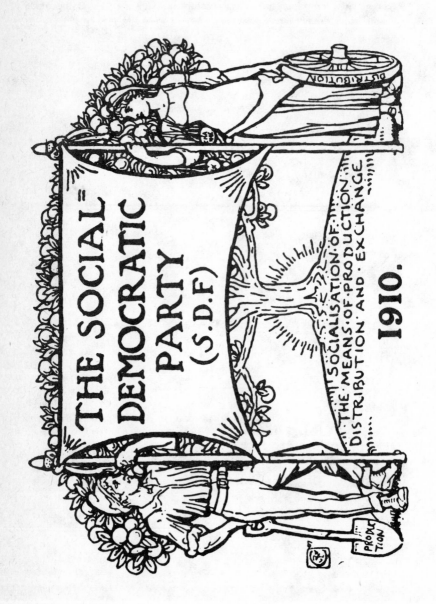

THE SOCIAL=
DEMOCRATIC
PARTY
(S.D.F.)

THE "SOCIALISATION" OF
THE MEANS OF PRODUCTION
DISTRIBUTION AND EXCHANGE

1910.

DISTRIBUTION

PRODUC=
TION

11
Social Democracy

HENRY MAYERS HYNDMAN (1842–1921)

Introduction

Hyndman was the eldest son of a wealthy London businessman and, like his father, received his degree from Trinity college, Cambridge. In spite of his background, the young Hyndman absorbed and adopted the main elements of socialist thought through reading Marx. Though Hyndman mentioned his indebtedness to a 'great thinker and original writer' in a pamphlet he wrote entitled *England for All*, in which he drew extensively on Marx's work, he failed to mention his source by name, an omission which caused Marx and Engels to view him with suspicion.

Hyndman acted as special correspondent in Italy during the war that led to the unification of the Italian principalities, and during this time he met Mazzini and Garibaldi. He then travelled for about ten years, visiting Australia, New Zealand and the United States. He returned to Europe in 1871 at the start of the events of the Paris Commune, the development and outcome of which served to reinforce his nascent socialist leanings.

Hyndman did not in fact acknowledge his conversion to socialism until his late thirties, when he took the decision to devote himself to the organisation of a social democratic party in England. He began by writing an article which was published in the *Nineteenth Century* in January 1980 entitled 'The Dawn of a Revolutionary Epoch'. It was probably the first summary of Marx's views to appear in English. Soon he set about organising the English socialist movement by inviting a group who had been meeting as the Rose Street Club to join him in forming a Democratic Party. These overtures led to the formation of the Democratic Federation in 1881.

This organisation formulated a programme calling for the remedy of social ills, and which included demands for an eight-hour working day, free and compulsory education, cheap transport for workers and the provision of working-class housing. It was in the manifesto of the Federation drawn up by Hyndman that the slogan 'Educate, Agitate, Organise' was first used. In 1884 he financed the publication of *Justice*, a journal which continued through the last decade of the century.

Like many of the stalwarts of the socialist revival of the 1880s, Hyndman viewed the Labour Party with suspicion. However, during the First World War, when he joined the War Emergency Workers' National Committee, and later the Consumers' Council, working alongside Sydney Webb, he modified his opinions.

In spite of his personal ambition to become an MP, and though he 'nursed' the Burnley constituency for many years, Hyndman never managed to enter Parliament.

He joined the British Socialist Party at its inception in 1911 and left it in 1916 at the Fifth Party Conference, as he opposed the anti-war attitude of the majority of party members. His break with socialism was cemented by his condemnation of the Russian Revolution. Though he disapproved of British troops being sent to intervene in Russia on the side of the counter-revolutionaries, at the same time he expressed his intention to do all he could to prevent any attempts at peace by negotiation. In 1920 he decided to ignore the formation of the British Communist Party. His last years were spent writing and speaking.

The pamphlet *Social Democracy*, reproduced here, which was one of his lectures, shows both the strengths and weaknesses of Hyndman's understanding of scientific socialism as expounded by Karl Marx. Marx in fact had described Hyndman many years before the publication of *Social Democracy* as a 'well-meaning petit bourgeois'.

Hyndman's lectures and writing did in fact stimulate people to read and discuss Marx's writings, and many socialists had a copy of *Capital* on their bookshelves as a result of his efforts. Moreover, *Social Democracy* enjoyed a readership which extended beyond the membership of the SDF: it reached members of the ILP and other organisations. In this way the basic propositions of scientific socialism won wide acceptance through the whole of the socialist movement in that period.

Hyndman's lecture was delivered in the Queen's Hall, London on 14 April 1904.

Sources

C. Tsuzuki, *H.M. Hyndman and British Socialism*, Oxford University Press, 1961. *The Labour Magazine*, vol. 1, no. 5, September 1922, p. 195.

* * *

Mr. Chairman, Friends, and Fellow Citizens – If I had wanted evidence of the fact that the people of London and English people generally are not fond of looking into matters of principle which closely affect themselves, as compared with something of passing interest, I need only contrast the aspect of this hall tonight with that which greeted me when I was addressing this audience, or an audience in this hall, on the subject of the Fiscal Policy. That which is a comparatively minor matter, a thing which is of passing interest in the main, not only crowded this hall completely, but we turned two thousand people away; whereas tonight, when we have to deal with questions of principle that come home to every man, woman, and child in this country; with matters that are concerning at this instant the whole civilised world, there are comparatively few who are interested therein. There is something else which I would like to say. I see many of you here in this hall tonight are in possession of the syllabus to which our comrade and friend the chairman, Burrows, has referred, and I think you will sympathise with me when I endeavour to perform that remarkable juggler's feat of getting five pints into a quart pot, because there is enough here for about twelve nights of addresses, rather than for the time I shall be able to devote to it on this occasion. Also I think I may say that in speaking now, as our comrade has said, I am speaking at a moment when both the other parties, at any rate, are thoroughly well played out, and if there was ever a period in our history when Tory and Liberal, Liberal and Tory, had utterly failed to put before the people any principles or programme which can be really beneficial to them for the future, this is the time when that may be said to be the case. But it is of no use to criticise both these parties and proclaim where they are wrong unless we are prepared to propound something ourselves; and unless, further, we are able to say that not only have we a theory as regards the past and a policy as regards the present, but a distinct intention of putting forward measures which will carry us through the future.

One other thing. In speaking here tonight, I think I may claim that I am speaking on behalf of the International Social-Democratic Party of the whole civilised world. I am, myself, a member of the International Socialist Bureau. I have worked a great many years in this movement, and I think there is not a Socialist in this hall, nor do I think there are many on the Continent of Europe, who would not accept this syllabus as being in the main a summary of the views which they all collectively and individually hold upon the principles of the party to which they belong.

Now, friends and fellow citizens, in dealing with this matter I will, as far as I possibly can − as you know I am not in the habit of speaking from notes, and tonight I feel a little as if I were tied by the notes before me, but I want as far as I possibly can, for those of you who do not agree with us, who are of opinion that we Socialists are all in the air − I want as far as I possibly can to keep to this syllabus, and you must excuse me if I do not speak with the fluency which at times you have heard from me on the platform.

I believe one of the great reasons why Socialism in England holds the unsatisfactory place it does today, is the fact that our education is extremely bad. If you take the education of the ordinary school boards and elementary schools of this country what will you discover? You will find it is precisely of that character which will induce a habit of snippety reading and very little else. Nearly all our board school teaching has no ultimate end before it; nothing is aimed at beyond teaching the children a certain amount of reading, writing and arithmetic. Until recently there was no conception which went beyond that. I am only saying now what is said commonly by men who have no interest in saying it, because they have been responsible for all the education that has been given. England today has fallen behind to a large extent because we have not given to the children of the people the education they ought to have in view of the competition from other parts of the world. I do not think anybody who knows the condition of public education will doubt that is the case. In addition to that there are many other reasons why England today has not that vigour which even our forefathers had in the matter of the democratic feelings and democratic claims of the people. Emigration in this country has played almost as fatal a part as it did in the days of old Spain; the most active, vigorous, intelligent of the working-class population have gone into other fields to earn their living, and have stayed there away from the main stock, while only the less adventurous have remained at home. There are other causes that seem to me to have played a part. For instance, we were the first in capitalism, and for the last three or four generations practically the whole nation has been taught the doctrines of political economy, not from the point of view of the people but from that of the capitalists. And we accept this. I have found men who live by working with their hands as intolerant and bigoted upholders of the present system, and as incapable of appreciating what co-operation as a whole would mean, as any member of the classes who live upon their labour. We owe the present position of this country largely to the apathy of the mass of the people of England. In addition to that there is in this country a large number of people who form what I may call a 'buffer' class – a class not strictly concerned in keeping wages low, which, in the main, does not wish wages to be kept low, and which, when difficulties arise, not infrequently take the side of the workers against the larger capitalists. That class to a certain extent shades off the antagonism which otherwise would come to the front between the wage-earner on the one side, and the landlord and the capitalist on the other. And then there is the aristocracy of labour – the trade unionists – who have lost contact with their poorer brethren, and have been satisfied to benefit themselves a little under capitalism, instead of working for that complete change which they might have undertaken. This was predicted by Bronterre O'Brien and other Chartists, who foresaw the dangerous results of making a schism in the ranks of labour when they had against them a great class interested in keeping wages as low as possible.

Lastly, there has been a physical deterioration in the mass of the people. Taking one thing with another, a man physically well-developed is mentally and morally stronger than the man who is not. There are exceptions; but take a population which as a whole is well built up, physically strong, capable, and in every respect well trained, that will be as a whole a better population for all purposes than one which is not. Unfortunately, the inhabitants of our great cities have undergone an amount of physical deterioration which renders it extremely difficult for them to have initiative in any direction whatever.

If we turn to the other side, the educated classes, I think there also you see reasons why, even supposing Social-Democracy to be what we thoroughly, earnestly, and fully believe it to be, and can prove it to be – namely, completely true – why they refuse to look into the matter, and accept what could be proved to them. As a matter of fact the educated classes who come from our public schools and universities are also extremely lacking in initiative. Nothing is more remarkable than the commonplace of the educated man. I do not think any educated man here will deny that England in that respect has fallen remarkably behind the continent of Europe. Take the professors of our Universities. With few exceptions they are content to go on in the old ruts. Particularly is this so in the case of political economy. Whereas on the Continent young professors are adopting the theories of Marx so far as they can without losing their Chairs, in this country no man has come forward; and one of the most distinguished of our accredited teachers, having his second volume ready for eight or ten years, will not publish it, because he is not certain of the conclusion he has arrived at, or, perhaps, because they are of such a nature that he dare not publish them. That is Professor Marshall.

The Public School and University education of this country is not a scientific education in any sense. It is an education to a large extent of the past – languages of the past, thoughts of the past, ideals of the past, conduct of the past are what it treats of. And these are the days of modern thought, when we have got to sweep away a great deal of that old rubbish.

At present we have not swept it away, and this is one reason we are so far behind the continent of Europe and America.

I contend that modern Socialism is the science of sociology, and not merely an expression of the feeling and desires of the people; and the best evidence is that if you take any department of history and look at it in the light of the doctrines and theories which are propounded by the men of this school, you will find to your surprise that you have keys to all sorts of problems that have been practically insoluble, and the better you understand history and the more you read it from the scientific point of view the more completely will you be convinced that the Socialist doctrines comprise the only sound and solid view of the development of humanity. If that is so, and we can claim at the present moment, as we can, the most distinguished men in almost every department of art and science in Europe, surely it is worth the while of those who do not agree with us to see why we are attaining to this position. It is of no use for the men who happen to be in the front rank of politics to say we are utterly incompetent and ignorant when they will never meet us on any public platform, or, if they can help it, in the columns of a magazine or newspaper. If our views are so foolish, surely it would be an evening's entertainment for somebody in the front rank of the Tory or Liberal Party to come here and smash us some evening. I wish they would try to do it. The hall would be fuller than it is tonight to see the operation, and I venture to say we should survive. I doubt whether the other man would.

I say the growth of Socialism is primarily due to social and economic conditions. That is to say, it is perfectly impossible for a feudal society to breed modern scientific Socialism; the conditions would not admit it. Socialism is a growth necessarily coming out of the society of the time. Prior to that there may have been ideals of co-operation, of a few bodies of men sequestering themselves from the rest of the world; but an ideal of a Socialist society where all shall be for each and each for all, growing out of a competitive system, could not have arisen in the primitive communist period, the slave period, the feudal period, or prior to the capitalist period. We contend, therefore, that there is an inevitable fatalism running through the development of humanity, and that what we have to do is to appreciate what is occurring, and, having appreciated, to influence; not to imagine we can influence before we have appreciated or understood.

At the present moment, if you look at any of the countries where Socialism has made way this will strike you. It has been argued by our school persistently that the economic development of a country as a rule has conditioned its social progress, and that it attained to Socialism in so far as it did so by the scale of development of its industries and general social standing. That, in the main, has proved to be true, and the exception in the case of England will not, I think, be permanently enduring. But if you turn now to countries coming to the front in the social development you will see an extraordinary contrast. Germany is the best educated country in Europe, and Germany is the country where Socialism is most known at the present moment, and where it is best organised. We Social-Democrats cast there no fewer than three million votes. If Socialism were so entirely the property of the ignorant it would not have much hold upon Germany. But at the same time Germany is not so economically advanced as America, and America had ten years ago practically no Socialist Party at all; but with the extraordinary development of American industry, with the development of those trusts about which I shall have to say something later, and the terrible and vindictive action of the capitalist class in its monopoly-form in the last four or five years, the tendency of America in the direction of Socialism is so extraordinary that in a letter received from Simons this morning, speaking of the infamies committed in Colorado,[1] where atrocities like those of Russia are being committed under a democratic Government, he tells me it is his profound conviction that in 1908 they will poll only second to the German vote, and probably be in excess even of that.

What, therefore, has been the cause of this? Not necessarily the education of the American people, though they are a great deal better educated than we are; but the economical development, which has forced those who but yesterday were just as much opposed to us as anybody in this hall, by the logic of events, into the camp of the collectivists. You have on the one side the relentless economic development, which goes on, on, on, almost irrespective of those whom it crushes under its wheels, and on the other hand the necessary appreciation of that development which can only come with a sentient and educated population. Of the two, the development of the economic will overcome the development of the intellectual. It is my profound conviction that although the intelligent appreciation of surroundings will enable you to change and alter and modify them to.a certain extent, nevertheless the development of the economic and social conditions which you have not controlled and which have come upon you from centuries before have much more to do with your future than even your own action in your own time.

Socialism has three important departments: First, there is the historic. Now, our view of the historic conditions of human society and how they have come about, it would take much more than this evening's address alone to deal with – a course of lectures might be devoted to showing how each successive stage of human society arose in the main out of the material conditions for the production of wealth and the class wars resulting therefrom.

Take as example such a universal stage in the early history of man as cannibalism. Man ate man very commonly. I have been in countries where that peculiar form of obtaining indigestion was extremely common. All over the world the consumption of man by man has been almost a rule of human life. How did cannibalism come to an end? Cannibalism came to an end, as we contend, by the fact that the arts had advanced to such a stage that the captive was able to produce more than his keep, and that therefore, instead of eating him at once, it was more economical to eat him slowly; his life was used up for the benefit of the tribe which had enslaved him in place of their eating him there and then and I think the more you reflect upon that, the more you will see it is actually the case. And so consequently, going on to other illustrations, we come to this conclusion, that the development of mankind is not, as some have said, theological, positive, but economical, ethical, religious; that is to say, that when man had ceased to eat his fellow man – having done so for economic reasons – it became unethical to eat him from a moral point of view, and having become improper from a moral point of view, such abstention was sanctified from the religious point of view.

I delivered some years ago an address on 'Socialism and the Ten Commandments in the Vulgar Tongue.' If you take the fifth commandment – it is, you must honour your father and mother – it must be perfectly apparent you must know who your father is before you can honour him. In the early stages of society that was impossible, because the woman belonged to one gens and the man to another. Identification in that relation of life, which even today is not always easy, was then impossible; and it was therefore of no use to enunciate that commandment because the child could not identify the parent he was to honour. Thus social relations govern commandments and not commandments social relations.

Take another commandment: 'Thou shalt not steal.' If there was nothing to steal the commandment was superfluous, and under the communal system there was nothing to which stealing could be applied. You might say, 'Do not be greedy,' but it would be meaningless to say, 'Do not steal.'

Thus, to give an idea of the view we take, we believe the introduction of pigs and sheep to be a better means of suppressing cannibalism than the sending of missionaries.

Or take such a remarkable fact as the gradual decline of slavery – watch what brought about the decline of slavery. We are frequently told it was the Christian Church or the Catholic religion. I have no prejudice against any religion; though I feel a little in the condition of the Emperor of China, who, having examined the three religions of his Empire issued a rescript telling his people to believe in none of them. But that, at the same time, is not a matter we are concerned with. We interfere with no man's private belief under any circumstances whatever. Whether a man be Buddhist, fetish worshipper, Catholic – so long as he is a Socialist we go no further.

It is supposed, however, slavery was uprooted by religious means; but the truth is slavery faded out when slaves could no longer be obtained by conquest and became dear in consequence. Their food also became dear, and the two dearnesses coming together, it became unprofitable to keep them. Later it became wrong to have them, and later still a religious duty to manumit them – when it was economically convenient.

We agree thoroughly with the religious man who came last, with the moral man who came before him, and primarily with the economist who saw the whole thing and did not know it.

There is also the economic side of Socialism. This I have partly touched upon in these last remarks. It gives the analysis of the methods of production and exchange, and especially of capitalism. I shall deal with that a little more at length further on, but I will say here that that economical analysis applies throughout the ages, only that at the initial point pecuniary relations were but a portion of society, whereas under the capitalist system pecuniary relations dominate the whole. It is this last analysis which is most important to us, because it is that of our own day.

The historic, which shows the economic development of mankind from its first rude condition, when it depended on the chase, fishing, and the like, onwards through the various forms till it reaches our own day. There already the class war plays a leading part. In all the history of antiquity you find three or four classes of men at war with one another: plebs at war with gentile families, slaves at war with both, various degrees of aristocratic society often at war amongst themselves.

Historic changes have brought us to our present point, through the nomadic tribes, clear through the early family slavery, which was a progress, to chattel slavery, likewise a progress and inevitable. Without it we should not have the finest parts of our civilisation today. Terrible as the cruelties were, especially under the Roman rule, when thousands of slaves were sacrificed along the Roman roads in the servile wars – nevertheless, humanity could not be where it is today but for the slave development which followed the break-up of the commune. It was those slaves who gave us the art of Greece, the jurisprudence of Rome, and the monuments of antiquity.

We consider the chattel slave period terrible, but we are ourselves the outcome of that period, and there is at the present moment perhaps as much actual slavery in this country as there was during the Roman period. If you look at matters without prejudice you will discover that through this long period of unconscious human development – when man, unknowing, unguided, incapable of appreciating, was gradually passing through these various phases of his social development – you will come to the conclusion that these inevitable processes have been achieved by the continuous martyrdom of man; and, moreover, as they have been our forerunners, we are inheriting all this, and it is our business to make use of it by appreciating what is going on around us. It is only by knowing what these powers have produced in the past that we can arrive at the conscious certainty of the development of the future.

It is as impossible for any phase of human society as it has grown up to have preceded any other phase as it is for smoke to come without fire.

Hence we find that through all this period, from the nomadic and primitive communism, when people lived for ages under a communistic system and divided the product, through chattel slavery which broke up the commune, and feudalism, it was quite as impossible for those who lived in any period to understand the one coming after as it is for the majority to apprehend the period coming after us. Aristotle, the greatest mind of antiquity, could barely apprehend that the doing away of slavery was possible. I am sure that the noble of the feudal period, with his grandeur and his nobility, and his power of life and death over his serfs and the inhabitants of his estate – who did not have the right to kill more than two serfs in order to warm his feet in their blood after hunting – I am sure that great noble could have no conception there was coming a time when he and his would be swept into the *Ewigkeit*.

It seemed to him incredible, and even when the aristocracy of France had been turned out of that country by the Revolution they could not imagine what the French people could do without them. They went to Coblentz and waited there expecting to be recalled.

The economic development was due in this, as it is due in every other period, to class decay. So long as the French nobility lived upon their estate and filled their part in the economic development of their time, they were cruel, lustful, everything abominable, but remained where they were. But when they became useless, when they lived in the cities and left agents to do their work, at the first movement down they went. They perished, not because they were wicked, but because they were economically useless.

As we pass through the survey tonight you will find that economic uselessness is the end practically of class rule. At the present moment, instead of feudalism or chattel slavery or primitive communism, we are living under capital as the ruling power of the world. Capital has as its one object the making of profit. If profit could be made without employing a human being, not a human being would be employed. If apes could be trained and developed so as to run the looms of Lancashire, all the Lancashire hands would be on the street, because the monkeys would be cheaper. The one object of capital is to get profit at as small an expenditure in wages as it is possible, and that is a development which has come by slow degrees out of the period of the past. It did not always pay to starve a slave, because if he died you might have to buy another one. Under the condition of capitalism where men are deprived of all property who have no land to fall back upon to till if they happen to be thrown out of work, who are bound to present themselves at the end of every week to re-hire the labour in bodies, there is always somebody to come along on the morrow and take the place of the man who has stepped out today. Therefore the lot of the slave under a good master was in many respects better than that of the proletariat in our great cities.

At the present moment this material fact comes to our eyes. There is a final class war between the capitalists and the wage-earners going on which the socialists are organising and leading in every civilised country. I do not think the full significance of this is appreciated by the majority of us. We Socialists in this hall do not amount to much, but as what we are a part of, we are the greatest party in the whole world. We are not only the most numerous by far, but the most active and growing of all the international parties. At the present moment, a Socialist who goes into any great city of the civilised world – Berlin, Paris, Vienna, Rome, New York, and even in far Japan – will find numbers of his own comrades ready to stand side by side with him, and understanding the principles which I am here announcing on this platform quite as well as most of the people in this hall.

That is a fact which there is no gainsaying. There is not in the whole world today any party whatsoever that can be compared in extent, significance, numbers, or activity with the Social-Democratic Party of the civilised world. We have our difficulties. We are brought up as individuals, and have to dominate our individualism in order to realise Socialist principles even among ourselves. Nevertheless, here we are, and here we are going to stay, and the dignity of that fact reflects itself back upon the smallest member of this Party. We feel – instinctively feel – the grandeur of the Party to which we belong, and the certainty of the triumph in the near future. And, mind you, that is something all have got to face and to deal with. If those in authority imagine we are to be suppressed, they are under a delusion. Bismarck thought that he could put back the wave of human progress, and it saw him under. It will see a good many others under too.

The origin and development of modern capital came, as has been pointed out, from slavery and piracy, and naturally enough we, having been the principal piratical race of the planet, took the lead in a particular period in that development. Anybody who doubts we are pirates had better read our history. It was piracy and slavery and appropriation without return in every direction that built up the capitalist system in Europe and in Great Britain.

The analysis of that capitalist system practically tells the tale of the development of Social-Democracy, and Social-Democracy could not have come to the front itself but for the economic development which thus was analysed.

Now, what are Marx's theories in the main? They are these: That at the present moment pecuniary relations dominate the whole of highly-civilised human society. In place of personal relations, whether of the slave to his master, serf to his lord, apprentice and journeyman to master-craftsman, co-operative work of monks in various communities, or different relations which previously subsisted of retainers and the like to great nobles, we have nothing but pecuniary relations which dominate the whole firmament of intelligence and everything else.

Further, the man who possesses capital in the shape of money goes forth on the market, and of all the things he buys only one produces a profit, that is the labour-power of the man he buys upon the street. He buys him at one price, takes him into the factory or workshop, sets him to work, pays him wages, and the difference between the wages he pays and the amount he realises constitutes profit, interest, and rent.

Outside of that Marx appreciated the whole development, and his main economic argument, wherein he practically showed where Adam Smith and Ricardo and his predecessors had gone wrong, is as to the constant capital which passes through the work that is done. If a man buys raw material, whether leather, cotton, silk, or whatever it is, the actual value of the leather, cotton, silk comes out the same way as before. The change is of form, not of value. The value of the raw material, oil, coal, etc., does not change. What does change is the value of the labour which is put in it and which is only partially paid for.

The man who goes to work for wages gets paid for, say, one-third, and two-thirds goes into the pockets of those who live upon labour.

The man who appreciates that, if he is labouring, rather wants to change it and get the other two-thirds. Consequently this doctrine is considered a revolutionary one. All doctrines are revolutionary if they are not consonant with the society which happens to exist. At the period of the Roman Empire the very men whom we now canonise as saints were the revolutionists of that period, and were martyred as such. If you read the doctrines of the Fathers of the Church, where will you read more scathing denunciations of usury, where greater denunciations of slavery? Saints now, they were revolutionists then. I see an aureole around our chairman's head already.

The object of the capitalist is to obtain a circulation of commodities in order to obtain a profit. Thus he produces not for use; he produces something which somebody else must use. The man who produces shoes, produces them to sell; so with everything else. Food is not produced for the people who produce it, but for other people thousands of miles away. In every department profit is everything; use has little to do with it, and adulteration has become a legitimate form of competition.

Under these circumstances, what of those who have no property? Old Cobbett[2] has said, 'What is a slave? A slave is a man who has no property.' Now I should like to know how many out of the many working men members of this audience have property? Most of them have not enough savings to last them three months if thrown out of work.

Consequently, if Cobbett's definition was correct, when we are denounced for using the word wage-slavery, we say no other word will apply, inasmuch as the man who has no property must necessarily be at the command of another man, or what is worse than a man, of another class. For whereas a man may have some feeling, a dominant class, like a company, has neither a soul to be damned nor a body to be kicked. It is one great whole that works together for its own emolument and benefit solely.

Hence that class war coming down through the centuries which we Social-Democrats call attention to. It is an antagonism between the man who lives by his labour, and the set of men who live upon that labour. Between these two it is impossible to bring about harmony, because the two are absolutely antagonistic positions. Anyone can see all that the one can gain is to the detriment of the other, and must be so. We have been living through the period of the greatest development of the power of man over nature that the world has ever seen. Now what has been the result? Has the result been to benefit the workers anything at all in proportion to the benefit of their masters? We are at once told by economists of the capitalist school, 'Oh, yes; look how the workers have benefited by these great inventions.' Now there are inventions applied in various departments of human life, producing one hundredfold what was produced one hundred years ago, with an equal amount of labour, and yet, at the present moment, the wages paid for that work are perhaps increased only 30 or 40 or 50 per cent! Not more, even taking into account the cheapening of commodities.

The advantages of the development go, not to the mass of mankind, but to the small minority who have taken possession of the means of production, and therefore of all the improvements which go to increase them. The rise of wages is out of all proportion in a smaller degree than the development of the power of man to make wealth, and therefore it is of no use to turn round upon us Socialists and say the condition of the people is better than it was. The condition of the people as respects those of the highly intelligent and highly skilled artisan class is to a certain extent better than it was when I was a boy; but take the whole population and take the power to make wealth which exists in any civilised country, and the amount of advantage the workers have derived is not worth talking of in comparison with that obtained by the capitalists.

It is no use talking of that as being a matter which can be arranged; because the people who are responsible for it are not so in themselves, but as a class. In one sense they are not to be blamed – in the sense that they cannot act otherwise as long as the system goes on. If a man is competing against his fellows he may try and give better conditions; frequently he does so because it pays, but in many other cases it will not pay, and he has either to get out of the business or rejoin the slave-driving majority.

Now, a word as to the survival of the fittest. As young men we are told the one thing was to develop our individuality. 'Go on and get others under. Do not co-operate. Compete, because competition means the survival of the fittest.' It may be the most miserable creatures possible that survive. That is where, as a matter of fact, the juggling of words comes in. When rats have survived or tape worms have survived they are the fittest, because they have survived; but we do not for that reason want the world peopled with vermin.

In certain portions of our great cities only the fittest can survive; and inevitably do survive because a really healthy person could not live there.

Competition has been preached to us even until now, and we have been told that this method of development was an absolute necessity and that anything else was undesirable and impossible; but I shall show in a minute or two that survival of the fittest has meant, in a large degree, the survival of the unfittest.

Then we have been told that over-population has been the cause of the terrible conditions that we see in large portions of our great cities. But the power of man to produce wealth is infinitely greater than any increase in population the world has ever heard of. Four men working on the soil in Western America can produce food enough for a thousand. People who talk about over-population frequently forget that every man and woman born into this world comes with two arms and two legs, and that with these arms and legs and machinery applicable today one man or woman working in co-operation can produce far more in food, clothing, housing – far more than any rate or population could overtake within our period; and, what is more, we see this today, that in good times we have not got people enough to do the work, we have got to work overtime in all our great factories in order to overtake the tremendous demand. Where is the over-population when you have got to work overtime in your factories to keep pace with the boom? There is no over-population then; the capitalist wants more men so as to get labour cheaper. But in a short time comes collapse, and then there is over-population, because, as a matter of fact, profit cannot be made out of the labour of these people. Then we hear of the law of Malthus, that you should accommodate your food and the amount of people to eat it, when all the time there are hundreds of thousands of people wasting the wealth they have previously accumulated all over the planet.

We have passed beyond the period of the survival of the fittest even from the ethical point of view; and, curiously enough, Fawcett himself made in one of his books this remarkable statement. He wrote: 'According to our present social arrangements scarcely any free scope is afforded for individuality. The careers of men and women are almost unalterably fixed before they are born. One man is born a peer and another a ploughman; and each must through life run in the groove that has been prepared for him, however unfitted for it his natural faculties may render him.' If the ploughman is a genius he remains a ploughman. If the peer is a fool he remains a peer.

The result of this competition has been the accumulation of enormous masses of wealth at one pole of society and the accumulation of unheard of and fearful poverty at the other end. As to the accumulation of the immense masses of wealth, the capitalist class, as a class, takes no risk. Individuals may run risks. But the class makes continuous gain. We have one example alone in the United States of America of a man in receipt this year of £20,000,000 sterling. Such a thing was never heard of in the history of the world before. Here in this country we have got the Park Lane gang, who at the present moment are possessed of millions sterling accumulated in their own lifetime. You will find also great landlords, especially landlords of great cities, in receipt of incomes of the most enormous dimensions, and the accumulations are amazing. They die worth colossal sums. On the other side you get an amount of deterioration and poverty almost unprecedented, I believe, in the history of the world. I know that history pretty well, and I know of no such accumulation of misery and squalor as exists in Glasgow today. On the other side of the Thames – in Bermondsey, Southwark, and so on – you can find there all the poverty, misery, degradation you can possibly want to discover; and if you wish to make a calculation as to what that poverty really is, you have only to take the statistics of the capitalist class formulated by a man like Giffen. Take his figures. Putting the wages of the people where he puts them, at £500,000,000 a year, and then deducting rent and the various expenses which go to cut down the amount really available to these people for existence and enjoyment, you will discover that the amount of return which, even on these figures, the wage-earner receives is not enough to keep the worker in health at any period of his career. Of course, I am perfectly well aware that you are told in a recent Blue Book there are fifteen trades in this country, the average wages of which are £2 2s. a week for everyone employed, but we have never been able to find any of these trades. We have had the figures and returns from all the great trade unions of this country at command, and we have not been able to find one single trade where the average wages approach £2 2s. a week. They don't exist. That an official department paid by us should give currency to such lies is really an abomination at a time like this when the class struggle is becoming so accentuated in this country.

This accumulation of wealth at one end of the social scale and misery at the other is especially to be noticed in England and America. In America it is becoming a danger to the State. The accumulation there is such that six men control the railway system, 30,000 people own more than six-sevenths of its whole wealth, seven-eighths it is confidently averred. Throughout that country 50 per cent of its total industry is in the hands of the Trust monopolists.

It is the same here, but we do not parade it. Here, also, more and more wealth is accumulating for the few, and the many are suffering in an untold degree. Sir Henry Campbell-Bannerman has told us 12,500,000 people in this country are in such a condition that a slight reduction from their weekly wage would reduce them to starvation. That is somewhat of an exaggeration, but not so much as people would suppose who have not looked into the facts. There are not a majority of the workers at the present moment receiving in actual wages enough to keep them in a state of health to enable them, for instance, to serve satisfactorily in the army.

Here, for instance, are men coming forward to perform an ordinary duty to the State, and 70 per cent of them are rejected as unfit to defend their country – which does not belong to them.

Now, I think you will admit, if there are any patriots here, it is not a patriotic condition when 70 per cent of these men are unable to take up the ordinary duties of citizenship; that is not a proof of what you call high civilisation. I think you would claim that capitalism has not produced an exhilarating effect upon a population brought to that condition. It is definite proof of deterioration.

But it is said if a trade union were properly handled the result would bring about the emancipation of the workers, and they themselves would be able to effect the change I am arguing for. But as a matter of fact, trade unionism exists for no purpose but to maintain the wage system, as well as it can be maintained. Trade unionists are for the most part engaged in a fight against capitalism without the slightest idea of progress. That has been the history of trade unionism up to the present moment. If we allow the wages system to continue it means continuance of oppression. The trade unionist is contented to maintain the wages at the highest point he can under the economic conditions of the time, but has never yet formulated a desire to obtain control in order to run the industrial machine on account of the whole population. The trade unions, from the point of view of Social-Democracy, are of no use except as organised bodies to be converted to the general purposes of the proletariat. The trade unionist, simply as a trade unionist, is not a real champion of the people in any way; he is arguing in favour of better conditions for himself, but without the tremendous force he would gain if he appealed to the whole people to back him for the transformation of society.

What is happening at the present moment to the trade unionists? They are doing all they can to fight against the introduction of the American driving system, and to limit the application of automatic machinery; but it is clear they cannot permanently resist these economic changes. It is just as impossible for a trade union permanently to fight on against the introduction of automatic machinery as it was for the Luddites to break down the introduction of machinery itself, and whether they like it or not they will have to look at this problem sooner or later from the Social-Democratic point of view.

The trade unionist himself is none too secure when such improved machinery comes in. He may be caught in one of those crises or collapses of trade which will throw him out of work. Strikes will be of no use; they rarely are. We contend the money spent on them should be spent on political work, but under present conditions even the most skilled trade unionist cannot possibly secure himself against want and trouble tomorrow or against old age; and I have known some of the most skilled and sober men obliged to go to the workhouse.

However much we respect the men who fought the battle of trade unionism in days gone by, or who do so today, they are behind the times. They are like men fighting with Brown Bess against repeating rifles. They have to change their conditions and consider matters as they are today. The strength of trade unionism is in its organisation, in the money it has accumulated, and the capitalists, seeing perfectly well that this is its strongest point, are taking pains to strike at those funds by decisions of the Courts, and to put them at the mercy of their class.

Now, in all this we have the class war of our time, and when men go out on strike, or are locked out, what does the class which is living by profit rely upon to win? They rely upon the misery of the women and children. In all great strikes one of the main causes of the victory of the capitalists has been the poverty and misery of the wives and children of the strikers. It is of no use to say there is no class war, when starvation is used to bring men into subjection. Starvation is the deadliest weapon of war, and the Russians are finding out today in Manchuria that the inability to supply themselves is the greatest difficulty they have to face. So in the class war of peace. The inability to feed the women and children has often been the cause of the men's defeat. When the workers endeavour to deal with these matters solely from the trade unionists' standpoint, they are playing into the capitalists' hands by leaving the economic and political situation unchanged.

The political situation is now being attacked. But, in the meantime, competition is manifestly decaying. The capitalists as a whole, the organisers of industry, have discovered that competition is not good enough for them, that if they compete they gradually lose. Although there was fierce competition when they entered upon their era, that was in the early days of capitalism. Then one man could be the architect of his own fortune – by kicking others down; but now companies are too big to kick each other down comfortably, so they have said: Let us cease competing and let us combine.

There were three great manufacturers of cotton thread in this country, named respectively Coats and Clarke and Brooks. Coats turned his concern into a company, but the competition between them still continued, and prices were kept down to a fairly low level. This was satisfactory to none of them, for in slack times they made no profit, and profit for the manufacturer is both the body and soul of business. After due reflection, therefore, and much private communing in spirit, Coats went unto Clarke and said unto him: 'Friend, it were meet that we two should no longer unrighteously strive the one against the other, but rather that we should come together and do business, which is better for us both.' And Clarke hearkened unto him, and they reasoned much on the matter, until they agreed as to how this thing should come about, and Clarke said unto Coats: 'Verily, so it shall be.' And they twain were made one flesh, and went forth to face the world and benefit humanity by competing no more. And they prospered much. But Brooks still withstood them. Thereupon Coats said further unto Clarke: 'Look, now, to that Brooks, how he doth deprive us of great advantage.' Whereupon Clarke answered and said: 'Let us go forth and reason with Brooks; mayhap he will listen unto us, and if he do not forthwith perceive the true bearing of fraternity in business, verily we may chastise him by underselling his goods in every market until the light of Christian truth shall break in upon his mind.' And they did so. Thus Brooks was persuaded to combine, and the duality of Coats and Clarke became the Trinity in unity of Coats and Clarke and Brooks, in which the three persons had one God, whom they have worshipped advantageously ever since. But they still preach the benefits of competition to their workers, though it does not suit them, and co-operation has so blessed their endeavours that they have prospered exceedingly, and their shares have increased in value a hundredfold.

Thus capitalist self-sacrifice conquers, and economic virtue is its own reward – which, unfortunately, you do not share.

That is modern combination as against old-world competition. You workers are adjured to compete because competition develops your faculties and expands your individuality. If, also, you compete on a starvation wage, that helps on tremendously the prosperity of your country and the growth of your glorious Empire. But capitalists do not so reason for themselves. They say, 'We have no call to compete for other people's benefit. Our glorious Empire is of no use to us unless it fills our pockets. We have come to the conclusion that we shall do better if we combine than if we compete.' So our Trinity in unity of Coats (inside him Clarke and Brooks) has become not only national but international. And every seamstress in Europe and America has to pay more for her sewing-cotton, while the cost of production is materially reduced. Here endeth the first lesson.

Now, that tale of trustification is only the story of what is going on all over the planet and in every department of industry at the present time.

A Trust begins by a combination constituted by some clever fellow in a comparatively small way. It is at first a local affair. No one is a big trustifier any more than a big sinner all at once. The capitalist co-operator starts by absorbing or beggaring his neighbour. And, having thus absorbed, he digests, getting bigger and bigger every day in the process. Like the Cerberus of Dante, this desire for more grows by what it feeds on, and the combiner more hungry after each meal than he was before.

That is how combination grows until it becomes a great company, embracing many firms which, being absorbed, no longer compete to the detriment of profit. Or a number of producing or distributing firms in the same trade agree, first not to compete below a certain price, establishing what is called a 'cartel,' which later develops into what is called a 'pool,' becoming still further on a complete combination or an incipient Trust. The process of development differs slightly in various cases, but the result is always the same. So, when competition is felt, the representatives of the bigger combination go to the competitor and say, 'Come in with us on good terms.' If he refuses they threaten to undersell him in his own goods at unremunerative prices, and gradually persuade him to listen to what they call reason. If he refuses to accept this view, ruin and liquidation almost certainly follow until the combination has its way and the Trust is formed.

But when larger foemen are encountered, when, that is to say, Trust meets Trust, both having reached the Ophiophagus or Trust-Eating-Trust stage of development, then comes the tug-of-war. Such a point was reached between the great billionaire potentates Rockefeller and Carnegie. Rockefeller, with the 'savings' of his huge income, due doubtless to abstinence and thrift, had been obliged for sheer lack of outlet to tumble some of them, almost against his will, into the steel industry. Enormous works were constructed in Illinois, near Chicago, filled with automatic machinery, to which, by organisation on an unheard-of scale, the finest of iron ore is supplied at an abnormally low cost. But the great iron and steel works of Homestead threatened competition. When Rockefeller had made all his arrangements, therefore, he suggested to Carnegie that he should either sell out or come in. Carnegie at first, so it is said, did not see this. But it was hinted to him that his rival controlled not only all his chief sources of ore supply, but the railways which led to them. Whereupon Carnegie was persuaded to be a combiner, and was bought at a great price of £40,000,000. Hence the Great Steel Trust of America. Many people imagine that because the Ordinary shares of that Trust are almost unsaleable, therefore the Trust itself has failed. Not a bit of it. The more they appear to fail financially, the more they really succeed economically: the big people buying up the shares.

That is the process which is going on steadily in every department of industry in the United States. I watched its beginnings in 1874, and I predicted what must inevitably take place and is now occurring in 1880 and 1881. At the present moment the Trusts of America own or control 50 per cent of the total production and distribution of the great plutocratic Republic.

But in 1825 Fourler, the economist and utopian idealist, predicted, when Marx was only seven years of age, that competition would inevitably find its logical term in monopoly. Things are turning out in practice as he foresaw they must in theory. The process of absorption goes relentlessly on. Put three pike of varying sizes in a tub: by and bye there is but one pike left.

It is the fashion to say, however, that nothing of this sort takes place here; that glorious Free Trade protects us against Trusts. This is not so. A few months ago I was travelling up from the country with an old friend of mine who is a banker. He said, 'There are no Trusts here.' 'Why,' I replied, 'you are a trustifier yourself. Do you suppose it is a mere accident that the London and Westminster Bank and the National Provincial Bank and your own bank and all the other banks name precisely the same rate of discount and the same rate of interest on deposits on the very same day at the very same hour immediately after the Bank of England has declared its rate of discount?' 'No,' he answered, 'I suppose not.' Just so. These great banks, which themselves are only the results of the combination or trustification of a lot of smaller banks, have reached already the 'cartel' stage of banking, and the Trust-Eating-Trust or Ophiophagus point of trustification is not far off. As indeed we see. The English banks are getting bigger and bigger all the time. 'Sharks eat the big fish, big fish eat little fish, little fish eat mud.' And as none of these banking philanthropists want to be mud-eaters they develop from big fish into sharks. They are, in fact, huge Trusts, and nothing less.

The railways are virtually Trusts in the same way. They agree to have no competition in rates to the same terminals. This means that they are arranged to get the better of the public.

If anybody in this audience wished to buy a few thousand tons of steel rails in this country, he would find himself looking into a 'pool.' A pool is a deep industrial arrangement in which those who have made it fish and draw much thereout. All the owners or combiners in the pool, that is to say, undertake not to sell to outsiders below a certain highly remunerative price. Trade after trade, whether steel rails, lead-piping, quicksilver, antimony, nickel, and so on, is organised in the same way. Producers combine nationally, and often now internationally, and if you try to get what you need below their price you will not get served. Flour is ruled as to its price by a combine. The fish supply of London is controlled virtually by three men, and when there is too much fish at Grimsby they use it for manure rather than bring down the price to us Londoners below a certain level.

In fact, Trusts, Combines, Pools, Cartels, etc., are nearly as powerful in Great Britain as they are in the United States, and use their power – witness the national Telephone Trust and its House of Commons 'persuasion' – almost with as little scruple as in America. But we English eels are more easily skinned if the skinners don't make any noise about it.

The truth is trustification, industrial monopoly, is an inevitable development. Those who think they can stop it by law may as well try to check the precession of the equinoxes by enactment. It is an economic and social progress growing up out of conditions existing before, and turned round the right way will ultimately be of great benefit to the human race.

Undoubtedly many abominable things have been and are being done by the Trusts, but this has been the invariable history of the development of human beings in society. Progress has been accompanied in every department by the martyrdom of man to the forms of production and exchange.

The Trust means economy of production and distribution. It is showing us how to socialise to the best advantage. Now we have got to the period when Trusts are dominating in every department we have reached the point where Socialism must come in. It is not possible to deal with a Trust from the old individualist standpoint. You cannot go back to individual production any more than you can go back to primitive communism or to the peasant proprietary of the fifteenth century. If you could you would be forfeiting all the advantages of the development of machinery of today. A railway must be run as a portion of a community; new automatic machinery, new steamers, cannot be handled by individuals; they must be handled by co-operative wholes. The question is: 'Shall they be left to the Rockefellers or shall the whole community take them over so that all shall reap the advantage of that which none as individuals made?' That is the question before this audience tonight, as it is before not only the workers but the educated classes of the whole civilised world.

But there is really no doubt which course will be followed. It is as inevitable we should proceed from capitalism to collectivism and Socialism as it was that our forbears should pass from feudalism into individualism and capitalism. But then some will say, 'If it is all inevitable, why trouble to do anything – why address this audience?' Because we are the true conservatives. Because we wish to avoid the hideous waste of today and to conserve the energy and vigour now uselessly expended in man competing against man, woman against woman, and class against class. Because we cannot help seeing the terrible difficulties and dangers which must come upon us in the near future if we drift on without understanding, and the problems of industrial and social revolution force themselves upon us before we are ready to deal with them and to transform existing arrangements for the benefit of all.

I do not think it will be denied that we are here in the period of cartels, pools, trusts, of agreements in every direction. Further, we are in a period of limitation of output. Why are the people of Lancashire in a condition of starvation today? It is the fault of the Anarchists of Labour, the so-called organisers, who, during the whole 40 years that have passed since the period of the American war, when they depended on the one source of supply, have failed to get a second source except to the amount of 20 per cent. They have seen the development of mills in Japan, Germany, America itself, and have had no foresight to make corresponding arrangements. Who suffers? Not the capitalists, but the men who are working short time, whose wives and children are starving.

The real state of the capitalist at the present moment is that of increasing imbecility. If you look at any department of English trade, what will you find? You will find that we have been to a large extent resting upon our laurels, and have refused to go forward with the development which is taking place in other countries. The American capitalists are brutal; the condition of Colorado, where every wrong that can be done is being done to American workmen, shows it. But unscrupulous and brutal as they are, they are also clever, quick and determined, and use all the resources of civilisation to keep themselves to the front. But the English manufacturer has fallen behind the times. I do not think even employers of labour will deny that the English capitalists are inferior as compared with those of other countries. If that be so, their time has come. As long as he was a useful person in the domain of human society, the capitalist remained dominant, and, in spite of the horrors which were inflicted upon children by unrestrained capitalism at the beginning of the last century, when children of four and five years old were worked to death in the mills and mines, he was the master of English society. Capitalists were scoundrels, especially in Lancashire and Yorkshire, but they were useful scoundrels in the economy of their time. Their brutality and callousness did not weaken their power.

What was said of even the best of the capitalists of those times? What did Lord Shaftesbury say of John Bright – a good man of his class? He said that his most bitter opponent in his endeavour to get some justice for the children and the women in the workshops of Lancashire was Mr. John Bright.

That shows the morals of a class practically overmaster the morals of the individual; the individual cannot maintain a high ethic when he is swept into the capitalism of his time. That has been the case with the capitalists all along. You could not have greater horrors than those of the period from 1780 to 1847, but they lived through it all and waxed fat. But today they are becoming incompetent; they are unable to handle the great forces of modern production and distribution, and you can see that even in America they are taking men of the working class to handle their industries.

But if the worker is used to handle industries for the capitalists surely he may as well be employed to handle them for the community. If he is a good man for the capitalists, it cannot be denied he might be used by the community for the benefit of all.

Under these circumstances we could do without the capitalists today as well as France did without the feudal nobility who ran away to Coblentz.

Whilst this decay is proceeding there is an increase of municipalism and co-operation and collectivism under the State. If you look back at the last 25 years that we Socialists have been carrying on our propaganda nothing will surprise you more than to find how many departments have fallen into the collective agency of the municipality and the State, gas, water, electric lighting, telephones, etc., and many departments of production have become subject to collective ownership.

This is no accident; it is a necessary endeavour to reorganise the anarchy around us, an unconscious protest against the conditions which obtain and the robbery of the community under the competitive system. But do not let us forget that, in so far as this tends simply to State control, it may mean the control of a bureaucracy and the domination of experts. That entails with it a sort of qualified slavery. I have a great fear of the expert. I never hear of an uncontrolled expert without thinking of the old Chancery lawyer who said there were three sorts of liars: a liar, a damned liar, and an expert witness. Whenever an expert is brought in to dominate the affairs of a country without popular control I think of the expert witness.

That is one of the misfortunes of the growth of collectivism without a definite Socialist object. You are liable to fall into the hands of the expert who thinks he knows everything, and in nine cases out of ten is a prig of an offensive breed. There is no more offensive prig than a bureaucrat; none more wholly impervious to reason when his conceit of himself is threatened.

Municipalism also is a good stepping-stone to the reorganisation of industry, but its scope is limited. A municipality is in itself a limitation. We desire to do away with all such limitations, and spread out those crowded in the cities into the country around. Wherever you concentrate upon the municipality you shut out the country. And all the time the competitive wage-earning system is upheld.

Again, if we take the Government departments for whose management we are all really responsible, what do we find? The Post Office, today, is an organised sweating-den. The government gets the largest possible amount of work for the lowest possible wages. That is not my ideal of State management. Exactly the same in government dockyards and clothing establishments. People ask, 'Do you want to extend and stereotype this under Socialism?' No, we do not; that is capitalist wage-slavery under Government control. We intend to do away with Government control by the dominant classes, and we want to replace it with an organised co-operative industry for the benefit of the whole community under the control of the whole people.

Incidentally I will say to those who do not belong to the working classes who are present, what we are striving for will hurt no man or woman, but will be a benefit to all.

What object in view has any man or woman in this hall who belongs to the class that lives upon Labour? What do they strive for? To have the full development of their mental, physical, and moral faculties, to be sure of the future, that he or she shall not find in old age they have nothing to depend upon – that they may hand on better education and better opportunities to their children.

We can secure all this and all that can conduce to the fullest happiness and enjoyment of life with the power over nature which man possesses today, without any of the endless striving and hopeless mischief which we see around us. If that is so, then I claim the support of every intelligent man and woman in this audience, no matter what class they belong to. If you aspire to be a greater man or woman than those around you, controlling them without their consent; if you wish for absurd distinctions or to wear diamonds as big as coat buttons round your neck, or any other things unseemly and grotesque, you shan't have them if we can help it. But all that reasonable human beings can desire for themselves and their offspring can be obtained by moderate service for the community through Social-Democracy and Social-Democracy alone. I appeal, therefore, to all who want nothing but that which will finally improve the lot of themselves and their children and relieve them – whether workers or well-to-do – from the uncertainty of the morrow, the greatest anxiety of our day, to be with us in the struggle of the near future. Social revolution is certain. It rests with us to decide what form that transformation shall take.

As bringing us to that, we are all in favour of political action. We are not so foolish as to say we would not use force if it would bring us to a better period more rapidly. We do not say we are such men of peace. We feel like the Quaker in 'Uncle Tom's Cabin.' When the slave-drivers were after Uncle Tom he got to the top of the precipice, and when the slave-owner climbed there the Quaker said, 'Friend, thee is not wanted here,' and he pushed him over the brink. We do not want anybody even to tumble down a precipice; all that we want possibly may be obtained in a peaceful manner; though, peaceably or not, the transformation of society will come about anyhow.

To transform society peacefully we need the complete political means for effecting a change. These do not exist here. The people have a certain amount of political power, but in the main the State is under the control of the well-to-do. Apart from his keep and some provision for the future, a man must have at his disposal from somewhere or another £400 or £500 in order to get a seat in the House of Commons. He starts with a fine to encourage him to do honest public work. There is no adult suffrage, no equality of voting, no payment of registration expenses or salary for services, no second ballot. 'Democracy' under such condition is mere humbug, and neither existing faction has the slightest intention of altering it – neither Liberal nor Tory. Let the Liberals be returned to power, and we shall be at the mercy of old Whigs instead of old Tories. Rosebery, Tweedmouth, Spencer, Fowler, Asquith, Haldane. Whigs and lawyers prey naturally together. They have control of the Liberal Party, and they are about as much democrats as the Duke of Devonshire. Why should they be? They make no pretence of being willing to serve the people. Their one object is to take all they can, and to stay pretty much where they are. It is your business to persuade them to move on. You can only do this if you talk the same talk in large numbers. In political affairs the eloquence of one man is of little use; the monosyllable of the million is astonishingly convincing.

A few may be run in. Many run the other fellows in. Successful revolution, peaceful or forcible, is the legalised expression of new social forms whose development has been arrested by ignorant or corrupt reaction at the top.

We have not the power to bring about a revolution peaceably because the people have neither the necessary education as yet nor the political opportunities. As Marx once said to me, 'England is perhaps the only country in which a peaceful revolution is possible – but history does not tell us so.'

That is my feeling today. Events move faster than minds. Such a problem as that of the unemployed may take a desperate shape at almost any moment. The growth of Trusts, the progress of automatic machinery, the increasing dependence upon foreign sources for supply of food and raw material, intensify the danger; while excessive extravagance alike in public and private life renders the situation more and more precarious. On all hands the hopeless incapacity and despicable social cowardice of our ruling classes are admitted, but none save the socialists dare formulate the policy of the future. Rottenness pervades every portion of our industrial, distributive, banking and social machinery, yet not a man in the front rank of politics has the pluck or the foresight to declare that speedy reconstruction of the entire fabric is essential.

Socialism alone is constructive as well as revolutionary. Socialism alone, while keeping the end steadily in view, does not reject useful palliatives of existing anarchy. True, we know that such palliatives, however attractive in appearance, will only provide better wage-slaves for capitalists under existing conditions. But several of them will serve to check degeneration and to bring up a more capable race to face the difficulties of the near future. Mere fiscal tinkering, mere land-tax burden-shifting, have, however, no charms for us. Free Trade means, today as ever, free exploitation of the labour of the workers for the benefit of the capitalists; protection means protection of the landlord and the capitalists against the workers. Under both, the mass of the people are still severed from the means of production and compete with one another for a subsistence wage. Similarly, no taxation of ground rents or pseudoland-nationalisation touches the basis of the system whereby the producers are at the mercy of the employers.

Palliatives, to be of any value even as palliatives, must touch directly upon the economic status of the workers themselves. Thus, eight hours in the day or 48 hours in the week should be the legal limit of labour in these days of intensive toil in all mines, factories and workshops, as well as the rule in other directions. By speeding up machinery and by 'driving' the hands the masters would soon cram more work into eight hours than is now done in nine or ten. But the gain of extra leisure would be maintained, and could be further extended.

Nationalisation of railways, though no more an emancipation of the workers than employment in the sweating-dens of the State Departments is today; where all the competition is at the bottom, and all the jobbery, favouritism, swindling, and overpay is at the top; nevertheless would constitute a direct economic advance; and the workers have only themselves to thank even now that the status of the employees of the government is so deplorable as it is, and their uncertainty of occupation in many branches so harassing. Today, at any rate, the railways of Great Britain are the worst managed in the world, and constitute the greatest system of Protection in favour of the foreigner ever heard of. A complete change in the direction of nationally-owned lines with freight tracks giving transport to goods at or near cost would, even under capitalism, lift an enormous weight from off the industry of the country. The same reasoning applies to genuine nationalisation of the land and the organisation of co-operative farming on the soil in connection with other industries; though here the economic difficulties are far greater, the divorce of the people from the land having gone further in Great Britain than in any other country. But in this case the housing of the people alone demands that the land question should at once be dealt with in a completely revolutionary spirit. It is impossible any longer to permit the overcrowding, lack of sanitation, and rack-renting of the wage-earners which is now going on, and getting worse in all our great cities, and in many of our country towns and villages as well. In effect, nothing whatever of importance has been done since the Royal Commission on Housing – that patent process for avoiding any real reform – of which the present King was a member, published its Report nearly a quarter of a century ago. On this point the proposal of the Social-Democrats that, regardless of vested interests and landlords' claims, houses should be built in town and country at public expense of the best quality, so as to provide by far the most valuable section of the people with comfortable and pleasant homes, to be let at the cost of construction and maintenance alone, still holds the field. Those who cannot pay even that amount of rent, as it has been proved there are thousands such in all our great cities, should be likewise removed from the dog-hutches which they inhabit today, and placed amid better surroundings. This palliative, adequately enforced, would in itself bring about a social revolution.

But we Social-Democrats attach most importance to the Free Maintenance of children in all the Common Schools of this country. At the present time in all our great cities tens of thousands, even hundreds of thousands, of children are undergoing physical degeneration of the most deplorable kind owing to lack of fresh air, want of food and insufficient clothing. This is not only cruelty and injustice to them, but it is an injury to the whole community. In Scotland the Physical Culture commission has just published a terrible indictment of this whole system of free trade in starvation and squalor. Here, in London, it has been proved over and over again that education is useless without food. Degeneration, mental and physical, must result from such a monstrous policy of systematic neglect. Individual effort has been constantly tried to avert the inevitable mischief, and has ignominiously failed. For more than 20 years the Social-Democratic Federation has advocated the only possible palliative under present circumstances – Free Maintenance of children at public cost. Degeneration, as is now universally admitted, is persistent, continuous, and is getting worse. It is our bounden duty to check it by all possible means. I do appeal, therefore, to all men and especially to all women to bring pressure to bear on members of the House of Commons to vote in favour of Free Maintenance as of necessity complementary to Free Education in the Common Schools.

It is absolutely impossible, as has long since been discovered, to teach starving children; impossible for the money spent on their training to be other than wasted; impossible that they should grow up sensible, capable members of the community. Whatever your political theories may be, whether you are Tories, Whigs, Liberals, or the most bigoted individualists ever known, I say no matter what your theories may be on political points you ought to be with us on this question, because you are asked to save many thousands of children from starvation and misery who cannot help themselves.

Children cannot be paupers. If they can, I was a pauper as a child, and the children of all those in this hall must of necessity be paupers, because they cannot provide for themselves. They must be provided for by somebody. We want to extend the area of such provision for the benefit of society at large.

Passing from home politics I come to foreign affairs. There we Socialists say we have the alliances of the world ready to our hand. We rejoice, as I think all rejoice, at the arrangements which have been come to between ourselves and France; it is a beneficial understanding for which we have agitated and worked for many a long day. We should rejoice to see similar arrangements between ourselves and Germany, or any civilised country which is under a free government. But out alliances are more complete than that; the alliances of the peoples of the world are practically at our disposal.

We stand for Justice, Humanity and Peace on every question that comes to the front. We denounce the raid in Tibet, because it is an outrage upon a community with which we have no quarrel, nor need have any. We denounced the Boer War because it was fought merely from a lust for gold mines. We denounce anything that tends to wars between peoples because we hold that the time has come when the workers of the world should be strong enough, banded together, to sweep aside those who make wars in their own interest and against the interest of the peoples.

In all questions of foreign politics in general we regard them from the point of view of the emancipation of the peoples. Our objects are the same as theirs. We look forward to the realisation of complete economic and social freedom, not only in England, but in France, Germany, Italy, the United States, all over Europe and America, and even in the Far East. Wherever we look we see the same class war, and we recognise that we stand side by side with our fellows in the greatest struggle for freedom that has occurred in the history of mankind.

As to our Colonies, we exercise over them a pecuniary domination, draining out of them wealth they can ill spare; while they for their part are equally selfish in accepting defence from the home country without payment. In Australia we see four millions of people shutting out the rest of mankind, though they can never hope to people that island-continent themselves. What an absurdity it was when six hatters went out there to earn their living and were not allowed to land! When the world has come to that, surely the system which produces such anomalies must be played out. At the present moment, too, our modern Colonial System is being brought in to dominate us at home, and to dictate our fiscal policy. A complete reorganisation is called for here, but not of an 'Imperialist' kind.

In India, even looking at things from the capitalist point of view, we are destroying the biggest market the world ever saw, draining away £30,000,000 of wealth every year for the benefit of but a small handful of people. If that wealth were left to fructify among the Indian people, those in England who are suffering from bad trade would have better trade than they ever had before. We are ruining that great empire with a cruelty and imbecility unknown since the Spanish conquest of South America, and exceeding in cold-blooded horror even the infamies of the inhuman Viceroys of that day.

The people of England, the people in this hall, are responsible for the famines in India and the plague which is engendered by poverty. They are responsible for allowing men like Curzon to manufacture famine in their name for tens of millions of people by a deliberate policy of bleeding to death. Any harm that comes upon this country for the wrong thus done will have been well deserved. The most hideous crime that has blackened the history of mankind is now being committed by us. As we have utterly failed to do anything but frightful mischief it is high time we left India to manage her own affairs.

Socialism, however, means emancipation everywhere. It will emancipate the workers as it will emancipate us all. It gives us new ideas of art, of pleasure, new ethical conceptions, better notions of what might be. It means a revolution, not merely economic, but ethical and religious. In place of competition, co-operation; in place of endeavouring to get the better of one another, will come continuous endeavour to uplift each other, knowing that this is best for ourselves also. Each for all and all for each becomes realisable for the first time on the planet.

And we English are behind in all this. We seem to have lost all those ideals which formerly inspired our race. At the present time Englishmen have resolved to put their noses into the mud rather than lift up their heads and see what might be. It is we who are holding back the movement of humanity throughout the world. We will not see that the growth of the power of man over nature which has been heretofore handled by individuals must, in the future, be handled by the people at large. The socialist ideal arises inevitably out of the conditions of our own time. The misery of our day is steadily preparing for a better state of things tomorrow. Monopoly, which has taken control today in private hands, must be collectivised, but placed under democratic control, not that of the capitalist State.

As for us Socialists, let us hearten one another. For my part I am glad that in the early days of this business we were so few. I like to look back on the time when we were a mere handful, and still doing the work. I know that I cannot hope to see compete realisation of what I am laying before this audience, but times move fast, and I may see some part. Who would have thought even a few months ago that little Japan would now be shaking the great despotism of Russia? Yet that was preparing all the time. Who then can say from what quarter may come the shock which shall arouse even the people of England? What we hope for is that when that shock from without shall come, and give them an opportunity of deciding what the future shall be, there may be here in this country a body of thoroughly capable men and women, holding out their hands to the nations of the world as their friends, determined to strive side by side − the workers of England with those of Europe, of America, of Asia − for the conquest of the future by the workers of the world.

Notes

1. The Rockefeller-controlled Colorado Fuel and Iron Company in Trinidad,

Colorado, had established a state of siege during a strike, and had evicted striking workers whose homes were owned by the company. These workers were living in tents, and had dug a hole under the largest tent in which the women and children took refuge at night. One night employees of the company doused the tent with petrol and set fire to it. Thirteen children were shot dead by soldiers as they tried to escape from the fire.

2. William Cobbett; radical writer and master of invective who advocated the reform of Parliament and championed the cause of the common people for almost 30 years.

12
Women and Socialism
ISABELLA FORD (1855–1924)

Introduction

Isabella Ford was born into a comparatively wealthy middle-class family in 1855. Her father was a solicitor and her mother came from a family which included bankers, colliery owners and stuff merchants. Her parents were Quakers and involved in radical liberal politics. They were also keenly interested in the women's rights movement from the 1860s onwards. Isabella was the youngest of eight children and she was very close to her sisters, Bessie and Emily.

Before she was 20, Isabella met Edward Carpenter and she and her sister Bessie started a correspondence with Walt Whitman in America. Isabella's interest in progressive causes resulted in her helping Emma Patterson, President of the Women's Provident and Protective League, together with members of Leeds Trades Council, to form a Machinists' Society for Leeds tailoresses.

In 1886 she set up a Workwomen's Society for Leeds tailoresses and textile workers and this trade union interest brought her into contact with members of the Leeds Socialist League. There she met Alf Mattison, Tom Maguire and Tom Paylor, all of whom remained her close personal friends and whose influence can be seen in her subsequent activity.

In 1888 Isabella formed another lifelong friendship with Ben Turner whom she met while participating in a weavers' strike at Wilsons in Leeds. A year later she was again involved with striking weavers at Alverthorpe and in October 1889 she helped establish the Leeds' Tailoresses Union which, together with members of the Socialist League, provided leadership during their strike from October to December of that year.

In recognition of this activity, Isabella Ford was made a life member of Leeds Trades Council in 1890 and president of the Tailoresses Union, a position that she held until 1899. But as well as giving her time and energy to the trades unions, she had started her writing career and 1890 saw the publication of her first novel, *Miss Blake of Monkshalton*. She also started her activity in the cause of women's suffrage and joined the Leeds Women's Suffrage Society.

During 1890–91, Isabella gave active support to the workers involved in a dispute at Mannigham Mills in Bradford. She took a further step along her political road by joining the Independent Labour Party in 1893. Two years later she was elected a parish councillor for Adel and Eccup. In spite of this activity she found time to write her second novel, *On The Threshold*, which was published in 1895. In 1896 she was a delegate to the Trades Union Congress and also to the women's meeting of the Second International which was held in London.

Soon after the turn of the century, her third novel, *Mr Elliott* was published. It was her last full-length work, but in 1904 she published the pamphlet *Women and Socialism* which was widely read. Continuing her political activity, Isabella was elected to the National Committee of the ILP and attended the Labour Party Annual Conference. At the following year's conference she made a contribution on women's suffrage. She attended the conference again in 1905, but did not stand for re-election in 1906.

She then turned increasingly to working for women's suffrage. In 1907 she was elected to the Executive Committee of the National Union of Women's Suffrage Societies, a position she retained until 1915, and accepted the position of vice-president of Leeds Women's Suffrage Society. She attended the Conference in Amsterdam of the International Women's Suffrage Alliance in 1908, and in 1911 became chairwoman of the West Riding Federation of Suffrage Societies.

Meanwhile she maintained her links with the working people. In 1904 she went as a delegate to the Textile Workers' Congress in Milan and in 1914 was a delegate to the International Textile Workers' Congress in Blackpool.

On the political front, she was a member of the Election Fighting Fund Committee in 1912, and a member of the Committee responsible for drafting the Labour Leaders' Suffrage Supplement in 1913. During the First World War peace became the focus of her activity and she became a member of the Executive of the British Section of the Women's International League and of the Union for Democratic Control, and in 1917 she helped form a Leeds branch of the women's Peace Crusade.

In 1920 she attended the meeting in Geneva of the International Women's Suffrage Alliance and was a delegate to the International Peace Congress at the Hague in 1922.

In addition to her political, trade union and suffrage activity, her writing and the time she devoted to her many friends, Isabella Ford managed to fit in such interests as her chairwomanship of the Leeds branch of the RSPCA, membership of the Anti-vivisection Society, the Leeds Arts Club and the 1917 Club. During her years before 1900, she was very active on behalf of the Friends of Russian Freedom; and throughout her busy life, she regularly wrote articles for the *Labour Leader* and *Common Cause*.

In *Women and Socialism*, which was published in 1906, Isabella Ford traces the development of the position of women in history, making a case for linking the labour movement with the struggle for women's emancipation on the basis that 'they both arise from the common evil of economic dependence, or rather economic slavery. They represent two sides of the very same question.'

Isabella Ford claimed that the social reforms called for by women were of the same kind as those being demanded by the Labour Party. She noted that though women were regarded as being conservative in outlook, they had taken part in all past struggles.

In *Women and Socialism* she analyses the need for women to be given the vote, and discusses what effect women's votes would have on the quality of life of the whole population. The pamphlet ends with an impassioned plea for women to trust the Labour Party and for the party to make full use of women in all its work. The appendix following the pamphlet lists useful information of the state of the women's movement internationally at the time.

Source
Bellamy and Saville, *Dictionary of Labour Biography*, Vol. VIII, article by June Hannam.

★　　★　　★

'The legislator ought to be whole and perfect, and not half a man only; he ought not to let the female sex live softly and waste money and have no order of life, while he takes the utmost care of the male sex, and leaves half of life only blest with happiness, when he might have made the whole state happy.'

Plato.[1]

'There has never been a labour question without a woman's question also.'

Karl Pearson.[2]

At this moment, when the women's movement has reached its present advanced stage, and when certainly the justice, if not always the expediency, of granting women's claim to possess equal political power with men is admitted by all intelligent persons, it may seem a little unnecessary to write further pamphlets, or revise old ones, on the subject. But it appears to me extremely important that just at this acute stage of the battle the absolute expediency for the welfare of the State, as well as the justice, of granting the vote to women should be made perfectly clear, and most particularly to those who desire to understand the Labour movement and what it really stands for, because unless the relation of the Labour movement – or perhaps it is better to use the wider term of the Socialist movement – to the Women's Movement, be clearly recognised, the real inner meaning of Socialism itself cannot be understood, for the two movements have the same common origin and the same aims.

The Meaning of Socialism

There are many people, even those in the Socialist ranks, who apparently forget, or perhaps have never quite realised, that Socialism demands more than that we should merely import Socialistic institutions into our midst, such as free meals for children, municipalisation, etc., and consider that they will regenerate society and turn us all into Socialists. It insists on a moral regeneration of society of the most complete and searching kind in order to make a lasting foundation for the political and social changes we many of us long to see.

Justice is to be the foundation on which we must build, not the kind of justice we have hitherto considered as sufficient for us, and which many countries pride themselves is their watchword and standard, but a justice that demands freedom for all. 'All men are free and equal,' declares the United States of America, but in only four of those States are women free, the industrial condition of the workers is not by any means one of freedom, and in the South the race question is still in a state of frightful chaos. Socialism, when it says that in order to have a great nation we must build on the sound foundation, also says that so long as any section of a State be left ignorant and fettered, and therefore powerless to help this immense work forward, that State will be incomplete, for its foundation will be incomplete, for since each and all of us alike are members of the State, it demands from us all an equal share of service. All hands must be on deck if we would save the ship.

Those who are left in voiceless ignorance and darkness cannot grow up lovers of justice and liberty, for having received neither, they can understand neither – slaves proverbially love their chains, and shrink from the burden of responsibility which freedom brings them – and the whole State can therefore only attain to the puny undeveloped idea we now possess of justice, and which now passes amongst us as the great goddess we imagine we worship and love. Her real image is graven on the hearts of some – of a few – but the mass of the earth's peoples do not know her; they still worship a figure whose face they cannot really see, for, like themselves, she is blindfolded. The justice of Socialism will see all things, and therefore understand all things.

The Importance of the Home

Now the relationship between men and women forms the core, the centre round which society grows for the family, the home, is the very heart of a nation. If that relationship be founded on justice such as I have described above, then we shall have a knowledge growing fuller and more complete as experience teaches each generation, of how to build our state out of this moral regeneration which Socialism calls for, since the two who form the home, understanding it equally in their own lives will teach each other and their families how to undertake it. As things are now, neither understands it (the man as occupying the more ignoble position, that of the oppressor, even less perhaps than the woman) for they stand in a false position of inequality towards each other, and that falseness spreads, as a fungus spreads its evil growth, into their relationship to others. Hence we have the world as we now see it; founded not on justice, not on freedom, but on a make-believe of both.

Socialism goes straight to the home, to the heart of the world, in its cry for freedom. Free the home, let the woman be no longer in political subjection, and free the worker, it says; bring light into all the dark homes of the earth so that each one like a torch may spread the light throughout all the world, and by that light we shall then see wisely and clearly how to bring about the social changes we so ardently desire. Reforms coming thus from the heart of a nation, must be and will be, of the strongest and most enduring kind.

Connection between the Woman's Movement and the Labour Movement

But now how is the woman's movement and the labour movement connected besides in this common demand for a State founded on the highest justice and the consequent reform of the home? They both arise from the common evil of economic dependence, or rather, economic slavery. They represent two sides of the very same question. As Karl Pearson puts it: 'The status of woman and the status of labour are intimately associated with the manner in which property is held and wealth inherited ... the position of woman is in the closest correlation with that of labour, and both vary with the nature of ownership. During the years of child bearing and child rearing, the woman in any but the most primitive stages of civilisation (where ownership is scarcely known) must be dependent upon the owner of property for subsistence.'

Early Civilisations

To show this connection a little more clearly let us see what, as far as we can tell, was the condition of women and the workers among early nations. All recent discoveries tend to show that before the owning of property became a nation's greatest ambition, neither women nor labourers were enslaved. If we carefully examine the most recent records of early Egyptian civilisation, we find (about 600 BC or earlier) no slavery, no impoverished class, and the women holding posts of equal responsibility with the men. There is no trace of the mothers of the nation having been classed with lunatics and imbeciles, as is the case in this enlightened age.

From the early histories of other nations, we find as a rule their women were more or less free and their workers prosperous. With increase of territory and wealth, came slavery, poverty, and a downfall in the position of women.

Plutarch[3] gives an interesting account of the Celtic women. He says: 'There arose a very grievous and irreconcilable contention among the Celts; the women, placing themselves between the armies, took up the controversies, argued them so accurately, and determined them so impartially that an admirable friendly correspondence and general amity ensued, both civil and domestic. Hence the Celts made it their practice to take women into consultation about peace or war, and to use them as mediates in any controversies that arose between them and their allies.'

The Romans were much struck by the high position held by the women amongst the Britons. Caesar says that the British women were made use of in Court, in Council, and in Camp, and that no distinction of sex was made in places of command or government.

The general prosperity of these nations also struck these early conquerors as remarkable.

The Guilds

When we come down to the fifteenth century the connection between the two movements is plain to read, for industrialism was becoming an important factor in the world's history.

The Guilds were then in their most prosperous stage, and the condition of the workers consequently in many ways superior to what it is now. So also was the position of women superior. As far back as the twelfth century we find records of women members who held positions and traded on equal terms with men. Mrs. Green[4] in her *History of Town Life in the Fifteenth Century*, says: 'Married women might become merchants on their own account and carry on trade, hold property and answer in all matters of business before the law as independent traders.' There are records of trading Guilds consisting of women members only.

Women also took a considerable part in the educational movement of this prosperous time, and the very first day-school of which we have any mention was founded at Wotton-under Edge, by a woman, in 1385. The grammar schools (both free and otherwise) which were founded during this period, very often (if not mostly) were for girls and boys alike. Some of the colleges at Cambridge and Oxford were founded or endowed by women. When one sees how jealously these Universities continue to exclude women from obtaining the degrees they have rightfully earned, and from holding fellowships, one cannot help thinking of those women to whom, in part, they owe their very existence!

With the decay and final extinction of the power of the Guilds by the

Crown and the Church, came a like fall in the position of women, and in James I's reign we find the lawyer, Sir Edward Coke[5] (whom James describes as 'the fittest engine for a tyrant ever was in England,') classing women as 'minors' and announcing that 'all women having freehold or no freehold must be henceforth excluded from voting for Parliament.' After this and similar pronouncements which eventually passed into law, began our gradual exclusion from all public affairs.

The position of the worker was, as we all know, permanently undermined by the destruction of the Guilds, and it was then also that both the poor and women began to lose their share in the educational institutions of the time. Until within comparatively recent years the knowledge even that girls were generally included in the foundation of our grammar schools, had vanished from people's minds, and there are few who know that Eton was originally founded for 'poor and indigent' scholars, yet such are the words in the foundation.

Beginning of the Capitalistic Era

Later again, during the sixteenth century, these two movements even more strikingly show their connection. The old organisations of labour and capital were, as just stated, being gradually destroyed, and the worker was falling into deeper and deeper poverty, for capitalism was beginning its 'long years of labour exploitation'; and it was during this very time that prostitution increased enormously and came to be recognised in some countries as a regular part of a nation's life. This was, of course, largely due to the decrease in the marriage rate which always follows on an increase in poverty. Capitalism always has been, and is now, a worse enemy to women than it can be to men for this very reason. Prostitution is chiefly – there are some who say entirely – an economic question. How terribly this evil corrupts the life and heart of a nation we all know and recognise in a general sort of copy-book fashion, just as we all know that 'unpunctuality is the thief of time,' or any other motto on which we do not act, but why is it that we do not as a nation rise up and insist that from every pulpit and lecture hall it be taught that every person who makes a living or a fortune out of the degradation of women be absolutely boycotted – that he shall never write M.P. after his name, and that his statue shall never be erected in any public place? We can have no socialistic state till this moral battle be begun, and it is women only who can begin it.

The dissolution of the monasteries also during this century, by turning adrift whole bands of men and women who possessed no means of livelihood whatsoever, struck another blow at the position of both the poor and women. Mrs. Green says of the labourers, the most destitute of all in those terrible days, 'their brotherhood was reinforced by the waifs and strays of town and country, that flocked into their sad fellowship on the dissolution of the monasteries.'

Martin Luther's Influence

Martin Luther,[6] by his teaching in his later life, was one of the worst enemies women (in Germany particularly where his influence was strongest) and the workers have had to contend with.

His attitude towards the peasants may be gathered from his tract entitled 'Against the murderous and rapacious rabble of Peasants,' in which he says 'a rebel is outlawed by God and Kaiser, therefore who can and will first slaughter such a man does right well ... O Lord God when such spirit is in the peasants, it is high time that they were slaughtered like mad dogs.'

This was written when the peasants, oppressed most intolerably by the nobility, rose in rebellion, and Luther, by his writing and preaching helped immensely to aid the oppressors during the ensuing 30 years of war. Of all wars it was one of the most wicked and cruel, and ended in such a complete repression of the peasantry that to this day the effects of its success are felt by the working-classes in Germany.

Of the position of woman he says 'where he (man) is there must she be, and bend before him as before her master whom she shall fear and to whom she shall be subject and obedient.' And of marriage he says, 'it is an outward bodily thing as any other worldly bargaining.' 'I must forsooth confess that I cannot prohibit any man from taking several wives.'

Witch superstition was rife at this time, and Luther spread it far and wide by his teaching. He says, 'No one should show mercy to such people, I would myself burn them.'

Witch burning and torturing spread rapidly all over Europe, and in later days reached America. Of all the world's sad pages this was one of the saddest. In France alone, during the reign of Francis I, more than 100,000 witches are said to have been put to death, and in Louis XIII's reign the proportion of witches burnt to wizards, is reckoned at 10,000 to one. From the pulpit people were exhorted to bring the witch to justice. The destruction of the peasants was also, as I have pointed out, preached from the pulpit.

An accusation of witchcraft served as a good excuse for weeding out any woman who was troublesome. A woman who was too clever, too ardent about reform, who refused to submit quietly to a husband's oppression or cruelty, who stood above her fellows in any manner to which the Church or her men-kind chose to object, was accused of witchcraft and her doom was sealed. This extermination of the cleverest and most original-minded women, women who dared to raise their voices, while it left mostly untouched the 'domestic doormat' species, and those who though rebels at heart became skilled in hypocrisy and deceitful silence, has undoubtedly degraded women and retarded the spread of their movement for education and freedom. It is largely responsible, more largely than we perhaps realise, for the type of domestic woman who says that submission to everything is 'womanly,' and also for the political woman who cares nothing about a vote, but who regards that dangerous and impure thing 'influence' as her noblest weapon (in those dark days it was her only hope and how continually it failed her if she was poor or obscure!) and who cannot see that every time she refuses to push forward her claim for freedom she most gravely injures the State she professes to love so well. By her refusal she is helping to keep half the State, her own half, bound in the old bonds of servitude, and is thus causing the whole to suffer.

Let those who love to rail at women for their foolishness, their ignorance, their submissive susceptibility to the opinions of others and so forth, be patient with us if they can, remembering that these were the very faults which were so bitterly enforced on our unhappy female forbears in those old days.

We have carried on the same process with our domestic animals, and with a complete success. In order to obtain a race of docile, brainless creatures, whose flesh and skins we can use with impunity, we have for ages past exterminated all those who showed signs of too much insubordination and independence of mind.

Karl Pearson describes this page in woman's history as her 'last struggle against complete subjection.' In Germany, just as in the case of the peasantry after the 30 years' war, the woman's struggle was entirely crushed. Woman became silent, for the dark waters of despair had closed over her, and in that country it is only within very recent years that she has really begun again to stir in good earnest.

The Present Day

Let us now turn to the present day. Is this connection between the movements, Labour and Women, still apparent, are the same powers still hostile to both?

In America, in the year 1830, when the anti-slavery movement was beginning, two sisters called Grimke freed their slaves, left their homes and retiring to the Northern States, began to fight for women's freedom as well as the negroes'. The clergy raised their voice in indignant protest against both doctrines. 'The enslavement of the negro and the woman,' they said, 'were alike the ordinance of God.'

In 1840, the great Anti-slavery Convention was held in London, and, with a few exceptions, our clergy took up the same line of argument, and announced their knowledge of the Almighty's views on women and negroes and their proper place in the world with a like explicitness. As we all know, they said it was 'in opposition to the plain teaching of the word of God' that 'females' should sit and deliberate in the Convention. It was because of this exclusion of women, some of whom had been his noblest colleagues, from the Conference, that Lloyd Garrison[7] refused to take any part in its proceedings, and sat alongside the despised 'females' behind the bar and curtain erected for them.

It was from this Convention that the Women's Suffrage movement arose in its present definite shape. Women began to see and understand the uselessness of trying, or even hoping to serve the State effectively, to give the nation their best work, unless they could do so with the same responsibility and power behind them that men possess. To depend on what is called 'woman's influence' was, they saw, to depend on an unworthy, and, in times of real stress, a useless, weapon; occasionally it might ameliorate a few of the lesser evils of the world, but it could never really touch or change them. They therefore made from henceforth the definite demand of an equal enfranchisement with men, their basis.

When the negroes' claim for enfranchisement was heard, the women's claim was thrust aside.

At the present moment the connection between the women's movement and the Socialist movement seems closer than ever. Before the last general election the ruling classes extended the antagonism they have always shown to the woman's cause, in an even more decided manner than usual, to the Trade Union cause, and whole Labour movement. The woman's cause received several blows too of a worse character than it had received for several previous years. Now, in Parliament, the Labour Party has definitely and decidedly espoused the cause of women's political enfranchisement, and the two causes are, therefore, in the House of Commons at least, distinctly joined together. Partly through the spread of the socialist trend of thought, partly through the slow upward growth of the women themselves, and the public work which they have achieved under immense difficulties, but chiefly through the terrible economic conditions which women wage earners have now to endure, the Labour Party realises that there can be no economic freedom for a country in which one half of the workers have no political freedom. The denial of such freedom to any one class must of necessity, as explained at the beginning, act disastrously on the progress of the whole community, and the more so when, as in this case, this class includes half the whole nation. The whole state, as Plato says, must be made happy, and not only half.

Women's Reform Work

The next point we come to is to show that women by their public work, both in countries where they have the vote and in those where they have not, make the same demands and have the same objects in view as the Labour Party.

In England on all public bodies on which women sit, they are insisting on proper cottage accommodation and a good water supply in rural and urban districts. They are urging that the lives of those who live in workhouses shall be made happy and useful, and that the children there must be trained to be good citizens, and that no 'taint of pauperism' be attached to them hereafter. They are asking that women shall receive equal pay with men for equal work. They have refused on more than one important occasion to support a candidate whose moral character was known to be bad.

These are all part of the Socialist creed.

If we turn to countries where women possess full political power we shall find this resemblance between the aims of Woman and Labour even still more apparent.

In Wyoming, where women have exercised the suffrage since 1869, in Utah and Idaho, where they were enfranchised in 1896, and in Colorado, in 1893, the women's vote raised the age of consent to 18. In this country it is still 16. In Wyoming women teachers must (by law) receive equal pay for equal work and when equally qualified, as men teachers receive. Excellent legislation against gambling has been passed. The employment of boys and girls in mines, and of children under 14 in public exhibitions is also forbidden there. Free Libraries, free kindergartens, the proper treatment of children, and also of animals, the cleaning of streets, and the care of the aged, the feeble-minded and insane, industrial conditions, and a host of other matters equally important, including temperance measures, have all been traced to the women's vote.

In New Zealand, as we all know, old age pensions were obtained in 1898, i.e. five years after women had obtained the franchise and, as everyone agrees, it was their vote mostly which passed it. Industrial reforms also of an important kind, both there and in Australia, have resulted from the women's vote. The presence too of women at the polling booth in those countries has been productive of nothing but good, as all the authorities combine in telling us; men have taken more interest in recording their votes, the public houses are closed on the election day in some parts, and neither the husband's shirt buttons nor the baby have been in the least neglected. Sir John Cockburn[8] says, in referring to South Australia, and the effect of the women's vote there, 'In the first place, legislators have to lead decent lives. Women won't put up with any nonsense ... The woman's vote in South Australia has been a vote for health, physical and moral, in the highest possible sense.'

Everywhere in England we see women fighting for reforms of the same kind as those for which the Labour Party is fighting, and arousing therefore the same opposition from those who prefer stagnation to reform. The women are, of course, generally unconscious as yet of the connection between their cause and the labour cause, and of the similarity of their respective aims, and, doubtless, the larger reforms we in the Socialist ranks desire, they do not always understand or wish for. Probably, the word Socialism arouses in some the same dread that it arouses within many men's minds. But, nevertheless, it was a non-Socialist woman Parish Councillor, the late Miss Jane Escombe, who first lead the way in the direction of land nationalisation in rural districts. She made her Council build and own cottages on their own land. Women's work is awakening people to see that society must be responsible for the welfare of the individual, because the individual, each one of us who fulfils a duty to the State, is the State (each of all, all for each, we say), and I am convinced they have thus helped immensely, even though unconsciously, to prepare the way for the growth of a Socialism of the best and most enduring kind. Unconscious reformers have sometimes achieved the strongest results. Mary Carpenter,[9] who began the idea of reformatory schools for the young, was no more a Socialist than was Lord Shaftesbury.[10]

Liberal and Tory Attitude to Women and their Work

The other two political parties know perfectly well that behind the women's demand for the vote lies the demand for a great economic and moral reform, and a reform which will immediately take its place amongst the practical politics of the day. Old-age pensions will not be left any longer on paper, adult suffrage will not have to wait another 40 long years, temperance reform will mean something beside mere tinkering, industrial reforms will come which will, doubtless, end, as in New South Wales, in a material improvement (unpleasant to the capitalist) in the conditions and wages of working women, when the women's voice is heard in Parliament.

In the struggle for the repeal of the Contagious Diseases Acts,[11] women and the then Labour Party (the trade unionists and the co-operators) joined hands, and won an immortal victory. Some of our opposers probably remember that great triumph. They know, in spite of denials and quibbling, that the women's suffrage agitation has never meant simply a demand for a property vote, otherwise, in their own interests, they would have granted it long ago.

Women are called conservative, but has there been any great struggle or revolution in which women have not taken a prominent and important part? What would the Russian revolution be without the women: whose women stood more nobly beside their men, even in the trenches, than the Boer women? Politicians know that when once the women of a nation come into political power, their day of quiet slumber or gentle obstruction is over, for, as Sir John Cockburn puts it, 'women won't put up with any nonsense.' The extension of men's vote, even if it be the manhood suffrage, they apparently do not dread at all, and one supposes they must argue from experience.

At the heart of every woman who now asks for the vote in all seriousness, lies the conviction that until women possess this power, the deepest moral evils against which the world is perpetually battling can never be crushed or even touched. This is chiefly due to the increasing knowledge of industrial life and conditions which women have gained through their work as guardians, factory inspectors, sanitary inspectors, and so forth. It has shown them with a fearful distinctness, that the barbarous state of our marriage and divorce laws, of our laws concerning the custody of children, illegal motherhood and fatherhood, the condition of our streets and factories, etc.: all press most heavily on the lives of *poor* women. It is this knowledge which has stirred in so many women's minds an enthusiasm strong as a religion – to many it is a religion – and a desperate determination that these things shall no longer continue, and, therefore they have brought the question forward in such a manner that it now has acquired a position of enormous importance in all thinking minds.

The Labour Party has found its political voice, the women insist that theirs be heard, too. The Labour Party, understanding economic slavery as no other class can, understands the women's need, and the two stand together now, in this demand for political freedom, which alone brings economic freedom. This is what the other two political parties have to recognise at this moment.

Effect of the Franchise on Women

So much has been said about the manner in which women have used their vote, on progressive lines, in those places where they possess political freedom, that it hardly seems necessary to describe what the effect of the vote will have in England on women themselves. But there is one point which is at times overlooked. Wherever an extension of the franchise has been granted, increased facilities for education have followed. It is, I feel convinced, only where women are citizens that the importance of training and educating the mothers of the nation in their duties as such, will be recognised.

A man is trained for this trade or profession; nature is not considered as a sufficient guide for him if he wishes to be for instance, an engineer. A woman receives no special training when she undertakes the fearfully important role of motherhood. Nature is supposed to teach her everything. She is taught neither chemistry nor hygiene – nor domestic economy,

except in a most incomplete and desultory manner. Consequently we have
our present high rate of infantile mortality, an increase of anaemia amongst
our growing girls particularly, and our miserable housing conditions.

The supreme importance of teaching physical control of every kind to
their children is never explained or mentioned to women, and therefore we
have certain moral evils increasing, instead of diminishing, and to an
alarming extent.

It is a little misleading, too, to say we trust nature. We have lost all
connection with nature through our industrial life, and we no longer
understand her. The mother wild animal, as those who read Long's books
will see, teaches her children how to conduct themselves, and how to avoid
the dangers and difficulties of life. Our mothers, particularly those in the
poorest classes where life's dangers are most keenly felt, cannot do this.
The instincts which free wild animals possess they now know nothing of,
and we have not given them any training which can take their place.

Attitude of the Labour Party to the Women's Movement

In the past, and indeed in some measure at the present day too, there has
been a prejudice against the women's movement amongst Socialists on the
ground that it owes its origin and growth, mostly if not entirely, to middle-
class women. Surely it is anti-Socialistic and futile to argue in this position.
Our present Socialist party was in the beginning formed chiefly by middle-
class men and women. William Morris was a middle-class man. Lord
Shaftesbury was not of the 'working class,' as we term it, but the Factory
Acts he initiated nevertheless marked the beginning of a socialistic
industrial era. The very reason why the Labour movement of the present
day is superior to all similar movements in the past, and why it has before
it a future of endless growth and development, is because it has swept into
its great current followers of all classes. It has got beyond the earlier stages
of mere class warfare, it has lost that old provincial spirit, and is now
international, cosmopolitan in its demands. It aims at binding the workers
of all nations, regardless of sex or race or caste into one great whole, and
in that word Workers it includes all who contribute their share of service
to the world. Mutual service is an imperative condition. It appeals to all
to join its ranks, solely on this condition.

Just so is the woman's movement now expanding out of its narrow origin
and appealing to all classes of women to take their share in the crusade.
The Trade Union woman sees that she is entitled to political representation
in return for her political fund levy. Discontent is everywhere spreading
amongst women workers, and they are desiring to put their case
themselves before the world, in their own way. Their standard of living has
been slowly raised by the sanitary and housing and factory reforms the

middle-class woman has been ceaselessly advocating since she attained a place in the local government of the country, and they are therefore beginning to wish for better conditions in their lives.

The middle-class woman, as I have pointed out, bases her demand for justice, primarily of the needs of the working woman, now that her knowledge of those needs has grown clearer.

It is impossible, therefore, any longer to brand the woman's movement as only a middle-class affair.

Women's Attitude to the Labour Party

It is perfectly true that hitherto women have mistrusted the Labour Party. It is only recently that the latter has really understood what the women's party is fighting for underneath its cry for a vote. The working women's economic demands and needs have made them see its meaning and its connection with their own aims. Before this, women have seen that each time an extension of the franchise has been granted to the male workers, their own claim, on even the most modest scale, has been pushed ruthlessly aside, and all promises to the contrary broken unhesitatingly, because the safety of the Bill, they were told, must not be endangered by the addition of less important matter. Now no one likes to be described as 'less important matter,' especially as none of the State's pecuniary burdens are lifted from our shoulders on that ground, but only its privileges, and a distrust of the working-class voter has grown up in many women's minds, particularly since the last Reform Bill of 1884. The steady decrease in women's local government powers since that date has produced this mistrust. The Judge's decision that as the word 'person' did not include women, they could not sit on County Councils, made these suspicious-minded ones conclude that an extended male franchise must continually bring them further loss of liberty. Moreover, the socialist cry of Adult Suffrage (the word Adult now does not include woman), which when put into shape as a Bill for Parliament shrinks into Manhood Suffrage only, makes them think, and naturally I hold, that Socialism means nothing more for them than Liberalism has ever meant, with its empty cry of 'no taxation without representation,' or Toryism, with its 'property vote,' which has always ignored women's property claims.

Manhood suffrage in Germany, in France, in America (excepting always those four States where women possess the vote) has not brought freedom to women. In all these countries the position of women, industrial and otherwise, is inferior to their position in this country. In New South Wales women waited ten years before manhood suffrage was altered to adult suffrage. In some of the American States it took it away from them, and in Victoria in Australia, where, since 1857 men have had manhood suffrage, even yet women are not fully enfranchised. Manhood suffrage they have dreaded here, believing it would, as things are now, and looking at these countries as an instance, deliver them even more completely into the hands of the capitalist and exploiter. Those who desire a true adult suffrage consider that it will come infinitely quicker when together men and women can work for it. Men alone have certainly not achieved it here as yet.

To destroy the justice of sex disability will, many of us hold, so immensely help to clear the world's vision, will sweep away so many old superstitions and foolish prejudices, that we shall then be able to see how to establish a true enfranchisement for all, and bring an ever widening justice, in which we shall then include love of the human race, into all the relationships of life. As I said at the beginning of this pamphlet, if justice (and love) be brought into our home life, it will become part of the whole nation's life.

Result of the Two Movements Working Together

We must I think, surely gather from a clear understanding of the common origin and aims of these two movements, that the more they work alongside or together, the more each will strengthen the other. The Labour Party will always keep the economic side well to the front, and this is a side women are apt to overlook since all women do not yet grasp the intimate connection between morals and economics. Women will help to keep more clearly before our eyes, than is perhaps always possible now, those great ideals for the accomplishment of which Labour representation is only a means. History shows us that no cause can be far reaching or eternal that has not within it a religious enthusiasm, using the word in its very widest sense. The loyalty of women to priest and parson, for which they are continually ridiculed, has its foundation (distorted as is its shape at present) in a dim, unconscious recognition of this. Turned into wide and wholesome channels this enthusiasm will be invaluable to the Labour movement.

We think now that we understand and worship love, justice and compassion, but our present understanding of them is a mere blurred vision compared with what, in the future, it will be when men and women stand together, helping and teaching one another as equals and friends, instead of as now often living alongside one another as strangers, sometimes even as enemies. Our lives at present are mostly quite different from our ideals, poor as our ideals are – we worship poverty in our churches, and we scorn it in our daily life and our laws, which class the lunatic and the pauper together; we reverence woman and motherhood in our poetry, whilst we underpay and enslave women, and motherhood leads to untold misery and degradation in the lives of innumerable women; we talk much about the beauty of compassion for the weak and helpless, and at the same time think we are justified in torturing animals, of all things the most helpless, for our own use and comfort. All this, and infinitely more of a like nature, we do in a stupid, blind fashion, not knowing that we do it. Slowly our eyes are opening and we begin to feel our lives are wrong and we long to do better; but it is not until woman, strong and free, stands beside man, helping him to reach this better life, and not as now often holding him back from it, that we shall begin in real earnest to walk towards the full light of day.

May it not be that this very subjection has in itself so chastened, so trained her (woman) to think of others rather than of herself, that after all it may have acted more as a blessing than as a curse of the world? May it not bring her to the problems of the future with a purer aim and a keener insight than is possible for man?

Appendix

Guilds

In 1388 (12 Richard II) an order was given that all Guilds and Brotherhoods should give returns of their foundations. Women appear as founders of some of these Guilds, which were partly of a social and religious character, and which taught an equal moral standard for both sexes. This is a remarkable indication of woman's influence in those early times.

The large trading Guilds, Clothworkers, Drapers, Brewers, Fishmongers, Weavers, besides many smaller ones, admitted women members. In Edward IV's reign we find mention of a Guild of 'Silkewomen and Throwsters,' consisting of women only. (*See* 'British Furwoman,' by E. C. Stopes. Also Mrs. Green's 'History of Town Life in the Fifteenth Century.')

'Prostitution began to play a great part in the social life of the medieval cities. It must also be noted that at the same time the line between capitalist and worker became more prominent, and a town proletariat made its influence felt.'

(*See* 'The Sex-Relations in Germany,' by Karl Pearson. Also 'Martin Luther,' both in 'The Ethic of Freethought,' by Pearson.)

Witchcraft

The following is an account of materials and other expenses attending the execution of two witches in Scotland. These matter-of-fact records bring the horror of the whole thing clearly before one's mind.

	£	s.	d.
For ten loads of coal to burn the witches	3	16	8
,, a tar barrel	0	14	0
,, towes	0	6	0
,, hurdles to be jumps for them	3	0	0
,, making of them	0	8	0
For one to go to Tinmouth for the Lord to sit upon the assize as judge	0	6	0
,, the executioner for his pains	8	14	0
,, his expenses there	0	16	4

The clergy and kirk sessions appear to have been the unwearied instruments of 'purging the land of witchcraft.' Many women were driven to suicide in fear of the tortures in store for them, for tortures of the most atrocious kind were applied to make them 'confess.'

In Germany, during the reign of Duke Heinrich Julius 'ten or twelve witches were often burnt in one day, so that the place of execution, before the Lechenholz near Wolfenbüttel, the stakes stood like a small forest.' (Pearson's translation of Tittmann.) Two of the signs of a witch were, 'a strong intellect, or remarkable beauty.'

These accusations laid against women, partly (if not chiefly in France) arose from the horrible feudal claim, called Marquette, a claim in most countries invariably enforced. This was the right every feudal lord possessed to the first 48 hours of every bride's life on his estate.

So desperate were the women, 'God Himself seemed to have forsaken women,' says one writer, that they, together with their husbands, met together secretly at nights, to pray to God for help, and with their prayers they presented offerings of corn, etc. – the remains of early Pagan offerings of fruits of the earth. These offerings were attended by old rites of a harmless character, but which were construed by the feudal lords and the church into 'Black Acts,' and the poor worshippers were denounced as witches.

The Pilgrim Fathers took the idea of witchcraft over to America, and the prosecutions there were terrible.

For the attitude of the early *Christian Fathers* towards women, see the prayer of St. Chrysostom, in which he describes women as a 'necessary evil, a natural temptation, a desirable calamity, a domestic peril, a deadly fascination, and a painted evil.'

'In the Laws and Resolutions of Women's Rights' (London 1632), we find: 'The reason why women have no control in Parliament, why they make no laws, consent to none, abrogate none, is their Original Sin'!

New Zealand

Women had a long fight to gain their enfranchisement, after Manhood Suffrage was established.

A National Council of Women was established 1896, three years after the granting of the Franchise. This Council considers all political matters, and draws up Bills for the Legislature.

A resolution was passed by it in 1896 urging the need for old age pensions, subject to the following conditions: '(1) The cost to be a charge on the consolidated Revenue; (2) the qualification of the recipients to be 20 years' residence in the country and a certified age of 65 years.' This meant universal old age pensions, and was objected to in the Legislature, and the present Bill, which has an income limitation, was passed. The women continue to urge their Bill, because by it no stigma of pauperism would be attached to the recipients.

The Women's Temperance Union is affiliated with the National Council and the subject has been in evidence at every Council meeting. The abolition of licences in five fresh electorates at the last Licensing Election is attributed by 'the Trade' to the women's vote. – Mrs. Sheppard.

Sir John Cockburn says, 'I believe the success of that measure (Old Age Pensions) was largely owing to the influence of the women's vote.'

The 'Lyttleton Times' (New Zealand) says in 1903, 'One good effect of the extension of the Franchise to women is seen in the increased activity of the male electors. When the men had the field to themselves it was a rare thing for 60 per cent of those on the rolls to record their votes. It is now about 78 to 79 per cent. About 75 per cent of the women vote.'

Women are paid in factories, etc.; for all public holidays.

Australia

Women were enfranchised in South Australia in 1894. In Western Australia in 1900. In New South Wales in 1902, i.e., ten years after the granting of Manhood Suffrage. In Queensland women obtained full suffrage in 1905.

Sir John Cockburn says of the women's vote in South Australia, 'With regard to Temperance, that cause has had a great accession of strength. A Bill providing a greater measure of local option has been passed into law. Sunday closing has been made more effective. It was the law before, but it was not strictly observed, and the women said, "We are going to have it kept." Women have set their faces against gambling and betting.'

Tasmania

Women obtained full suffrage in 1903.

United States

An interesting report published in America of a Committee on the Judiciary House of Representatives of the United States throws light on the effect of the women's vote in America, where they possess it. They have made the mothers the co-equal guardians of their children. Very stringent laws for the prevention of cruelty to children and to animals have been passed. The insurance of children under 10 is forbidden in order to prevent the murder of babies.

It is a criminal offence for any person, parent or otherwise, to encourage, cause, or contribute to the delinquency of any child.

Between the ages of 14 and 16 no one may work more than 8 hours a day.

Free kindergartens, in Utah, are provided in all school districts having a population of 2,000.

The report shows that the 'corrupt vote' is biggest in those districts where are the fewest women voters, and it goes on to state that in the States '11 per cent of the total male voters cannot read their own ballots' – they are entirely illiterate. These are the persons, it is considered, who continue to withhold the franchise from women.

In 14 States women have no suffrage of any kind whatsoever, for any local affairs even. In 1807, in New Jersey, women were deprived of the vote. In Massachusetts also women were turned off the register in 1820. Previously, they had voted in these States.

Germany

No property qualification exists for voters for the Reichstag. Women have no vote.

France

No property qualification for male voters. Women have no vote.

Finland

Women now vote on equal terms with men, since 1906.

England

The first petition in favour of women's suffrage was presented in 1832, and was from Mary Smith, of Stanmore, Yorks. In it she stated that as women were liable to all the penalties of the laws, including death, they ought to have a share in making those laws.

In May, 1866, a petition of 1,499 signatures was presented by John Stuart Mill, and received in the House of Commons with shouts of laughter.

1868: A petition of 21,000 signatures, headed by Florence Nightingale and Mrs. Somerville was presented, 'a heavy but delightful burden which Mr. Mill could hardly carry to the table.'

1873: Memorials from 11,000 women presented to Mr. Gladstone and Mr. Disraeli.

1881: Suffrage granted to women in the Isle of Man for the House of Keys.

1888: A memorial signed by 169 Members of Parliament presented to the First Lord of the Treasury asking Government to give a day for a Women's Suffrage Bill.

From 1870 to 1897 Bills or resolutions have been brought before the House of Commons almost annually. In 1897, 1,285 petitions were presented.

1901: A petition presented signed by 29,300 Lancashire textile women workers; and a memorial signed by 1,168 workers.

1902: A petition presented signed by 33,184 women textile workers in Yorkshire, and one signed by 4,300 women textile workers in Cheshire. A petition signed by 750 women graduates of Universities.

1903: Petition presented signed by 8,600 tailoresses in West Riding of Yorks.

Petition presented from 71 Trades and Labour Councils and 62 Trade Unions, representing over 100,000 working-men.

Petition presented from the I.L.P.

1905: Petitions bearing 25,708 signatures.

1906: Deputation representing over 100,000 women to Sir Henry Campbell Bannerman.

Petition from 8,000 women in the Rossendale Division.

In 1874 and 1875 petitions of 845,965 signatures were presented. In 1895 250,000 women signed one petition.

Before the passing of the Local Government Act, there were about 200 women Poor Law Guardians, but after 1894 the number immediately rose to 850, and is now about 1,000, of whom about 100 are Rural District Councillors, and two Urban District Councillors. Of women Parish Councillors there are about 100. No complete list has ever been compiled. There are 212 women physicians, surgeons, or general practitioners. Of women schoolmasters, teachers, professors, and lecturers, 171,670, as compared with 58,675 men.

Notes

1. Plato (427(?)–347 BC); Greek idealist Philosopher, taught philosophy, mathematics and government.
2. Karl Pearson (1857–1936); mathematician and idealist philosopher.
3. Plutarch; biographer and philosopher noted particularly for his *Parallel Lives* of Greek and Romans.
4. Alice Stopford Green (d. 1929); writer on historical subjects. A neighbour of the Webbs. A passionate Irish Nationalist, she became a member of the first Senate of the Irish Free State.
5. Sir Edward Coke (1552–1634); judge, and law writer and supporter of Oliver Cromwell. Attorney General who was also active in Parliament.
6. Martin Luther (1483–1546); leader of the Reformation and founder of Protestantism who translated the Bible into German.
7. William Lloyd Garrison (1805–79); American reformer, printer and journalist. Active in the cause of the abolition of slavery and an admirer of Thomas Paine.
8. Sir John Cockburn (born 1850); chairman of the Austral/Asian Chamber of Commerce.
9. Mary Carpenter (1807–77); social reformer interested in Ragged Schools and Reformatories as well as in prison reform.
10. Lord Shaftesbury (1801–85); Tory philanthropist and Parliamentary spokesman

for the Factory Movement for the Ten Hour Bill.

11. The Contagious Diseases Acts. The campaign led by Josephine Butler for a repeal of the Acts which discriminated against women was an early step in the emancipation of women. The protest, signed by a number of prominent women and presented in Parliament in 1870, alerted society to the need for reform of such discriminatory legislation.

13

This Misery of Boots

H.G. WELLS (1866–1946)

Introduction

H.G. Wells was born in Kent in 1866 and attended a private school followed by Midhurst Grammar School. He continued his education at the London Royal College of Science where he obtained a B.Sc. with first class honours in zoology.

His early work was in the field of science fiction and scientific romances but in all his work there was evidence of his socialist leanings. With maturity, this aspect of his interests developed and he became known for his forecasts of the future and his constructive idealism.

His rise to the rank of first rate novelist came with the publication in 1909 of *Ann Veronica*. This was the first of a number of social-ethical studies which caught the mood of the time and made him famous. His work sold in large quantities. Towards the end of his life, Wells turned to a liberal theism, though never considered himself a religious man.

His pamphlet output was considerable and generally written in accessible and comprehensible terms. He was anxious to reach people with his writing and went to some lengths to find ways of expressing the ideas of socialism so that the ordinary reader would understand.

Wells was considered to be rather an outsider by the original Fabian circle of the Webbs, Shaw and their friends, though they appreciated that his writing commanded a wider audience than theirs at the time. But it was Wells who realised that the Fabian Society was too conservative and set in its ways and needed bringing up to date, an assessment that was accepted by Shaw and the younger members.

It was agreed that there should be an airing of opinions as to the best way of bringing about the necessary changes. As his contribution Wells wrote *This Misery of Boots*, which was published in the *Independent Review*, December 1905, as an example of what socialist propaganda should be. The text satirised England from the bottom up.

This Misery of Boots was reprinted as a pamphlet by the Fabian Society in 1906, during a general election campaign. The Liberals won the election by a landslide and 30 Labour candidates were also elected. The result was a reflection of the wave of radical feeling sweeping the country at the time, in part generated by pamphlets such as this.

Sources
Vincent Brome, *H.G. Wells*, Longman's, Green and Co. 1951.
The Labour Who's Who 1927, Labour Publishing Co. Ltd.

★   ★   ★

The World as Boots and Superstructure

'It does not do,' said a friend of mine 'to think about boots.' For my own part, I have always been particularly inclined to look at boots, and think about them. I have an odd idea that most general questions can be expressed in terms of foot-wear – which is perhaps why cobblers are often such philosophical men. Accident, it may be, gave me this persuasion. A very considerable part of my childhood was spent in an underground kitchen; the window opened upon a bricked-in space, surmounted by a grating before my father's shop window. So that, when I looked out of the window, instead of seeing – as children of a higher upbringing would do – the heads and bodies of people, I saw their under side. I got acquainted indeed with all sorts of social types as boots simply, indeed, as the soles of boots; and only subsequently, and with care, have I fitted heads, bodies, and legs to these pediments.

There would come boots and shoes (no doubt holding people) to stare at the shop, finicking, neat little women's boots, good sorts and bad sorts, fresh and new, worn crooked in the tread, patched or needing patching; men's boots, clumsy and fine, rubber shoes, tennis shoes, goloshes. Brown shoes I never beheld – it was before that time; but I have seen pattens. Boots used to come and commune at the window, duets that marked their emotional development by a restlessness or a kick.

... But anyhow, that explains my preoccupation with boots.

But my friend did not think it *did*, to think about boots.

My friend was a realistic novelist, and a man from whom hope had departed. I cannot tell you how hope had gone out of his life; some subtle disease of the soul had robbed him at least of any enterprise, or belief in coming things; and he was trying to live the few declining years that lay before him in a sort of bookish comfort, among surroundings that seemed peaceful and beautiful, by not thinking of things that were painful and cruel. And we met a tramp who limped along the lane.

'Chafed heel,' I said, when we had parted from him again; 'and on these pebbly byways no man goes barefooted.' My friend winced; and a little silence came between us. We were both recalling things; and then for a time, when we began to talk again, until he would have no more of it, we rehearsed the miseries of boots.

We agreed that to a very great majority of people in this country boots are constantly a source of distress, giving pain and discomfort, causing trouble, causing anxiety. We tried to present the thing in a concrete form to our own minds by hazardous statistical inventions. 'At the present moment,' said I, 'one person in ten in these islands is in discomfort through boots.'

My friend thought it was nearer one in five.

'In the life of a poor man or a poor man's wife, and still more in the lives of their children, this misery of the boot occurs and recurs – every year so many days.'

We made a sort of classification of these troubles.

There is the TROUBLE OF THE NEW BOOT.

(I) They are made of some bad, unventilated material; and 'draw the feet,' as people say.

(II) They do not fit exactly. Most people have to buy ready-made boots; they cannot afford others, and, in the submissive philosophy of poverty, they wear them to 'get used' to them. This gives you the little-toe pinch, the big-toe pinch, the squeeze and swelling across the foot; and, as a sort of chronic development of these pressures, come corns and all the misery of corns. Children's feet get distorted for good by this method of fitting the human being to the thing; and a vast number of people in the world are, as a consequence of this, ashamed to appear barefooted. (I used to press people who came to see me in warm pleasant weather to play Badminton barefooted on the grass – a delightful thing to do – until I found out that many were embarrassed at the thought of displaying twisted toes and corns, and such-like disfigurements.)

(III) The third trouble of new boots is this: they are unseasoned and in bad condition, and so they squeak and make themselves an insulting commentary on one's ways.

But these are but trifling troubles to what arises as the boots get into wear. Then it is the pinch comes in earnest. Of these TROUBLES OF THE WORN BOOT, I and my friend, before he desisted, reckoned up three principal classes.

(I) There are the various sorts of chafe. Worst of the chafes is certainly the heel chafe, when something goes wrong with the upright support at the heel. This, as a boy, I have had to endure for days together; because there were no other boots for me. Then there is the chafe that comes when that inner lining of the boot rucks up – very like the chafe it is that poor people are always getting from over-darned and hastily-darned socks. And then there is the chafe that comes from ready-made boots one has got a trifle too large or long, in order to avoid the pinch and corns. After a little while, there comes a transverse crease across the loose-fitting forepart; and, when the boot stiffens from wet or any cause, it chafes across the base of the toes. They have you all ways. And I have a very lively recollection too of the chafe of the knots one made to mend broken laces – one cannot be always buying new laces, and the knots used to work inward. And then the chafe of the crumpled tongue.

(II) Then there are the miseries that come from the wear of the sole. There is the rick of ankle because the heel has gone over, and the sense of insecurity; and there is the miserable sense of not looking well from behind that many people must feel. It is almost always painful to me to walk behind girls who work out, and go to and fro, consuming much foot-wear, for this very reason, that their heels seem always to wear askew. Girls ought always to be so beautiful, most girls could be so beautiful, that to see their poor feet askew, the grace of their walk gone, a sort of spinal curvature induced, makes me wretched, and angry with a world that treats them so. And then there is the working through of nails, nails in the shoe. One limps on manfully in the hope presently of a quiet moment and a quiet corner in which one may hammer the thing down again. Thirdly, under this heading I recall the flapping sole. My boots always came to that stage at last; I wore the toes out first, and then the sole split from before backwards. As one walked it began catching the ground. One made fantastic paces to prevent it happening; one was dreadfully ashamed. At last one was forced to sit by the wayside frankly, and cut the flap away.

(III) Our third class of miseries were made of splitting and leaks. These are for the most part mental miseries, the feeling of shabbiness as one sees the ugly yawn, for example, between toe cap and the main upper of the boot; but they involve also chills, colds, and a long string of disagreeable consequences. And we spoke too of the misery of sitting down to work (as multitudes of London school children do every wet morning) in boots with soles worn thin or into actual holes, that have got wet and chilling on the way to the workplace...

From these instances my mind ran on to others. I made a discovery. I had always despised the common run of poor Londoners for not spending their Sundays and holidays in sturdy walks, the very best of exercises. I had allowed myself to say when I found myself one summer day at Margate: 'What a soft lot all these young people must be who loaf about the band-stand here, when they might be tramping over the Kentish hills inland!' But now I repented me of that. Long tramps indeed! Their boots would have hurt them. Their boots would not stand it. I saw it all.

And now my discourse was fairly underway. *'Ex pede Herculem,'* I said; 'these miseries of boots are no more than a sample. The clothes people wear are no better than their boots; and the houses they live in far worse. And think of the shoddy garment of ideas and misconceptions and partial statements into which their poor minds have been jammed by way of education! Think of the way *that* pinches and chafes them! If one expanded the miseries of these things... Think, for example, of the results of poor, bad, unwise food, of badly-managed eyes and ears and teeth! Think of the quantity of toothache.'

'I tell you, it does not *do* to think of such things!' cried my friend, in a sort of anguish; and would have no more of it at any price ...

And yet in his time he had written books full of these very matters, before despair overtook him.

People Whose Boots Don't Hurt Them

Well, I did not talk merely to torment him; nor have I written this merely to torment you. You see I have a persistent persuasion that all these miseries are preventable miseries, which it lies in the power of men to cure.

Everybody does not suffer misery from boots.

One person I know, another friend of mine, who can testify to that; who has tasted all the miseries of boots, and who now goes about the world free of them, but not altogether forgetful of them. A stroke of luck, aided perhaps by a certain alacrity on his own part, lifted him out of the class in which one buys one's boots and clothes out of what is left over from a pound a week, into the class in which one spends seventy or eighty pounds a year on clothing. Sometimes he buys shoes and boots at very good shops; sometimes he has them made for him; he has them stored in a proper cupboard, and great care is taken of them; and so his boots and shoes and slippers never chafe, never pinch, never squeak, never hurt nor worry him, never bother him; and, when he sticks out his toes before the fire, they do not remind him that he is a shabby and contemptible wretch, living meanly on the dust heaps of the world. You might think from this he had every reason to congratulate himself and be happy, seeing that he has had good follow after evil; but, such is the oddness of the human heart, he isn't contented at all. The thought of the multitudes so much worse off than himself in this matter of foot-wear, gives him no sort of satisfaction. Their boots pinch *him* vicariously. The black rage with the scheme of things that once he felt through suffering in his own person in the days when he limped shabbily through gaily busy, fashionable London streets, in split boots that chafed, he feels now just as badly as he goes about the world very comfortably himself, but among people whom he knows with a pitiless clearness to be almost intolerably uncomfortable. He has no optimistic illusion that things are all right with them. Stupid people who have always been well off, who have always had boots that fit, may think that; but not so, he. In one respect the thought of boots makes him even more viciously angry now, than it used to do. In the old days he was savage with his luck, but hopelessly savage; he thought that bad boots, ugly uncomfortable clothes, rotten houses, were in the very nature of things. Now, when he sees a child sniffing and blubbering and halting upon the pavement, or an old country-woman going painfully along a lane, he no longer recognises the Pinch of Destiny. His rage is lit by the thought, that there are fools in this world who ought to have foreseen and prevented this. He no longer curses fate, but the dullness of statesmen and powerful responsible people who have neither the heart, nor courage, nor capacity, to change the state of mismanagement that gives us these things.

Now do not think I am dwelling unduly upon my second friend's good fortune, when I tell you that once he was constantly getting pain and miserable states of mind, colds for example, from the badness of his clothing, shame from being shabby, pain from the neglected state of his teeth, from the indigestion of unsuitable food eaten at unsuitable hours, from the insanitary ugly house in which he lived and the bad air of that part of London, from things indeed quite beyond the unaided power of a poor overworked man to remedy. And now all these disagreeable things have gone out of his life; he has consulted dentists and physicians, he has hardly any dull days from colds, no pain from toothache at all, no gloom of indigestion...

I will not go on with the tale of good fortune of this lucky person. My purpose is served if I have shown that this misery of boots is not an unavoidable curse upon mankind. If one man can evade it, others can. By good management it may be altogether escaped. If you, or what is more important to most human beings, if any people dear to you, suffer from painful or disfiguring boots or shoes, and you can do no better for them, it is simply because you are getting the worse side of an ill-managed world. It is not the universal lot.

And what I say of boots is true of all the other minor things of life. If your wife catches a bad cold because her boots are too thin for the time of the year, or dislikes going out because she cuts a shabby ugly figure, if your children look painfully nasty because their faces are swollen with toothache, or because their clothes are dirty, old, and ill-fitting, if you are all dull and disposed to be cross with one another for want of decent amusement and change of air – don't submit, don't be humbugged for a moment into believing that this is the dingy lot of mankind. Those people you love are living in a badly-managed world and on the wrong side of it; and such wretchednesses are the daily demonstration of that.

Don't say for a moment: 'Such is life.' Don't think their miseries are part of some primordial curse there is no escaping. The disproof of that is for any one to see. There are people, people no more deserving than others, who suffer from none of these things. You may feel you merit no better than to live so poorly and badly that your boots are always hurting you; but do the little children, the girls, the mass of decent hard-up people, deserve no better fate?

At This Point a Dispute Arises

Now let us imagine some one who will dispute what I am saying. I do not suppose any one will dispute my argument that a large part of the misery of civilised life – I do not say 'all' but only a 'large part' – arises out of the network of squalid insufficiencies of which I have taken this misery of boots as the simplest example. But I do believe quite a lot of people will be prepared to deny that such miseries can be avoided. They will say that every one cannot have the best of things, that of all sorts of good things, including good leather and cobbling, there is not enough to go round, that lower-class people ought not to mind being shabby and uncomfortable, that they ought to be very glad to be able to live at all, considering what they are, and that it is no good stirring up discontent about things that cannot be altered or improved.

Such arguments are not to be swept aside with a wave of the hand. It is perfectly true that every one cannot have the best of things; and it is in the nature of things that some boots should be better and some worse. To some people, either by sheer good luck, or through the strength of their determination to have them, the exquisitely good boots, those of the finest leather and the most artistic cut, will fall. I have never denied that. Nobody dreams of a time when every one will have exactly as good boots as every one else; I am not preaching any such childish and impossible equality. But it is a long way from recognising that there must be a certain picturesque and interesting variety in this matter of foot-wear, to the admission that a large majority of people can never hope for more than to be shod in a manner that is frequently painful, uncomfortable, unhealthy, or unsightly. That admission I absolutely refuse to make. There is enough good leather in the world to make good sightly boots and shoes for all who need them, enough men at leisure and enough power and machinery to do all the work required, enough unemployed intelligence to organise the shoemaking and shoe distribution for everybody. What stands in the way?

Let us put that question in a rather different form. Here on the one hand – you can see for yourself in any unfashionable part of Great Britain – are people badly, uncomfortably, painfully shod, in old boots, rotten boots, sham boots; and on the other great stretches of land in the world, with unlimited possibilities of cattle and leather and great numbers of people, who, either through wealth or trade disorder, are doing no work. And our question is: 'Why cannot the latter set to work and make and distribute boots?'

Imagine yourself trying to organise something of this kind of Free Booting expedition; and consider the difficulties you would meet with. You would begin by looking for a lot of leather. Imagine yourself setting off to South America, for example, to get leather; beginning at the very beginning by setting to work to kill and flay a herd of cattle. You find at once you are interrupted. Along comes your first obstacle in the shape of a man who tells you the cattle and the leather belong to him. You explain that the leather is wanted for people who have no decent boots in England. He says he does not care a rap what you want it for; before you may take it from him you have to buy him off; it is his private property, this leather, and the herd and the land over which the herd ranges. You ask him how much he wants for his leather; and he tells you frankly, just as much as he can induce you to give.

If he chanced to be a person of exceptional sweetness of disposition, you might perhaps argue with him. You might point out to him that this project of giving people splendid boots was a fine one that would put an end to much human misery. He might even sympathise with your generous enthusiasm; but you would, I think, find him adamantine in his resolve to get just as much out of you for his leather as you could with the utmost effort pay.

Suppose now you said to him: 'But how did you come by this land and these herds, so that you can stand between them and the people who have need of them, exacting this profit?' He would probably either embark upon a long rigmarole, or, what is much more probable, lose his temper and decline to argue. Pursuing your doubt as to the rightfulness of his property in these things, you might admit he deserved a certain reasonable fee for the rough care he had taken of the land and herds. But cattle breeders are a rude, violent race; and it is doubtful if you would get far beyond your proposition of a reasonable fee. You would in fact have to buy off this owner of the leather at a good thumping price – he exacting just as much as he could get from you – if you wanted to go on with your project.

Well, then you would have to get your leather here; and, to do that, you would have to bring it by railway and ship to this country. And here again you would find people without any desire or intention of helping your project, standing in your course, resolved to make every possible penny out of you on your way to provide sound boots for everyone. You would find the railway was private property, and had an owner or owners; you would find the ship was private property, with an owner or owners; and that none of these would be satisfied for a moment with a mere fee adequate to their services. They too would be resolved to make every penny of profit out of you. If you made inquiries about the matter, you would probably find the real owners of railway and ship were companies of shareholders, and that the profit squeezed out of your poor people's boots at this stage went to fill the pockets of old ladies at Torquay, spendthrifts in Paris, well-booted gentlemen in London clubs, all sorts of glossy people . . .

Well, you get the leather to England at last; and now you want to make it into boots. You take it to a centre of population, invite workers to come to you, erect sheds and machinery upon a vacant piece of ground, and start off in a sort of fury of generous industry, boot-making... Do you? There comes along an owner for that vacant piece of ground, declares it is his property, demands an enormous sum for rent. And your workers all round you, you find, cannot get house room until they too have paid rent – every inch of the country is somebody's property, and a man may not shut his eyes for an hour without the consent of some owner or other. And the food your shoe-makers eat, the clothes they wear, have all paid tribute and profit to land-owners, cart-owners, house-owners, end-less tribute over and above the fair pay for work that has been done upon them...

So one might go on. But you begin to see now one set of reasons at least why every one has not good comfortable boots. There could be plenty of leather; and there is certainly plenty of labour and quite enough intelligence in the world to manage that and a thousand other desirable things. But this institution of Private Property in land and naturally produced things, these obstructive claims that prevent you using ground, or moving material, and that have to be bought out at exorbitant prices, stand in the way. All these owners hang like parasites upon your enterprise at its every stage; and, by the time you get your sound boots well made in England, you will find them costing about a pound a pair – high out of the reach of the general mass of people. And you will perhaps not think me fanciful and extravagant when I confess that when I realise this, and look at poor people's boots in the street, and see them cracked and misshapen and altogether nasty, I seem to see also a lot of little phantom land-owners, cattle-owners, house-owners, owners of all sorts, swarming over their pinched and weary feet like leeches, taking much and giving nothing, and being the real cause of all such miseries.

Now is this a necessary and unavoidable thing? That is our question. Is there no other way of managing things than to let these property-owners exact their claims, and squeeze comfort, pride, happiness, out of the lives of the common run of people? Because, of course, it is not only the boots they squeeze into meanness and badness. It is the claim and profit of the land-owner and house-owner that make our houses so ugly, shabby, and dear, that make our roadways and railways so crowded and inconvenient, that sweat our schools, our clothing, our food – boots we took merely by way of one example of a universal trouble.

Well, there are a number of people who say there is a better way, and that the world could be made infinitely better in all these matters, made happier and better than it ever has been in these respects, by refusing to have private property in all these universally necessary things. They say that it is possible to have the land administered, and such common and needful things as leather produced, and boots manufactured, and no end of other such generally necessary services carried on, not for the private profit of individuals, but for the good of all. They propose that the State should take away the land, and the railways, and shipping, and many great organised enterprises from their owners, who use them simply to squeeze the means for a wasteful private expenditure out of the common mass of men, and should administer all these things, generously and boldly, not for profit, but for service. It is this idea of extracting *profit* they hold which is the very root of the evil. These are the Socialists; and they are the only people who do hold out any hope of far-reaching change that will alter the present dingy state of affairs, of which this painful wretchedness of boots is only one typical symbol.

Is Socialism Possible?

I will not pretend to be impartial in this matter, and to discuss as though I had an undecided mind, whether the world would be better if we could abolish private property in land and in many things of general utility; because I have no doubt left in the matter. I believe that private property in these things is no more necessary and unavoidable than private property in our fellow-creatures, or private property in bridges and roads. The idea that anything and everything may be claimed as private property belongs to the dark ages of the world; and it is not only a monstrous injustice, but a still more monstrous inconvenience. Suppose we still admitted private property in high roads, and let every man who had a scrap of high road haggle a bargain with us before we could drive by in a cab! You say life would be unendurable. But indeed it amounts to something a little like that if we use a railway now; and it is quite like that if one wants a spot of ground somewhere upon which one may live. I see no more difficulty in managing land, factories, and the like, publicly for the general good, than there is in managing roads and bridges, and the post office and the police. So far I see no impossibility whatever in Socialism. To abolish private property in these things would be to abolish all that swarm of parasites, whose greed for profit and dividend hampers and makes a thousand useful and delightful enterprises costly or hopeless. It would abolish them; but is that any objection whatever?

And as for taking such property from the owners; why shouldn't we? The world has not only in the past taken slaves from their owners, with no compensation or with a meagre compensation; but in the history of mankind, dark as it is, there are innumerable cases of slave-owners resigning their inhuman rights. You may say that to take away property from people is unjust and robbery; but is that really so? Suppose you found a number of children in a nursery all very dull and unhappy because one of them, who had been badly spoilt, had got all the toys together and claimed them all, and refused to let the others have any. Would you not dispossess the child, however honest its illusion that it was right to be greedy? That is practically the position of the property-owner today. You may say, if you choose, that property-owners, land-owners for example, must be bought out and not robbed; but since getting the money to buy them out involves taxing the property of some one else, who may possibly have a better claim to it than the land-owner to his, I don't quite see where the honesty of that course comes in. You can only give property for property in buying and selling; and if private property is not robbery, then not only Socialism but ordinary taxation must be. But if taxation is a justifiable proceeding, if you can tax me (as I am taxed) for public services, a shilling and more out of every twenty shillings I earn, then I do not see why you should not put a tax upon the land-owner if you want to do so, of a half or two thirds or all his land, or upon the railway shareholder of ten or fifteen or twenty shillings in the pound on his shares. In every change some one has to bear the brunt; every improvement in machinery and industrial organisation deprives some poor people of an income; and I do not see why we should be so extraordinarily tender to the rich, to those who have been unproductive all their lives, when they stand in the way of the general happiness. And though I deny the right to compensation I do not deny its probable advisability. So far as the question of method goes it is quite conceivable that we may partially compensate the property owners and make all sorts of mitigating arrangements to avoid cruelty to them in our attempt to end the wider cruelties of today.

But, apart from the justice of the case, many people seem to regard Socialism as a hopeless dream, because, as they put it, 'it is against human nature.' Every one with any scrap of property in land, or shares, or what not, they tell us, will be bitterly opposed to the coming of Socialism; and, as such people have all the leisure and influence in the world, and as all able and energetic people tend naturally to join that class, there never can be any effectual force to bring Socialism about. But that seems to me to confess a very base estimate of human nature. There are, no doubt, a number of dull, base, rich people who hate and dread Socialism for purely selfish reasons; but it is quite possible to be a property-owner and yet be anxious to see Socialism come to its own.

For example, the man whose private affairs I know best in the world, the second friend I named, the owner of all those comfortable boots, gives time and energy and money to further this hope of Socialism, although he pays income tax on twelve hundred a year, and has shares and property to the value of some thousands of pounds. And that he does out of no instinct of sacrifice. He believes he would be happier and more comfortable in a

Socialistic state of affairs, when it would not be necessary for him to hold on to that life-belt of invested property. He finds it – and quite a lot of well-off people are quite of his way of thinking – a constant flaw upon a life of comfort and pleasant interests to see so many people, who might be his agreeable friends and associates, detestably under-educated, detestably housed, in the most detestable clothes and boots, and so detestably broken in spirit that they will not treat him as an equal. It makes him feel he is like that spoilt child in the nursery; he feels ashamed and contemptible; and, since individual charity only seems in the long run to make matters worse, he is ready to give a great deal of his life, and lose his entire little heap of possessions if need be, very gladly lose it, to change the present order of things in a comprehensive manner.

I am quite convinced that there are numbers of much richer and more influential people who are of his way of thinking. Much more likely to obstruct the way to Socialism is the ignorance, the want of courage, the stupid want of imagination of the very poor, too shy and timid and clumsy to face any change they can evade! But, even with them, popular education is doing its work; and I do not fear but that in the next generation we shall find Socialists even in the slums. The unimaginative person who owns some little bit of property, an acre or so of freehold land, or a hundred pounds in the savings bank, will no doubt be the most tenacious passive resister to Socialistic ideas; and such, I fear, we must reckon, together with the insensitive rich, as our irreconcilable enemies, as irremovable pillars of the present order. The mean and timid elements in 'human nature' are, and will be, I admit, against Socialism; but they are not all 'human nature,' not half human nature. And when, in the whole history of the world, have meanness and timidity won a struggle? It is passion, it is enthusiasm, and indignation that mould the world to their will – and I cannot see how any one can go into the back streets of London, or any large British town, and not be filled up with shame, and passionate resolve to end so grubby and mean a state of affairs as is displayed there.

I don't think the 'human nature' argument against the possibility of Socialism will hold water.

Socialism Means Revolution

Let us be clear about one thing: that Socialism means revolution, that it means a change in the everyday texture of life. It may be a very gradual change, but it will be a very complete one. You cannot change the world, and at the same time not change the world. You will find Socialists about, or at any rate men calling themselves Socialists, who will pretend that this is not so, who will assure you that some odd little jobbing about municipal gas and water is Socialism, and back-stairs intervention between

Conservative and Liberal the way to the millennium. You might as well call a gas jet in the lobby of a meeting-house, the glory of God in Heaven!

Socialism aims to change, not only the boots on people's feet, but the clothes they wear, the houses they inhabit, the work they do, the education they get, their places, their honours, and all their possessions. Socialism aims to make a new world out of the old. It can only be attained by the intelligent, outspoken, courageous resolve of a great multitude of men and women. You must get absolutely clear in your mind that Socialism means a complete change, a break with history, with much that is picturesque; whole classes will vanish. The world will be vastly different, with different sorts of houses, different sorts of people. All the different trades and industries will be changed, the medical profession will be carried on under different conditions, engineering, science, the theatrical trade, the clerical trade, schools, hotels, almost every trade, will have to undergo as complete an internal change as a caterpillar does when it becomes a moth. If you are afraid of so much change as that, it is better you should funk about it now than later. The whole system has to be changed, if we are to get rid of the masses of dull poverty that render our present state detestable to any sensitive man or woman. That, and no less, is the aim of all sincere Socialists: the establishment of a new and better order of society by the abolition of private property in land, in natural productions, and in their exploitation – a change as profound as the abolition of private property in slaves would have been in ancient Rome or Athens. If you demand less than that, if you are not prepared to struggle for that, you are not really a Socialist. If you funk that, then you must make up your mind to square your life to a sort of personal and private happiness with things as they are, and decide with my other friend that 'it doesn't do to think about boots.'

It is well to insist upon one central idea. Socialism is a common-sense, matter-of-fact proposal to change our conventional admission of what is or is not property, and to rearrange the world according to these revised conceptions. A certain number of clever people, dissatisfied with the straightforwardness of this, have set themselves to put it in some brilliant obscure way; they will tell you that Socialism is based on the philosophy of Hegel,[1] or that it turns on a theory of Rent, or that it is somehow muddled up with a sort of white Bogey called the Overman, and all sorts of brilliant, nonsensical, unappetising things. The theory of Socialism, so far as English people are concerned, seems to have got up into the clouds, and its practice down into the drains; and it is well to warn inquiring men, that neither the epigram above nor the job beneath are more than the accidental accompaniments of Socialism. Socialism is a very large, but a plain, honest, and human enterprise; its ends are to be obtained neither by wit nor cunning, but by outspoken resolve, by the self-abnegation, the enthusiasm, and the loyal co-operation of great masses of people.

The main thing, therefore, is the creation of these great masses of people out of the intellectual confusion and vagueness of the present time. Let me suppose that you find yourself in sympathy with this tract, that you, like my second friend, find the shabby dullness, the positive misery of a large proportion of the population of our world, make life under its present conditions almost intolerable, and that it is in the direction of Socialism that the only hope of a permanent remedy lies. What are we to do? Obviously to give our best energies to making other people Socialists, to organising ourselves with all other Socialists, irrespective of class or the minor details of creed, and to making ourselves audible, visible, effectual as Socialists, wherever and whenever we can.

We have to think about Socialism, read about it, discuss it; so that we may be assured and clear and persuasive about it. We have to confess our faith openly and frequently. We must refuse to be called Liberal or Conservative, Republican or Democrat, or any of those ambiguous things. Everywhere we must make or join a Socialist organisation, a club or association or what not, so that we may 'count.' For us, as for the early Christians, preaching our gospel is the supreme duty. Until Socialists can be counted, and counted upon by the million, little will be done. When they are – a new world will be ours.

Above all, if I may offer advice to a fellow-Socialist, I would say: Cling to the simple essential idea of Socialism, which is the abolition of private property in anything but what a man has earned or made. Do not complicate your cause with elaborations. And keep in your mind, if you can, some sort of talisman to bring you back to that essential gospel, out of the confusions and warring suggestions of everyday discussion.

For my own part, I have, as I said at the beginning, a prepossession with boots; and my talisman is this: The figure of a badly fed but rather pretty little girl of ten or eleven, dirty, and her hands coarse with rough usage, her poor pretty child's body in ungainly rags, and, on her feet, big broken-down boots that hurt her. And particularly I think of her wretched sticks of legs and the limp of her feet; and all those phantom owners and profit-takers I spoke of, they are there about her martyrdom, leech-like, clinging to her as she goes...

I want to change everything in the world that made that; and I do not greatly care what has to go in the process. Do you?

(Here is just a bit of hard fact to carry out what I say. It is a quotation from a letter from a workman to my friend Mr. Chiozza Money, one of the best informed writers upon labour questions in England:

I am a railway man, in constant work at 30*s*. per week. I am the happy, or otherwise, father of six healthy children. Last year I bought twenty pairs of boots. This year, up to date, I have bought ten pairs, costing £2; and yet, at the present time, my wife and five of the children have only one pair each. I have two pairs, both of which let in the water; but I see no prospect at present of getting new ones. I ought to say, of course, that my wife is a thoroughly domesticated woman, and I am one of the most temperate of men. So much so, that if all I spend in luxuries was saved it would not buy a pair of boots once a year. But this is the point I want to mention. During 1903 my wages were 25s. 6d. per week; and I then had the six children. My next-door neighbour was a boot-maker and repairer. He fell out of work, and was out for months. During that time, of course, my children's boots needed repairing as at other times. I had not the money to pay for them being repaired, so had to do what repairing I could myself. One day I found out that I was repairing boots on one side of the wall, and my neighbour on the other side out of work, and longing to do the work I was compelled to do myself...

The wall was a commercial organisation of society based on private property in land and natural productions. These two men must work for the owners or not at all; they cannot work for one another. Food first, then rent; and boots, if you can, when all the owners are paid.)

Notes

1. Georg Wilhelm Friedrich Hegel (1770–1831); one of the German classical philosophers, an objective idealist. As a young man, he welcomed the French Revolution and rebelled against the feudal order of the Prussian monarchy. Marx took the dialectical method from Hegel.

14
Socialism Made Easy

JAMES CONNOLLY (1868–1916)

Introduction

James Connolly was born in an Edinburgh slum and received his first political education in Scotland. He became involved in the socialist movement through the Scottish Socialist Federation and the Independent Labour Party when he returned from military service at the end of the 1880s, and the whole of his short life was spent in furthering the socialist cause.

In 1896, he moved to Dublin where he lived until 1903. There he tried to reconcile socialism with the national question, and helped form the Irish Socialist Republican Party. The party's programme identified the 'national and economic freedom of the Irish people' with 'the establishment of an Irish Socialist Republic'.

Connolly spent seven years, 1903–10, in the United States of America where he established connections with Daniel de Leon's Socialist Labour Party. Although he was critical of De Leon's sectarianism, he became one of the founder members of the Industrial Workers of The World, the IWW. Under De Leon's influence, he became convinced of the correctness of syndicalism and adopted a syndicalist approach.

As a socialist propagandist, Connolly spent much of his time in poverty. Returning from America in 1910, he immediately found himself involved in the working-class struggles in Belfast and then in the Dublin lock-out, one of the highest points in the class struggle in Europe in the period leading up to the First World War.

When war broke out, Connolly refused to consider Germany as the enemy, declaring 'We serve neither King nor Kaiser, but Ireland.' From the outbreak of war, Connolly devoted his time to preparing for the 1916 Easter rising. Though his ideas of syndicalism had been somewhat eroded during his participation in the Irish nationalist struggles, he still maintained that they had 'succeeded in creating an organisation that will willingly do more for Ireland than any other trade union movement in the world has attempted to do for its national government.'

Realising the potential revolutionary situation that was developing in Ireland he used all his influence and skill as a propagandist to increase and hasten the preparations. The story of the Easter Rising and its defeat is well documented. Unfortunately, although there was evidence of opposition to the war in a number of countries, nowhere was it strong enough to include support for the Irish, and they therefore stood alone on the international scene. It was a foregone conclusion that the forces of reaction would rally to demonstrate that revolution was not a solution to world problems. It took another year, and activities of the Russian people, for them to be proved wrong.

James Connolly played a significant part in the uprising and was present at the reading of the Proclamation of the Declaration of the Irish Republic, but he was badly injured a couple of days later and was captured. After a mockery of a trial, he was condemned to be shot. Because of his injuries he was unable to stand and was strapped in a chair. His final words were, 'I will say a prayer for all brave men who do their duty according to their lights.'

Had Connolly been able to educate sufficient people in Ireland to understand the need for a scientific socialist party, the story of Ireland's subsequent struggle for independence could have been very different. His ability to relate the national problem to the industrial one might have guided the Irish people to a united struggle. Connolly's death at the age of 47, however, ended an era in Irish history which has still to see the triumph of the cause for which he gave his life.

Charles H. Kerr, socialist publishers in Chicago, first published *Socialism Made Easy* in 1909, when Connolly was in America. It was not published in Britain until the Socialist Labour Party in Edinburgh reprinted it in 1917. In the intervening years however, copies of the Kerr edition had circulated in the British Isles.

Connolly advocated industrial unionism in place of craft unionism, because he saw it as a more effective weapon for the workers against the growing menace of trusts. Industrial unity was paramount and industrial unions were the embryo of the new socialist society. They also provided the revolutionary instrument with which the change could be effected.

He also argued that the day-to-day struggles within industry would lead to the working class gaining the power to control it. Action at the ballot box, he maintained, would only supplement action in the workshops, and he questioned whether the ruling class would ever concede power as a result of a socialist victory in a Parliamentary election. He regarded the general strike as the most effective weapon in the worker's armoury.

Sources

C. Desmond Greaves, *The Life and Times of James Connolly*, Lawrence & Wishart, 1961.
David Howell, *A Lost Left*, Manchester University Press, 1986, pp. 11–12.

*   *   *

Foreword

Since the execution of James Connolly, many of his admirers have written to us asking our press to print some of his works. In response to their wishes, we publish the following pamphlet, which shows Connolly at his best as a Socialist writer. As it is not generally known that Connolly was a gifted song writer, we also reprint his now famous 'Rebel Song,' which he contributed to 'The Socialist' (the organ of the SLP) many years ago.

For permission to reprint the following pamphlet we are indebted to Chas. H. Kerr & Co., of Chicago,[1] in whose magazine, 'The International Socialist Review,' portions of the pamphlet appeared; but we also wish to point out that the chapter entitled 'The Political Action of Labour' first appeared in 'The Socialist,'[2] the official organ of the SLP.

Connolly's Work on Behalf of the SLP

James Connolly was one of the band of able young Marxians which severed its connection with the then existing SDF.[3] The rupture that led to the formation of the SLP[4] was not the result of personal bitterness. It was due to the autocratic attitude adopted by such 'revolutionaries' as H. M. Hyndman,[5] etc., and it was due also to the fact that the old SDF was saturated with compromise and had no policy to show how Capitalism could be destroyed and the Socialist Republic erected. James Connolly at once helped to form the SLP. He was chairman of the first conference, and was the party's first organiser. Due in great measure to his activity then, the SLP adopted that policy which has made it the clearest exponent of Socialist tactics in Britain regarding industrial and political action. During his connection with the SLP Connolly contributed many articles and songs to 'The Socialist.'

After Connolly left Britain, to take up work in America, he remained in sympathetic touch with the party. When he returned a few years ago to Ireland, Connolly asked the S.L. Press to publish the 'Irish Worker'[6] of which he was editor, and which the Government sought to suppress. The S.L. Press, at the risk of being dismantled and destroyed by the State, not only printed the banned paper but succeeded in getting the 'Irish Worker' into Dublin.

The story of the circumstances that led to the Rebellion, and the position of Connolly regarding it, is a tale that is yet to be told.

When the British Government shot James Connolly – wounded and dying as he was – it killed one of the most generous and intelligent of men. He died as all Socialists would fain die – with a wish 'that all noble men would do their duty.'

Socialist Labour Press

SECTION I   WORKSHOP TALKS

Internationalism

Socialism is a foreign importation!
I know it because I read it in the papers. I also know it to be the case

because in every country I have graced with my presence up to the present time, or have heard from, the possessing classes, through their organs in the press and their spokesmen upon the platform, have been vociferous and insistent in declaring the foreign origin of Socialism.

In Ireland Socialism is an English importation, in England they are convinced it was made in Germany, in Germany it is a scheme of traitors in alliance with the French to disrupt the Empire, in France it is an accursed conspiracy to discredit the army which is destined to reconquer Alsace and Lorraine, in Russia it is an English plot to prevent Russian extension towards Asia, in Asia it is known to have been set on foot by American enemies of Chinese and Japanese industrial progress, and in America it is one of the baneful fruits of unrestricted pauper and criminal immigration.

All nations today repudiate Socialism, yet Socialist ideas are conquering all nations. When anything has to be done in a practical direction toward ameliorating the lot of the helpless ones, or towards using the collective force of society in strengthening the hands of the individual, it is sure to be in the intellectual armoury of Socialists the right weapon is found for the work.

Well, I am not interested in internationalism. This country is good enough for me.
Is that so? Say: Are you taking a share in the Moscow-Windau-Rydinsk Railway?

The Moscow-Windau-Rydinsk railway is, as its name indicates, a railway running, or proposed to be run, from one part of Russia to another. You would think that that concerned the Russian people only, and that our patriotic capitalist class, always so ready to declare against working-class Socialists with international sympathies, would never look at it or touch it.

You would not think that Ireland, for example – whose professional patriots are forever telling the gullible working men that Ireland will be ruined for the lack of capital and enterprise – would be a good country to find money in to finance a Russian railway.

Yet, observe the fact. All the Dublin papers of Monday, June 12, 1899, contained the prospectus of this far-away Russian railway, offered for the investment of Irish capitalists, and offered by a firm of London stockbrokers who are astute enough not to waste money in endeavouring to catch fish in waters where they were not in the habit of biting freely.

And in the midst of the Russian revolution of 1905 the agents of the Czar succeeded in obtaining almost unlimited treasures in the United States to pay the expenses of throttling the infant Liberty.

As the shares in Russian railways were sold in Ireland, as Russian bonds were sold in America, so the shares in American mines, railroads and factories are bought and sold on all the stock exchanges of Europe and Asia by men who never saw America in their lifetime.

Now, let us examine the situation, keeping in mind the fact that this is but a type of what prevails all round; you can satisfy yourself on that head by a daily glance at our capitalist papers.

Capital is International

The shares of Russian railways, African mines, Nicaraguan canals, Chilian gas works, Norwegian timber, Mexican water works, Canadian fur trappings, Australian kanaka slave trade, Indian tea plantations, Japanese linen factories, Chinese cotton mills, European national and municipal debts, United States bonanza farms, are bought and sold every day by investors, many of whom never saw any one of the countries in which their money is invested, but who have, by virtue of so investing, a legal right to a share of the plunder extracted under the capitalist system from the wage workers whose bone and sinew earn the dividends upon the bonds they have purchased.

When our investing classes purchase a share in any capitalist concern, in any country whatsoever, they do so, not in order to build up a useful industry, but because the act of purchase endows them with a prospective share of the spoils it is proposed to wring from labour.

Therefore every member of the investing classes is interested to the extent of his investments, present or prospective, in the subjection of Labour all over the world.

That is the internationality of capital and capitalism.

The wage worker is oppressed under this system in the interest of a class of capitalist investors who may be living thousands of miles away and whose very names are unknown to him.

He is, therefore, interested in every revolt of Labour all over the world, for the very individuals against whom that revolt may be directed may – by the wondrous mechanism of the capitalist system – through shares, bonds, national and municipal debts – be the parasites who are sucking his blood also.

That is one of the underlying facts inspiring the internationalism of Labour and Socialism.

Confiscation

Would you confiscate the property of the capitalist class and rob men of that which they have, perhaps, worked a whole lifetime to accumulate?

Yes, sir, and certainly not.

We would certainly confiscate the property of the capitalist class, but we do not propose to rob anyone. On the contrary, we propose to establish honesty once and forever as the basis of our social relations. This Socialist movement is indeed worthy to be entitled 'The Great Anti-Theft Movement of the Twentieth Century.'

You see, confiscation is one great certainty of the future for every business man outside of the trust. It lies with him to say if it will be confiscation by the Trust in the interest of the Trust, or confiscation by Socialism in the interest of All.

If he resolves to continue to support the capitalist order of society he will surely have his property confiscated. After having, as you say, 'worked for a whole lifetime to accumulate' a fortune, to establish a business on what he imagined would be a sound foundation, on some fine day the Trust will enter into competition with him, will invade his market, use their enormous capital to undersell him at ruinous prices, take his customers from him, ruin his business, and finally drive him into bankruptcy, and perhaps to end his days as a pauper.

That is capitalist confiscation! It is going on all around us, and every time the business man who is not a Trust Magnate votes for capitalism he is working to prepare that fate for himself.

On the other hand, if he works for Socialism it also will confiscate his property. But it will only do so in order to acquire the industrial equipment necessary to establish a system of society in which the whole human race will be secured against the fear of want for all time – a system in which all men and women will be joint heirs and owners of all the intellectual and material conquests made possible by associated effort.

Socialism will confiscate the property of the capitalist and in return will secure the individual against poverty and oppression; it, in return for so confiscating, will assure to all men and women a free, happy, and unanxious human life. And that is more than capitalism can assure anyone today.

So you see the average capitalist has to choose between two kinds of confiscation. One or the other he must certainly endure. Confiscation by the Trust and consequently bankruptcy, poverty and perhaps pauperism in his old age, or confiscation by Socialism and consequently security, plenty, and a care-free life to him and his to the remotest generation.

Which will it be?

But it is their property. Why should socialists confiscate it?
Their property, eh? Let us see: here is a cutting from the *New York World* giving a synopsis of the Annual Report of the Coats Thread Company of Pawtucket, Rhode Island, for 1907. Now, let us examine it, and bear in mind that this company is the basis of the Thread Trust, with branches in Paisley (Scotland) and on the continent of Europe.

Also bear in mind that it is not a 'horrible example,' but simply a normal type of a normally conducted industry, and therefore what applies to it will apply in a greater or less degree to all others.

This report gives the dividend for the year at 20 per cent per annum. Twenty per cent dividend means four shillings in the pound profit. Now, what is a profit?

According to Socialists, profit only exists when all other items of production are paid for. The workers by their labour must create enough wealth to pay for certain items before profit appears. They must pay for the cost of raw material, the wear and tear of machinery, buildings, etc. (the depreciation of capital), the wages of superintendence, their own wages, and a certain amount to be left aside as a reserve fund to meet all possible contingencies. After, and only after, all these items have been paid for by their labour, all that is left is profit.

With this company the profit amounted to four shillings on every pound invested.

What does this mean? It means that in the course of five years – five times four shillings equals one pound – the workers in the industry had created enough profit to buy the whole industry from its present owners. It means that after paying all the expenses of the factory, including their own wages, they created enough profit to buy the whole building, from the roof to the basement, all the offices and agencies, and everything in the shape of capital. All this in five years.

And after they had so bought it from the capitalists it still belonged to the capitalists.

It means that if a capitalist had invested £1,000 in that industry, in the course of five years he would draw out £1,000, and still have £1,000 lying there untouched; in the course of ten years he would draw £2,000, in fifteen years he would draw £3,000. And still his first £1,000 would be as virgin as ever.

You understand that this has been going on ever since the capitalist system came into being; all the capital in the world has been paid for by the working class over and over again, and we are still creating it, and recreating it. And the oftener we buy it the less it belongs to us.

The capital of the master class is not their property; it is the unpaid labour of the working class – 'the hire of the labourer kept back by fraud.'

Socialism and Nationalism

Well, you won't get the Irish to help Socialism. Our Irish leaders tell us that all we Irish in this country ought to stand together and use our votes to free Ireland.

Sure, let us free Ireland!

Never mind such base, carnal thoughts as concern work and wages, healthy homes, or lives unclouded by poverty.

Let us free Ireland!

The rackrenting landlord – is he not also an Irishman, and wherefore should we hate him? Nay, let us not speak harshly of our brother – yea, even when he raises our rent.

Let us free Ireland!

The profit-grinding capitalist, who robs us of three-fourths of the fruits of our labour, who sucks the very marrow of our bones when we are young, and then throws us out in the street, like a worn-out tool, when we are grown prematurely old in his service – is he not an Irishman, and mayhap a patriot, and wherefore should we think harshly of him?

Let us free Ireland!

'The land that bred and bore us.' And the landlord who makes us pay for permission to live upon it.

Whoop it up for liberty!

'Let us free Ireland,' says that patriot who won't touch Socialism.

Let us all join together and cr-r-rush the br-r-rutal Saxon. Let us all join together, says he, all classes and creeds.

And, says the town worker, after we have crushed the Saxon and freed Ireland, what will we do?

Oh, then you can go back to your slums, same as before.

Whoop it up for liberty!

And, say the agricultural workers, after we have freed Ireland, what then?

Oh, then you can go scraping around for the landlord's rent or the money-lender's interest, same as before.

Whoop it up for liberty!

After Ireland is free, says the patriot who won't touch Socialism, we will protect all classes, and if you won't pay your rent you will be evicted, same as now. But the evicting party, under command of the sheriff, will wear green uniforms and the Harp without the Crown, and the warrant turning you out on the roadside will be stamped with the arms of the Irish Republic.

Now, isn't that worth fighting for?

And when you cannot find employment, and, giving up the struggle of life in despair, enter the Poorhouse, the band of the nearest regiment of the Irish army will escort you to the Poorhouse door to the tune of 'St. Patrick's Day.'

Oh; it will be nice to live in those days!

'With the green Flag floating o'er us,' and an ever-increasing army of unemployed workers walking about under the Green Flag, wishing they had something to eat. Same as now!

Whoop it up for liberty!

Now, my friend, I also am Irish, but I'm a bit more logical. The capitalist, I say, is a parasite on industry – as useless in the present stage of our industrial development as any other parasite in the animal or vegetable world is to the life of the animal or vegetable upon which it feeds.

The working class is the victim of this parasite – this human leech; and it is the duty and interest of the working class to use every means in its power to oust this parasite class from the position which enables it to thus prey upon the vitals of Labour.

Therefore, I say, let us organise as a class to meet our masters and destroy their mastership; organise to drive them from their hold upon public life through their political power; organise to wrench from their robber clutch the land and workshops on and in which they enslave us; organise to cleanse our social life from the stain of social cannibalism, from the preying of man upon his fellow-man.

Organise for a full, free, and happy life *for all or for none.*

SECTION II   **POLITICAL ACTION OF LABOUR**

Industrial and Political Unity

At meetings throughout this country one frequently hears speakers labouring to arouse the workers to their duty, exclaiming:

'You unite industrially; why, then, do you divide politically? You unite against the bosses in strikes and lock-outs, and then you foolishly divide when you go to the ballot-box. Why not unite at the ballot-box as you unite in the workshop? Why not show the same unity on the political field as you do on the industrial battlefield?'

At first blush this looks to be an exceedingly apt and forcible form of appeal to our fellow-workers, but when examined more attentively it will be seen that in view of the facts of our industrial warfare this appeal is based upon a flagrant mis-statement of facts. The real truth is that the workers do not unite industrially, but on the contrary are most hopelessly divided on the industrial field, and that their division and confusion on the political field are the direct result of their division and confusion on the industrial field. It would be easy to prove that even our most loyal trade unionists habitually play the game of the capitalist class on the industrial field just as surely as the Liberal and Conservative workers do it on the political field. Let us examine the situation on the industrial field and see if it justifies the claim that economically the workers are united, or if it justifies the contention I made that the division of the workers on the political field is but the reflex of the confused ideas derived from the practice of the workers in strikes and lock-outs.

Quite recently we had a great strike of the workers employed on the subway and elevated systems of street car service in New York. The men showed a splendid front against the power of the mammoth capitalist company against which they were arrayed. Conductors, motormen, ticket-choppers, platform men, repairers, permanent way men, ticket-sellers – all went out together, and for a time paralysed the entire traffic on their respective system. The company, on the other hand, had the usual recourse to scabs, and sought to man the trains with those professional traitors to their class. The number of scabs was large, but small in proportion to the men on strike, yet the strike was broken. It was not the scabs, however, who turned the scale against the strikers in favour of the masters. That service to capital was performed by good union men with union cards in their pockets. These men were the engineers in the powerhouses which supplied the electric power to run the cars, and without whom all the scabs combined could not have run a single trip. A scab is a vile creature, but what shall we say of the men who helped the scab to commit his act of treason? The law says that an accessory before the fact is equally guilty of a crime with the actual criminal. What, then, are the trade unionists who supplied the power to scabs to help them break a strike? They were unconsciously being compelled by their false system of organisation to betray their struggling brothers. Was this unity on the industrial field? And is it any wonder that the men accustomed to so scab upon their fellow-workers in a labour struggle should also scab it upon their class in a political struggle? Is it not rather common sense to expect that the *recognition of the necessity for concerted common action of all workers against the capitalist enemy in the industrial battle ground must precede the realisation of the wisdom of common action as a class on the political battlefield*? The men who are taught that it is all right to continue working for a capitalist against whom their shopmates of a different craft are on strike are not likely to see any harm in continuing to vote for a capitalist nominee at the polls even when he is opposed by the candidate of a Labour organisation. Political scabbery is born of industrial scabbery; it is its legitimate offspring.

Instances of this industrial disunion could be cited indefinitely. Can men who are trained and taught to believe that such a course of conduct is right and proper be expected to realise the oneness of the interests of the working class as a whole against the capitalist class as a whole, and vote and act accordingly? In short, can their field of vision be so extensive that it can see the brotherhood of all men, and yet so restricted that it can see no harm in a brother labour organisation in their own industry being beaten to death by capital?

Contrast this woeful picture of divided and disorganised 'unionism' in America with the following account from the *New York Sun* of the manner in which the Socialist unionists of Scandinavia stand together in a fight against the common enemy, irrespective of 'craft interests' or 'craft contracts'.

A short sojourn in Scandinavia, particularly in Copenhagen and the southern part of Sweden, gives one an object-lesson in Socialism. In some way or other the Socialists have managed to capture all the trade unions in these parts, and between them have caused a reign of terror for everybody who is unfortunate enough to own a business of any sort. Heaven help him if he fires one of his help or tries to assert himself in any way. He is immediately declared in 'blockade.'

This Socialist term means practically the same as a boycott. If the offending business man happens to be a retail merchant, all workmen are warned off his premises. The drivers for the wholesale houses refuse to deliver goods at his store; the truckmen refuse to cart anything to or from his place, and so on; in fact, he is a doomed man unless he comes to terms with the union. It is worth mentioning that boycotting bulletins and also the names and addresses of those who are bold enough to help the man out are published in leaded type in all the Socialistic newspapers. A law to prevent the publication of such boycotting announcements was proposed in the Swedish Riksdag this year, but was defeated.

If the boycotted person be a wholesale dealer the proceedings are much the same, or, rather, they are reversed. The retailers are threatened with the loss of the workmen's trade unless they cease dealing with such a firm; the truckmen refuse to haul for it. It has even happened that the scavengers have refused to remove the refuse from the premises. More often however, the cans are 'accidentally' dropped on the stairs. These scavengers belong to the cities' own forces, as a rule, and receive pensions after a certain length of service, but they have all sworn allegiance to the Socialistic cause.

In reading the foregoing it is well to remember that practically all the working men of such cities – that is, practically all Sweden and Denmark – are union men (i.e., Socialists) and are, therefore, able to carry out their threats.

Here we have a practical illustration of the power of Socialism when it rests upon an economic organisation, and the effectiveness and far-reaching activity of unionism when it is inspired by the Socialist ideal. Now, as an equally valuable object-lesson in craft unionism, an object-lesson in how not to do it, let us picture a typical state of affairs in the machine industry. The moulders' contract with the boss expires and they go out on strike. In a machine shop the moulder occupies a position intermediate between the patternmaker and the machinist, or, as they are called in Ireland, the engineers. When the moulders go out, the boss who has had all his plans laid for months beforehand brings in a staff of scabs and installs them in the places of the striking workers. Then the tragi-comedy begins. The union patternmaker makes his patterns and hands them over to the scab moulder; the scab moulder casts his moulds and when they are done the union machinist takes them from him and placidly finishes the job. Then, having finished their day's work, they go to their union meetings and *vote donations to help the strikers to defeat the boss, after they had worked all day to help the boss to defeat the strikers*. Thus they exemplify the solidarity of labour. When the moulders are beaten, the machinists and the patternmakers, and the blacksmiths, and the electricians, and the engineers, and all the rest, take their turn of going up against the boss in separate bodies to be licked. As each is taking its medicine its fellows of other crafts in the same shop sympathise with it in the name of the solidarity of labour, and continue to work in the service of the capitalist, against whom the strike is directed, in the name of the sacred contract of the craft union.

Need I go on to prove the point that industrial division and discord is the order of the day amongst the workers, and that this disunion and confusion on the economic field cannot fail to perpetuate itself upon the political field? Those orators who reproach the workers with being divided on the political field, although united on the industrial, are simply mis-stating facts. The workers are divided on both, and as political parties are the reflex of economic conditions, it follows that industrial unity once established will create the political unity of the working class. I feel that we cannot too strongly insist upon this point. Political division is born of industrial division; political scabbery is born of industrial craft scabbery; political weakness keeps even step with industrial weakness. It is an axiom enforced by all the experience of the ages that they who rule industrially will rule politically, and therefore they who are divided industrially will remain impotent politically. Failure to unite politically the forces of Labour is the inevitable outcome of the policy of division on the industrial battle ground. The natural lines of thought and action lead from the direct to the indirect, from the simple to the complex, from the immediate to the ultimate. Labour leaders ignore this natural line of development and preach the separation into craft organisations, with separate craft interests, of the workers, and then expect them to heed the call to unity on the less direct and immediate battleground of politics. They inevitably fail, as even the Socialists would fail if they remained equally blind to the natural law of our evolution into class consciousness. That natural law leads us as individuals to unite in our craft, as crafts to unite in our industry, as industries in our class, and the finished expression of that evolution is, we believe, the appearance of our class upon the political battle ground with all the economic power behind it to enforce its mandates. Until that day dawns our political parties of the working class are but propagandist agencies, John the Baptists of the new Redemption; but when that day dawns our political party will be armed with all the might of our class; will be revolutionary in fact as well as in thought.

To Irish men and women, especially, I should not need to labour this point. The historic example of their Land League bequeaths to us a precious legacy of wisdom, both practical and revolutionary, outlining our proper course of action. During Land League days in Ireland, when a tenant was evicted from a farm, not only his fellow-tenants but practically the whole country united to help him in his fight. When the evicted farm was rented by another tenant, a land-grabber or 'scab,' every person in the countryside shunned him as a leper, and, still better, fought him as a traitor. Nor did they make the mistake of fighting the traitor and yet working for his employer, the landlord. No, they included both in the one common hostility.

At the command of the Land League every servant and labourer quit the service of the landlord. In Ireland, it is well to remember, in order to appreciate this act of the labourers, that the landlords were usually better paymasters and more generous employers than the tenant farmers. The labourers, therefore, might reasonably have argued that the fight of the tenant farmers was none of their business. When the landlord had declared war upon the tenant by evicting him, the labourers responded by war upon the landlord. Servant boy and servant girl at once quit his service, the carman refused to drive him, the cook to cook for him, his linen remained unwashed, his harvest unreaped, his cows unmilked, his house and fields deserted. The grocer and the butcher, the physician and the schoolmaster, were alike hostile to him; if the children of the land-grabber (scab) entered school all other children rose and left; if the land-grabber or his landlord attended Mass every one else at Mass walked out in a body. They found it hard to get anyone to serve them or feed them in health, to attend them in sickness, or to bury those dear to them in death. It was this relentless and implacable war upon the land-owning class and traitors among the tenant class which gave the word 'boycott' to the English language through its enforcement against an Irish landowner, Captain Boycott. It was often horrible, it was always ugly in appearance to the superficial observer, but it was marvellously effective. It put courage and hope and manhood into a class long reckoned as the most enslaved in Europe. It broke the back of the personal despotism of the Irish landlord, and so crippled his social and economic power that Irish landed estates, from being a favourite form of investment for the financial interests, sank to such a position that even the most reckless moneylender would for a time scarce accept a mortgage upon them. That it failed of attaining real economic freedom for the Irish people was due not to any defect in its method of fighting but rather to the fact that economic questions are not susceptible of being settled within the restricted radius of any one small nation, but are acted upon by influences world-wide in their character.

But how great a lesson for the worker is to be found in this record of a class struggle in Ireland! The British worker was never yet so low in the social and political scale as the Irish tenant. Yet the Irish tenant rose and by sheer force of his unity on the economic field shattered the power of his master, whilst the British worker remaining divided upon the economic field sinks day by day lower toward serfdom. The Irish tenant had to contend against the overwhelming power of a foreign empire backing up the economic power of a native tyranny, yet he conquered, whilst the British worker able to become the political sovereign of the country remains the sport of the political factions of his masters and the slave of their social power.

The Irish tenant uniting on the economic field felt his strength, and, carrying the fight into politics, simply swept into oblivion every individual or party that refused to serve his class interests, but the toilers remain divided on the economic field, and hence are divided and impotent upon the political – zealous servants of every interest but their own.

Need I point the moral more? Every one who has the interests of the working class at heart should strive to realise industrial unity as the solid foundation upon which alone the political unity of the workers can be built up and directed toward a revolutionary end. To this end all those who work for industrial unionism are truly co-operating even when they least care for political activities.

Industrial Unionism and Constructive Socialism

There is not a Socialist in the world today who can indicate with any degree of clearness how we can bring about the co-operative commonwealth except along the lines suggested by industrial organisation of the workers.

Political institutions are not adapted to the administration of industry. Only industrial organisations are adapted to the administration of a co-operative commonwealth that we are working for. Only the industrial form of organisation offers us even a theoretical constructive Socialist programme. There is no constructive Socialism except in the industrial field.

The above extract from the speech of Delegate Stirton, editor of the 'Wage Slave,' of Hancock, Michigan, so well embodies my ideas upon this matter that I have thought well to take them as a text for an article in explanation of the structural form of Socialist Society. In a previous chapter I have analysed the weakness of the craft or trade union form of organisation alike as a weapon of defence against the capitalist class in the everyday conflicts on the economic field, and as a generator of class consciousness on the political field, and pointed out the greater effectiveness for both purposes of an industrial form of organisation. In the present article I desire to show how they who are engaged in building up industrial organisations for the practical purposes of today are at the same time preparing the framework of the society of the future. It is the realisation of that fact that indeed marks the emergence of Socialism as a revolutionary force from the critical to the positive stage. Time was when Socialists, if asked how society would be organised under Socialism replied invariably, and airily, that such things would be left to the future to decide. The fact was that they had not considered the matter, but the development of the Trust and Organised Capital in general, making imperative the Industrial Organisations of Labour on similar lines has provided us with an answer at once more complete to ourselves and more satisfying to our questioners.

Now to analyse briefly the logical consequences of the position embodied in the above quotation.

'Political institutions are not adapted to the administration of industry.'

Here is a statement that no Socialist with a clear knowledge of the essentials of his doctrine can dispute. The political institutions of today are simply the coercive forces of capitalist society; they have grown up out of and are based upon territorial divisions of power in the hands of the ruling class in past ages, and were carried over into capitalist society to suit the need of the capitalist class when that class overthrew the dominion of its predecessors. The delegation of the function of government into the hands of representatives elected from certain districts, states, or territories represents no real natural division suited to the requirements of modern society, but is a survival from a time when territorial influences were more potent in the world than industrial influences, and for that reason is totally unsuited to the needs of the new social order which must be based upon industry. The Socialist thinker when he paints the structural form of the new social order does not imagine an industrial system directed or ruled by a body of men or women elected from an indiscriminate mass of residents within given districts, said residents working at a heterogeneous collection of trades and industries. To give the ruling, controlling, and directing of industry into the hands of such a body would be too utterly foolish. What the Socialist does realise is that under a Socialist form of society the administration of affairs will be in the hands of representatives of the various industries of the nation, that the workers in the shops and factories will organise themselves into unions, each union comprising all the workers at a given industry; that said union will democratically control the workshop life of its own industry, electing all foremen, etc., and regulating the routine of labour in that industry in subordination to the needs of society in general, to the needs of its allied trades and to the department of industry to which it belongs. That representatives elected from these various departments of industry will meet and form the industrial administration or national government of the country. In short, Social-Democracy, as its name implies is the application to industry, or to the social life of the nation, of the fundamental principles of democracy. Such application will necessarily have to begin in the workshop, and proceed logically and consecutively upward through all the grades of industrial organisation until it reaches the culminating point of national executive power and direction. In other words, Socialism must proceed from the bottom upward, whereas capitalist political society is organised from above downward; Socialism will be administered by a committee of experts elected from the industries and professions of the land; capitalist society is governed by representatives elected from districts, and is based upon territorial division. The local and national governing or rather administrative bodies of Socialism will approach every question with impartial minds armed with the fullest expert knowledge born of experience; the governing bodies of capitalist society have to call in an expensive professional expert to instruct them on every technical question, and know that the impartiality of said expert varies with and depends upon the size of his fee.

It will be seen that this conception of Socialism destroys at one blow all the fears of a bureaucratic state, ruling and ordering the lives of every individual from above, and thus gives assurance that the social order of the future will be an extension of the freedom of the individual, and not a suppression of it. In short, it blends the fullest democratic control with the most absolute expert supervision, something unthinkable of any society built upon the political state. To focus the idea properly in your mind you have but to realise how industry today transcends all limitations of territory and leaps across rivers, mountains and continents, then you can understand how impossible it would be to apply to such far-reaching intricate enterprises the principle of democratic control by the workers through the medium of political territorial divisions.

Under Socialism states, territories or provinces will exist only as geographical expressions, and have no existence as sources of governmental power, though they may be seats of administrative bodies.

Now, having grasped the idea that the administrative force of the Socialist Republic of the future will function through unions industrially organised, that the principle of democratic control will operate through the workers correctly organised in such industrial unions, and that the workers correctly organised in such industrial unions, and that the political, territorial state of capitalist society will have no place or function under Socialism, you will at once grasp the full truth embodied in the words I have just quoted, that 'only the industrial form or organisation offers us even a theoretical constructive Socialist programme.'

To some minds constructive Socialism is embodied in the work of our representatives on the various public bodies to which they have been elected. The various measures against the evils of capitalist property brought forward by, or as a result of, the agitation of Socialist representatives on legislative bodies are figured as being of the nature of constructive Socialism. As we have shown, the political state of capitalism has no place under Socialism, therefore measures which aim to place industries in the hands of or under the control of such a political state are in no sense steps towards that ideal; they are but useful measures to restrict the greed of capitalism and to familiarise the workers with the conception of common ownership. This latter is indeed their chief function. But the enrolment of the workers in unions patterned closely after the structure of modern industries, and following the organic lines of industrial development, is par excellence the swiftest, safest, and most peaceful form of constructive work the Socialist can engage in. It prepares within the framework of capitalist society the working forms of the Socialist Republic, and thus while increasing the resisting power of the worker against present encroachments of the capitalist class it familiarises him with the idea that the union he is helping to build up is destined to supplant that class in the control of the industry in which he is employed.

The power of this idea to transform the dry detail work of trade union organisation into the constructive work of revolutionary Socialism, and thus to make of the unimaginative trade unionist a potent factor in the launching of a new system of society cannot be overestimated. It invests the sordid details of the daily incidents of the class struggle with a new and beautiful meaning, and presents them in their true light as skirmishes between the two opposing armies of light and darkness. In the light of this principle of Industrial Unionism every fresh shop or factory organised under its banner is a fort wrenched from the control of the capitalist class and manned with the soldiers of the Revolution to be held by them for the workers. On the day that the political and economic forces of labour finally break with capitalist society and proclaim the Workers' Republic these shops and factories so manned by Industrial Unionists will be taken charge of by the workers there employed, and force and effectiveness thus given to that proclamation. Then and thus the new society will spring into existence ready equipped to perform all the useful functions of its predecessor.

The Future of Labour

In choosing for the subject of this chapter such a title as 'The Future of Labour,' I am aware that I run the risk of arousing expectations that I shall not be able to satisfy. The future of labour is a subject with which is bound up the future of civilisation, and therefore a comprehensive treatment of the subject might be interpreted as demanding an analysis of all the forces and factors which will influence humanity in the future, and also their resultant effect.

Needless to say, my theme is a less ambitious one. I propose simply to deal with the problem of labour in the immediate future, with the marshalling of labour for the great conflict that confronts us, and with a consideration of the steps to be taken in order that the work of aiding the transition from Industrial Slavery to Industrial Freedom might be, as far as possible, freed from all encumbering and needless obstacles and expense of time, energy, and money.

But first, and as an aid to a proper understanding of my position, let me place briefly before you my reading of the history of the past struggles of mankind against social subjection, my reading of the mental development undergone by each revolting class in the different stages of their struggle, from the first period of their bondage to the first dawn of their freedom. As I view it, such struggles had three well-marked mental stages, corresponding to the inception, development, and decay of the oppressing powers, and as I intend to attempt to apply this theory to the position of labour as a subject class today, I hope you will honour me by at least giving me your earnest attention to this conception, and aid by your discussion in determining at which of these periods or stages the working class, the subject class of today has arrived. My reading, then, briefly is this: that in the first period of bondage the eyes of the subject class are always turned toward the past, and all its efforts in revolt are directed to the end of destroying the social system in order that it might march backward and re-establish the social order of ancient times − 'the good old days.' That the goodness of those days was largely hypothetical seldom enters the imagination of men on whose limbs the fetters of oppression still sit awkwardly.

In the second period the subject class tends more and more to lose sight and recollection of any pre-existent state of society, to believe that the social order in which it finds itself always did exist, and to bend all its energies to obtaining such ameliorations of its lot within existent society as will make that lot more bearable. At this stage of society the subject class, as far as its own aspirations are concerned, may be reckoned as a conservative force.

In the third period the subject class becomes revolutionary, recks little of the past for inspiration, but, building itself upon the achievements of the present, confidently addresses itself to the conquest of the future. It does so because the development of the framework of society has revealed to it its relative importance, revealed to it the fact that within its grasp has grown, unconsciously to itself, a power which, if intelligently applied, is sufficient to overcome and master society at large.

As a classic illustration of this conception of the history of the mental development of the revolt against social oppression, we might glance at the many present revolts recorded in European history. As we are now aware, common ownership of land was at one time the basis of society all over the world. Our fathers not only owned their land in common, but in many ways practised a common ownership of the things produced. In short, tribal communism was at one time the universally existent order. In such a state of society there existed a degree of freedom that no succeeding order has been able to parallel, and that none will be able to until the individualistic order of today gives way to the Industrial Commonwealth, the Workers' Republic, of the future. How that ancient order broke up it is no part of my task to tell. What I do wish to draw your attention to is that for hundreds, for a thousand years after the break-up of that tribal communism, and the reduction to serfdom of the descendants of the formerly free tribesmen, all the efforts of the revolting serfs were directed to a destruction of the new order of things and to a rehabilitation of the old. Take as an example the various peasant wars of Germany, the Jacquerie[7] of France, or the revolt of Wat Tyler[8] and John Ball[9] in England as being the best known; examine their rude literature in such fragments as have been preserved, study their speeches as they have been recorded even by their enemies, read the translations of their songs, and in all of them you will find a passionate harking back to the past, a morbid idealising of the status of their fathers, and a continued exhortation to the suffering people to destroy the present in order that, in some vague and undefined manner, they might reconstitute the old.

The defeat of the peasantry left the stage clear for the emergence of the bourgeoisie as the most important subject class and for the development of that second period of which I have spoken. Did it develop? Well, in every account we read of the conflicts between the nobility and the burghers in their guilds and cities we find that the aggressive part was always taken by the former, and that wherever a revolt took place the revolting guild merchants and artisans justified their act by an appeal to the past privileges which had been abrogated and the restoration of which formed the basis of their claims, and their only desire if successful in revolt. One of the most curious illustrations of this mental condition is to be found in the 'History of the Rise of the Dutch Republic' by Motley, in which that painstaking historian tells how the Netherlands in their revolt against the Spanish Emperor continued for a generation to base their claims upon the political status of the provinces under a former Emperor, made war upon the Empire with troops levied in the name of the Emperor, and led by officers whose commissions were made out by the rebel provinces in the name of the sovereign they were fighting against. This mental condition lasted in England until the great Civil War, which ended by leaving Charles I without a head, and the bourgeoisie, incarnated in Cromwell[10] firmly fixed in the saddle; in France it lasted till the Revolution. In both countries it was abandoned, not because of any *a priori* reasoning upon its absurdity nor because some great thinker had evolved a better scheme – but because the growth of the industrial system had made the capitalist class realise that they could at any moment stop the flow of its life-blood, so to speak, and from so realising it was but a short mental evolution *to frame a theory of political action which proclaimed that the capitalist class was the nation,* and all its enemies the enemies of the nation at large. The last period of that social evolution had been reached, the last mental stage of the transition from feudal ownership to capitalist property.

Now, let me apply this reading of history to the development of the working class under capitalism and find out what lessons it teaches us, of value in our present struggle. Passing by the growth of the working class under nascent capitalism, as it belongs more to the period I have just dealt with than to the present subject, and taking up working-class history from the point marked by the introduction of machinery to supplant hand labour – a perfectly correct standpoint for all practical purposes – we find in the then attitude of the workers an exemplification of the historical fidelity of our conception. Suffering from the miseries attendant upon machine labour, the displacement of those supplanted and the scandalous overworking of those retained, the workers rioted and rebelled in a mad effort to abolish machinery and restore the era of hand labour. In a word, they strove to revert to past conditions, and their most popular orators and leaders were they who pictured in most glowing terms the conditions prevalent in the days of their fathers.

They were thus on the same mental plane as those medieval peasants who, in their revolt, were fired by the hope of restoring the primitive commune. And just as in the previously cited case, the inevitable failure of this attempt to reconstruct the past was followed in another generation by movements which accepted the social order of their day as permanent, and looked upon their social status as wage-slaves as fixed and immutable in the eternal order of things. To this category belongs the trade union movement in all its history. As the struggles of the serfs and burghers in the middle ages were directed to no higher aim than the establishing of better relations between these struggling classes and their feudal overlords, as during those ages the division of society into ruling classes of king, lords, and church resting upon a basis of the serfdom of the producers, was accepted by all in spite of the perpetual recurrences of civil wars between the various classes, so, in capitalist society, the trade unionists, despite strikes, lock-outs, and black lists, accepted the employing class as part and parcel of a system which was to last through all eternity.

The rise of Industrial Unionism is the first sign that that − the second stage of the mental evolution of our class − is rapidly passing away. And the fact that it had its inception amongst men actually engaged in the work of trade union organisation, and found its inspiration in a recognition of the necessities born of the struggles of the workers, and not in the theories of any political party − this fact is the most cheering sign of the legitimacy of its birth and the most hopeful augury of its future. For we must not forget that it is not the theorists who make history; it is history in its evolution that makes the theorists. And the roots of history are to be found in the workshops, fields, and factories. It has been remarked that Belgium was the cockpit of Europe because within its boundaries have been fought out many of the battles between the old dynasties; in like manner we can say that the workshop is the cockpit of civilisation because in the workshop has been and will be fought out those battles between the new and old methods of production, the issues of which change the face and the history of the world.

I have said that the capitalist class became a revolutionary class when it realised that it held control of the economic heart of the nation. I may add when the working class is in the same position it will also as a class become revolutionary, it will also give effective political expression to its economic strength. The capitalist class grew into a political party when it looked around and found itself in control of the things needed for the life of the individual and the State, when it saw that the ships carrying the commerce of the nation were its own, when it saw that the internal traffic of the nation was in the hands of its agents, when it saw that the feeding, clothing, and sheltering of the ruling class depended upon the activities of the subject class, when it saw itself applied to to furnish finance to equip the armies and fleets of the kings and nobles; in short, when the capitalist class found that all the arteries of commerce, all the agencies of production, all the mainsprings of life in fact, passed through their hands as blood flows through the human heart − then and only then did capital raise the banner of political revolt and from a class battling for concessions became a class leading its forces to the mastery of society at large.

This leads me to the last axiom of which I wish you to grasp the significance. It is this, that the fight for the conquest of the political state is not the battle, it is only the echo of the battle. The real battle is the battle being fought out every day for the power to control industry, and the gauge of the progress of that battle is not to be found in the number of voters making a cross beneath the symbol of a political party, but in the number of these workers who enrol themselves in an industrial organisation with the definite purpose of making themselves masters of the industrial equipment of society in general.

That battle will have its political echo, that industrial organisation will have its political expression. *If we accept the definition of working-class political action as that which brings the workers as a class into direct conflict with the possessing class* AS A CLASS, *and keeps them there, then we must realise that* NOTHING CAN DO THAT SO READILY AS ACTION AT THE BALLOT BOX. Such action strips the working-class movement of all traces of such sectionalism as may, and indeed must, cling to strikes and lock-outs, and emphasises the class character of the Labour Movement. IT IS THEREFORE ABSOLUTELY INDISPENSABLE FOR THE EFFICIENT TRAINING OF THE WORKING CLASS ALONG CORRECT LINES THAT ACTION AT THE BALLOT BOX SHOULD ACCOMPANY ACTION IN THE WORKSHOP.

I am convinced that this will be the ultimate formation of the fighting hosts of Labour. The workers will be industrially organised on the economic field, and until that organisation is perfected, whilst the resultant feeling of class consciousness is permeating the minds of the workers, the Socialist Labour Party will carry on an independent campaign of education and attack upon the political field, and as a consequence will remain the sole representative of the Socialist idea in politics. But as industrial organisation grows, feels its strength, and develops the revolutionary instincts of its members, there will grow also the desire for a closer union and identification of the two wings of the army of Labour. Any attempt prematurely to force this identification would only defeat its own purpose, and be fraught with danger alike to the economic and the political wing. Yet it is certain that such attempts will be of continual recurrence and multiply in proportion to the dissatisfaction felt at the waste of energy involved in the division of forces. Statesmanship of the highest kind will be required to see that this union shall take place only under the proper conditions and at the proper moment for effective action. Two things must be kept in mind – viz., that a Socialist Political Party not emanating from the ranks of organised Labour is, as Karl Marx phrased it, simply a Socialist sect, ineffective for the final revolutionary act, but that also the attempt of craft organised unions to create political unity before they have laid the foundation of industrial unity in their own, the economic field, would be an instance of putting the cart before the horse. But when that foundation of industrial union is finally secured then nothing can prevent the union of the economic and political forces of Labour. I look forward to the time when every economic organisation will have its Political

Committee, just as it has its Organisation Committee or its Strike Committee, and when it will be counted to be as great a crime, as much an act of scabbery to act against the former as against any of the latter. When that time comes we will be able to count our effective vote before troubling the official ballot-box, simply by counting our membership in the allied organisations; we will be able to estimate our capacity for the revolutionary act of Social Transformation simply by taking stock of the number of industries we control and their importance relative to the whole social system, and when we find that we control the strategic industries in society, then society must bend to our will – or break. In our organisations we will have Woman Suffrage, whether governments like it or not, we will also have in our own organisations a pure and uncorrupted ballot, and if the official ballot of capitalist society does not purify itself of its own accord, its corruption can only serve to blind the eyes of our enemies, and not to hide our strength from ourselves.

Compare the political action of such a body with that of any party we know. Political parties are composed of men and women who meet together to formulate a policy and programme to vote upon. They set up a political ticket in the hope of getting people, most of whom they do not know, to vote for them, and when that vote is at last cast, it is cast by men whom they have not organised, do not know, and cannot rely upon to use in their own defence. We have proven that such a body can make propaganda, and good propaganda, for Socialist principles, but it can never function as the weapon of an industrially organised working class. To it such a party will always be an outside body, a body not under its direct control, but the political weapon of the *Industrially Organised Working Class will be a weapon of its own forging* and wielded by its own hand. I believe it to be incumbent upon organised Labour to meet the capitalist class upon every field where it can operate to our disadvantage. Therefore I favour direct attacks upon the control of governmental powers through the ballot-box, but I wish to see these attacks supported by the economic organisation. In short, I believe that there is no function performed by a separate political party that the economic organisation cannot help it perform much better and with greater safety to working-class interests. Let us be clear as to the function of Industrial Unionism. That function is to build up an industrial republic inside the shell of the political State in order that when that industrial republic is fully organised it may crack the shell of the political State and step into its place in the scheme of the universe. But in the process of upbuilding, during the period of maturing, the mechanism of the political State can be utilised to assist in the formation of the embryo Industrial Republic. Or, to change the analogy, we might liken the position of the Industrial Republic in its formative period towards political society to the position of the younger generation towards the generation passing away. The younger accepts the achievements of the old, but gradually acquires strength to usurp its functions until the new generation is able to abandon the paternal household and erect its own. While doing so it utilises to the fullest all the privileges of its position. So the Industrial Unionists will function in a double capacity in capitalist society. In his position as a citizen in a given geographical area he will use his political voting power in attacks upon the political system of capitalism, and in his position as a member of the Industrial Union he will help in creating the economic power which in the fullness of time will overthrow that political system, and replace it by the Industrial Republic.

My contentions along these lines do not imply by any means that I regard immediate action at the ballot-box by the economic organisation as essential, although I may regard it as advisable. As I have already indicated, the proletarian revolution will in that respect most likely follow the lines of the capitalist revolutions in the past.

In Cromwellian England, in Colonial America, in Revolutionary France, the real political battle did not begin until after the bourgeoisie, the capitalist class, had become the dominant class in the nation. Then they sought to conquer political power in order to allow their economic power to function freely. It was no mere coincidence, but a circumstance born of the very nature of things, woven, so to speak, in the warp and woof of fate, that in all the three countries the signal for the revolution was given by the ruling class touching the bourgeoisie in the one part that was calculated to arouse them as a class, and at the same time demonstrate their strength. That one sensitive part was their finance, their ownership of the sinews of war. In England it was over the question of taxes, of ship money, that Hampden[11] first raised the standard of revolt, whose last blow was struck at Whitehall when the king's head rolled in the gutter. In America it was over the question of taxes, and again the capitalist class were united, until a new nation was born to give them power. In France it was the failure of the king to raise taxes that led to the convocation of the States General which assembly first revealed to the French capitalists their power as a class and set their feet upon the revolutionary path. In all three countries the political rebellion was but the expression of the will of a class already in possession of economic power. This is in conformity with the law of human evolution, that the new system can never overthrow the old, until it itself is fully matured and able to assume all the useful functions of the thing it is to dethrone.

In the light of such facts, and judging by such reasoning, we need not exercise our souls over the question of the date of the appearance of the Industrial Organisations of Labour upon the electoral field. Whether we believe, as I believe, that the electoral field offers it opportunities it would be criminal to ignore, or believe, as some do, that electoral action on the part of the economic organisations is at present premature, one thing we can be agreed upon, if we accept the outline of history, I have just sketched – viz., that it is necessary to remember that at the present stage of development all actions of our class at the ballot-box are in the nature of mere preliminary skirmishes, or educational campaigns, and that *the conquest of political power by the working class waits upon the conquest of economic power*, and must function through the economic organisation.

Hence, reader, if you belong to the working class your duty is clear. Your union must be perfected until it embraces every one who toils in the service of your employer, or as a unit in your industry. The fact that your employers find it necessary to secure the service of any individual worker is or ought to be that individual's highest and best title to be a member of your union. If the boss needs him you need him more. You need the *open union* and the *closed shop* if you ever intend to control the means and conditions of life. And, as the champion of your class upon the political field, as the ever-active propagandist of the idea of the working class, as the representative and embodiment of the social principle of the future, you need the Socialist Labour Party. The Future of Labour is bound up with the harmonious development of those twin expressions of the forces of progress; the Freedom of Labour will be born of their happily consummated union.

Join the Socialist Labour Party
For years the Socialist Labour Party has preached the truth that our present-day society is divided into two hostile groups – one group (the capitalist class) owning practically everything in the country, yet performing no social service, and the other group (the working class) owning practically nothing, yet performing all the necessary social service – producing all the social wealth.

We have pointed out that the natural result of such a social system is poverty for the masses, social stagnation and feverish activity alternately, economic crises, industrial battles, *and international wars*.

The Socialist Labour Party is organised to end this social system. We propose to reorganise society in accordance with the interests of the working class. We propose to substitute the political State with the Industrial Republic of Labour. And we propose to do this on the basis of political action and industrial union organisation.

Do You Agree With This?

The Socialist Labour Party asserts the right of man to life, liberty, and the pursuit of happiness.

We hold that the purpose of government is to secure to every citizen the enjoyment of this right; but experience teaches us that such right is illusory to the majority of the people, the working class, under the present system of industrial bondage – a system destructive of *their* life, *their* liberty, and *their* happiness.

We hold that the true theory of economics is that the means of production must be owned, operated, and controlled by the people in common. Man cannot exercise his right to life, liberty, and the pursuit of happiness without the ownership of the land on, and the tool with which to work. Deprived of these, his life, his liberty, and his fate fall into the hands of that class which owns these essentials for work and production.

We hold that the existing contradiction between social production and capitalist appropriation – the latter resulting from the private ownership of natural and social opportunities – divides the people into two classes: the Capitalist Class and the Working Class; throws society into the convulsions of the Class Struggle; and perverts government in the interests of the Capitalist Class.

Thus Labour, robbed of the wealth which it alone produces, is often denied the means of employment, and, by the conditions of wage slavery, is even deprived of the necessaries of life.

Against such a system the Socialist Labour Party raises the banner of revolt, and demands the unconditional overthrow of the Capitalist system.

In place of such a system the Socialist Labour party aims to substitute a system of social ownership of the means of production, industrially administered by the Working Class – the workers to assume control and direction as well as operations of their industrial affairs.

This solution of necessity requires the organisation of the Working Class *as a class* upon revolutionary political and industrial lines.

We therefore call upon the wage-workers to organise themselves into a revolutionary political organisation under the banner of the Socialist Labour Party; and to organise themselves likewise upon the industrial field into a revolutionary industrial union in keeping with their political aims.

And we also call upon all other intelligent citizens to place themselves squarely upon the ground of Working Class interests, and join us in this mighty and noble work of human emancipation, so that we may put summary end to the existing barbarous class conflict by placing the land and all the means of production, transportation, and distribution into the hands of the people as a collective body, and substituting the Co-operative commonwealth for the present state of planless production, industrial war and social disorder – a Commonwealth in which every worker shall have the free exercise and full benefit of his faculties, multiplied by all the modern factors of civilisation.

JOIN THE SLP TODAY!

Notes

1. Socialist Publishing house in Chicago. Many Kerr books and pamphlets were imported into Britain.
2. *The Socialist*; official organ of the Socialist Labour Party from 1902 to 1924. It advocated Daniel de Leon, the American socialist's ideas of revolutionary political action and industrial unionism and concentrated on Marxist theory.
3. *SDF*; *see* Chapter 1.
4. *SLP*; *see* Appendix.
5. H.M. Hyndman; *see* Chapter 11.
6. *The Irish Worker*; edited by James Larkin, it was first published in Dublin in 1911 irregularly. It was suppressed in December 1914.
7. Jacquerie; French peasants' revolt against the tyranny of Charles the Bad of Navarre in May 1358. The name comes from Jacques (clowns), a derogatory term for peasants.
8. Wat Tyler, the leader of the peasants' revolt in 1381.
9. John Ball, a hedge priest who played a prominent part in the peasants' revolt in 1381.
10. Oliver Cromwell (1599–1658); Lord Protector of England under the Commonwealth, 1653–58. Leader of the Parliamentary forces against Charles I, 1640.
11. Hampden Clubs; named after John Hampden, one of the leaders of the Parliamentary forces in the English Revolution. His fame derived from his courageous fight against King Charles's imposition of yet another tax called Ship Money.

Appendix:
Organisations and Publications

The Clarion

When Robert Blatchford left *The Sunday Chronicle* towards the end of 1891, he and the group of friends who left with him determined to start their own paper. Before the end of the year, on 12 December 1891, *The Clarion* first appeared on the street, priced 1*d*.

In his leading article in the first number, Blatchford said, 'The essence of this new journalism; for it is new journalism created by the men now risking this venture, is variety ... The policy of *The Clarion* is the policy of humanity; a policy not of party, sect or creed; but of justice, of reason and mercy.'

That intention was kept and *The Clarion* maintained a steady circulation of 30,000 for many years. At first the journalists went without pay, and even when it started to pay its way, they would normally make do with £4 each.

The Clarion had an influence far beyond its circulation. It was read with interest and approval in many working-class homes as soon as it appeared on a Friday evening. It was certainly the most interesting and lively radical paper ever published and it had a considerable effect on the development of the socialist revival.

The paper was the focus of a number of clubs and clubhouses. Perhaps the best known were the *Clarion* Cyclists who went around the country in a group spreading the word about socialism on their way. But the Glee Clubs, Cinderella Clubs and Drama Groups all played their part and helped to spread the message.

Among *The Clarion* activities were the Vans and the Clarion Press. The propaganda vans toured the country selling the pamphlets written by the Clarion journalists and published by the Press. The Clarion Fellowship, as it was known, was an excellent example of participation by many people working through their interests for the cause which they all supported. It had not happened before and it has not happened since.

Source
Laurence Thompson, *Robert Blatchford*, Gollancz, 1951.

220

The Fabian Society

The Fabian Society was founded in 1884. It had begun as a 'Fellowship of the New Life', set up by a group of people who contemplated founding a colony in South America. However, they decided to concentrate on transforming society at home in preference and formed themselves into the Fabian Society. They called themselves Fabian after the Roman General Quintus Maximus Fabius, who was noted for his philosophy of delaying taking action until the exact moment arrived when it would be most effective. Then, he said, the blow should be swift and hard. The Fabians adopted similar tactics of non-confrontation for an indefinite period.

At first there was little difference between the Social Democratic Federation Marxists and the Fabians. But from the time of the publication of the Fabian Essays in 1889, it can be seen that the Marxism had become diffused in middle-class aspirations for a peaceful progress towards socialism.

Some of the most able propagandists such as George Bernard Shaw, Annie Besant and Sidney and Beatrice Webb, were members of the Fabian Society in its early years.

Source
Margaret Cole, *The Story of Fabian Socialism*, Heinemann, 1961.

The Freethought Publishing Company

Charles Bradlaugh and Annie Besant started their own Freethought Publishing Company in the early 1880s. Under the management of W.J. Ramsey, business was good, and in 1882 it was possible to move to larger premises in 63 Fleet Street. They were opposite Richard Carlile's old Bouverie Street shop. Carlile was one of the best known of the earlier generation of radical and freethought printers and had been prosecuted many times for his fearless publishing.

In 1884 Arthur Bonner, who later married Bradlaugh's daughter, Hypatia, became manager. The following year, the landlord of the property became bankrupt and Bradlaugh took over the whole lease rather than risk being moved.

When Annie Besant and Charles Bradlaugh parted company the business came to an end. Arthur Bonner continued printing from the same address and the publishing passed to Robert Forder.

The company published many books and pamphlets under the title, *The International Library of Science and Freethought*. These covered authors such as Aveling, Winwood Reade and Ernest Haeckel. A wide range of subjects was covered. Annie Besant wrote on *Landlords and Tenant Farmers and Labourers, Civil and Religious Liberty* and *English Republicanism* among many other topics.

Sources

Edward Royle, *Radicals, Securalists and Republicans, Popular Freethought in Britain 1866–1915*, MUP, 1908.
A Selection of the Social and Political Pamphlets of Annie Besant, Kelley, New York, 1970.

The Independent Labour Party

The Independent Labour Party (ILP) was formed at a conference in Bradford in 1893 from a number of groups which had previously been acting on a local basis. The main policy was to secure the collective ownership of the means of production, distribution and exchange. The immediate demands were for an eight-hour day and the provision of work for the unemployed.

The National Administrative Council consisted of four elected members from the Annual Conference, plus the Chairpersons of each of the party's nine divisions. From its inception, the party aimed, and succeeded, in influencing the trade unions.

Because the party had little theoretical basis, it could accommodate many trends of thought within its ranks. What it lacked in theory, it made up for in fervour and enthusiastic emotion.

The most prominent and best known leaders were Ramsey MacDonald and Philip Snowden. But the most flamboyant figure was Victor Grayson who, despite the refusal of the National Administrative Council to endorse his candidature, won a resounding and popular victory in the parliamentary by-election at Colne Valley in 1907. He stood on a militant socialist policy.

Following this episode, a rift developed between the rank and file and the leadership. The policy of accommodation with the Liberals, advocated by Keir Hardie and MacDonald, was sharply criticised. From 1909, membership of the ILP declined and during the years of the 'Great Unrest' immediately preceding the First World War, it was the syndicalists who led the labour movement in militant industrial action.

The Manchester Labour Press Society

The Manchester Labour Press Society was established in 1892 as a co-operative whose object was to supply working people with books and pamphlets on the labour question.

At first the business was run by Harry Henshall on a small hand platen machine. The venture prospered, and by 1896 had a turnover of £5,000 annually and employed 30 people on an eight-hour day.

In 1897 new premises were obtained at Arkwright Mills and the co-operative had 115 members. However, when the Independent Labour Party (ILP), the Fabian Society and *The Clarion* organisation all developed their own publishing and printing facilities, the basis of support for the press dried up, and in June 1901 there was a net deficit of £2,080. The managing director was bankrupt and the firm in voluntary liquidation.

In its heyday the society produced a variety of well printed and designed books and pamphlets. In the four years to 1897 it printed one and a half million pamphlets. The 1897 list included 27 pamphlets and 17 books.

The work of the Manchester Labour Press Society that has survived shows that it was among the best designed and printed work done for the labour movement.

Sources
Society for the Study of Labour History Bulletin no. 28, Spring 1974, pp. 22–7.
M.J. Harkin, *The Manchester Labour Press Society.*

The Modern Press

The Modern Press was the creation of Henry Hyde Champion and J.C. Foulger.

In 1883 the Democratic Federation decided to advocate socialism and changed its name to the Social Democratic Federation. It published its creed in the pamphlet *Socialism Made Plain.* This was the first of many pamphlets published by the Modern Press between 1883 and 1888.

On 14th January 1884, the Modern Press printed the first number of *Justice,* the organ of the Social Democratic Federation. It was a weekly newspaper and was financed to the extent of £300 by Edward Carpenter.

Champion ensured that the ideals of socialism were carried out within the Modern Press. He introduced an eight-hour day and won the support of his compositors. However, despite the efforts of William Morris and H.M. Hyndman who sold *Justice* on the streets of London, a loss of £10 a week was incurred.

Early in 1888 Champion was expelled from the SDF after a disagreement with the leadership, and in June of that year he printed the first number of the *Labour Elector* at the Modern Press. Although he tried to broaden the financial basis of the press in 1889 by the formation of a Press Society, when the *Labour Elector* failed, the Modern Press came to an end.

Sources
Society For The Study Of Labour History Bulletin 31, Autumn 1975,
pp. 62–5.
R. and E. Frow, *The Modern Press and the Social Democratic Federation*.

The Socialist Labour Party

The Socialist Labour Party was formed on 7 June 1903 by dissident
Scottish members of the Social Democratic Federation. They were
strongly influenced by the American socialist, Daniel de Leon and were
supported by James Connolly.

The *Socialist* had been published from August 1902 as the organ of the
Scottish District Council of the Social Democratic Federation and it was
taken over by the newly formed SLP.

The SLP remained a mainly Scottish organisation although there were
groups in a few large industrial centres and on the coalfields. But the
Socialist and the SLP pamphlets imported from America were widely sold
and read by socialists throughout the movement. De Leon's pamphlets,
Reform or Revolution, What Means This Strike and *Two Pages From Roman
History* were printed and reprinted in Edinburgh in editions of 10,000.

The SLP was comprised of a group of dedicated revolutionaries whose
influence was considerably greater than their numerical strength.

The Socialist League

Towards the end of 1884, a crisis developed in the Social Democratic
Federation partly on political and partly on personal issues. William
Morris and a group of his friends therefore seceded and formed the
Socialist League.

The League immediately issued a manifesto advocating the principles of
revolutionary international socialism. Strenuous political and educational
propaganda was conducted. A new paper, *The Commonweal* was launched
and a series of penny pamphlets, many of which were written by Morris,
were published.

The League proved popular with those class-conscious workers to whom
Hyndman's top-hat and frock coat image appeared out of keeping with
their idea of revolutionary socialism. They were anxious to conduct
propaganda and accepted the leadership of Morris and his comrades.

However, in such important struggles as the London Dock Strike of
1889, the League was on the outside rather than among the workers giving
leadership. Moreover, the seed of the destruction of the League was sown
at its inception when a group of anarchists attracted by Morris joined and

started organising to establish their influence. At the sixth Annual Conference in 1890, with only fourteen delegates present, the Anarchist-Communists elected their own group onto the Executive Council and removed Morris and Sparling from the editorship of *Commonweal*.

Morris dropped out of membership of the League and his Hammersmith Branch seceded to form the Hammersmith Socialist Society in which he conducted his socialist activity for the rest of his life.

Index

Acts of Parliament, 36, 101n
  Artisans Dwellings, 36
  Contagious Diseases, 116, 176n
  Education, 36
  Employers' Liability, 36
  Ground Game, 36
  Land, 36
  Local Government, 175
  National Insurance, xv
  Shipping, 36
  Trade Board, xv
Africa, 50, 88, 196
  Boer War, 152, 166
  Dahomey, 50
Amalgamated Engineering Union, 71
Amalgamated Society of Engineers, 70, 71
Anarchism, 49, 59, 64, 69n, 225
Anti-Corn Laws, 6n
Anti-Slavery Convention 1840, 163, 164
Anti-Vivisection Society, 156
Asia, 195, 196
Asquith, Rt Hon H.H., 148
Association of All Classes of All Nations, xvi
Atheism, 90, 91
Australia, 152, 165, 173, 196
  New South Wales, 166
  Victoria, 169
Austria, Vienna, 134
Aveling, Edward, xiii, xiv, 32, 59, 221
Aveling, Eleanor Marx, xiii, 59

Balfour, Arthur James, 91, 93, 101n
Ball, John, 210, 218n
Bartley, James, 86
Bax, Ernest Belfort, 59, 64, 69n

Belgium, 15, 212
  Brussels, 45
Bell's Life, 85
Besant, Annie, xiv, xviii, xviiin, 32, 70, 122n, 221
  Biography, 32–3
  Civil and Religious Liberty, 222
  English Republicanism, 222
  Landlords and Tenant Farmers, 221
  Why I am A Socialist, 32, 33
Besant, Rev. Frank, 32
Birmingham, xvi, 45, 70, 84n
  Bull Ring, xvi
Bismarck, Prince Otto von, 33, 135
Blackpool, 156
Blatchford, Robert, xviii, 85, 86, 221
  Biography, 85–6
  God and my Neighbour, 86
  Merrie England, 86, 93
  Not Guilty, 86
  Real Socialism, 85, 86
Bolton, 70
Bonner, Hypatia Bradlaugh, 221
Booth, Charles, 41
  Survey of London, 41
Boycott, Captain, 204
Bradford, 155, 223
Bradford Labour Union, 85, 86
Bradlaugh, Charles, xiv, 32, 70, 91, 101n, 221
Bray, John Francis, xiii
Bright, John, 6n, 19, 31, 146
British Socialist Party, xv, 2, 126
Broadhurst, Henry, 62
Brooks, Rev. George, 93, 101n
Büchner, Professor Alexander, 35, 40n

Burnley, 63, 126
Burns, John, xiii, xiv, 70, 86,
122n
Burrows, Herbert, 6, 32, 127
Byron, Lord, xviiin

Caesar, Julius, 160
Cairnes, John Elliott, 43, 48, 49, 52n
*Some Leading Principles of
Political Economy*, 48
Campbell-Bannerman, Sir Henry,
139, 175
Canada, 196
Carlile, Richard, 221
Carlyle, Thomas, 65, 69n, 77, 84n
Carpenter, Edward, 62, 155, 223
Carpenter, Mary, 166, 175n
Chamberlain, Joseph, 84n
Champion, Henry Hyde, 2, 6, 62,
223
Charles I, 211, 218n
Cheshire, 175
Child labour, 82, 146, 151
Chile, 196
China, 81, 121, 132, 195, 196
Christian Socialist, 8
Clarion, 87, 219, 223
Clarion Clubs, xv, 86, 219
Clark, W. John, 6
Cobbett, William, 136, 154n
Cobden, Sir John, 165, 167, 175n
Coke, Sir Edward, 161, 175n
Common Cause, 156
Communist, 50, 54, 91, 100
Communist Party of Great Britain, 2,
71, 126
Connolly, James, 192, 193, 194, 224
Biography, 192–3
Socialism Made Easy, 192
Conservatives, 2, 3, 10, 86, 190, 200
Consumers' Council, 125
Co-operation, 95, 96
Co-operative Societies, 13
Corn Laws, 2, 6n
Coventry, Foleshill, 70
Cromwell, Oliver, 211, 215, 218n
Curzon, Lord, 152

Darwin, Charles, 35, 40n

Dason, A.J., 6
Democratic Federation, xii, 1, 3, 6,
59, 62, 64, 125, 223
Devonshire, Duke of, 149
Disraeli, Benjamin, Lord
Beaconsfield, 174
Drysdale, Charles Robert, 46
Durham, 43
Seaholme Harbour, 43
Dutt, Ranji Palme, 53

Education, 5, 118, 122n, 151
Engels, Frederick, ix, xi, xii,
xiii, xiv, xviiin, 9, 59, 101n,
125
England, 3, 5, 33, 36, 37, 43, 45, 46,
47, 54, 90, 95, 96, 98, 100, 105,
125, 127, 128, 129, 130, 139,
146, 152, 153, 165, 167, 174,
185, 195, 211
Civil War, 211
Escombe, Miss Jane, 166
Essex, 98
Europe, 17, 81, 125, 127, 129, 130,
135, 152, 153, 162, 192, 196,
204, 210, 212
Evolution, 35
Exeter, Bishop, xvi

Fabian Society, 32, 33, 41, 43, 44,
53, 54, 57n, 85, 177, 221, 223
Far East, 152
Fawcett, Henry, 26, 31, 138
Fiji Islands, 36
Finland, 174
Food Reform Magazine, 8
Ford, Bessie, 155
Ford, Emily, 155
Ford, Isabella, 155, 156
Biography, 155–7
Novels: *Miss Blake*, 155;
Mr Elliott, 156; *On The
Threshold*, 156
Forder, Robert, 222
Fortnightly Review, 64
Foulger, J.C., 2, 224
Fourier, Baron Jean Baptiste, 64,
69n, 143
Foxwell, Herbert Somerton, 45, 52n

France, 34, 36, 134, 146, 162, 169, 174, 195, 211, 215, 218n
  Paris, 134, 151, 152, 184
Free Love, 91, 92
Freedom Library, 102
Freethought Publishing Company, 221
Friends of Russian Freedom, 156

Garibaldi, Giuseppe, 125
Garrison, William Lloyd, 164, 175n
Gas Workers and General Labourers Union, 115
George, Henry, *Progress and Poverty*, 8, 70
Germany, xii, xiv, 34, 101n, 152, 162, 163, 171, 172, 174, 191n, 192, 195, 210
  Berlin, 134, 145, 151, 169
  Kaiser, 74, 75, 130, 162
  Peasant Wars, 210
Giffen, Robert, 73, 139
Gladstone, William Ewart, 174
Glasgow, xvi, 1, 97, 139
  Glasgow Green, xvi
Gray, John, xiii
Grayson, Victor, 222
Great Britain, 1, 2, 3, 75, 76, 80, 81, 122, 135, 144, 183, 193, 205
Great Unrest, xv, 222
Greece, 133
  Athens, 189
Green, Mrs Alice Stopford, 160, 161, 171, 175n
Guilds, 150, 161, 171

Haeckel, Professor Ernst Heinrich, 35, 40n, 221
Haldane, Lord, 148
Hall, Leonard, 85
Hammersmith, 60, 62
Hammersmith Socialist Society, 59, 102, 225
Hampden, John, 215, 218n
Hampden Clubs, 218n
Harcourt, Sir William, 92, 101n
Hardie, James Keir, 222
Harrison, Frederick, 46, 52n
Hegel, Georg, Wilhelm, Friedrich, 189, 191n

Hennessy, Patrick, 6
Henshall, Harry, 222
Historical Materialism, xiii
Hone, William, xixn
Holland, Amsterdam, 156
  The Hague, 156
Holyoake, George, Jacob, xvi, 70
Homer, 66
Hours of labour, 5, 62, 67, 70, 71, 78, 79, 118, 150, 176n, 222
House of Commons, 3, 56, 57, 83, 84, 114, 118, 148, 151, 174
House of Lords, xvi, 1, 3, 43
Hutchinson, Henry, 41
Huxley, Thomas Henry, 35, 36, 40n, 66, 91, 101n
Hyndman, Henry Mayers, xii, 1, 2, 6, 7, 9, 53, 59, 60, 63, 64, 85, 125, 126, 194, 218n, 223, 224,
  Bibliography, 125–6
  Social Democracy, 125, 126

Independent Labour Party, xiv, xv, 71, 86, 126, 155, 156, 174, 222, 223
  Administrative Council, 222
  Manchester Branch, 85
Independent Review, 177
India, 2, 33, 62, 81, 152, 196
Industrial Remuneration Conference 1886, 46, 47, 52n
Industrial Revolution, xi, xv
Industrial unionism, 193, 208, 212, 213, 214, 215, 222
Industrial Workers of The World, 192
International Library of Science and Free Thought, 221
International Peace Congress, The Hague, 1922, 156
International Socialist Bureau, 127
International Women's Suffrage Alliance, 156
Investigator, 101n
Ireland, 1, 3, 7, 17, 175n, 192, 193, 194, 195, 198, 199, 200
  Belfast, 192
  Dublin, 53, 192, 194, 195, 203, 204, 205, 218n
  Easter Rising, 192, 193

Land League, 204
Irish Coercion Bill, 1
Irish Socialist Republican Party, 192
Irish Worker, 194, 218n
Isle of Man, 174
Italy, 34, 125, 152
  Milan, 156
  Rome, 133, 134, 189

Jacquerie, 210, 218n
James I, 161
Japan, 81, 134, 145, 153, 195, 196
Jevons, H. Stanley, 43
Johnson, Samuel, xvii, xviii, xviiin, xixn
Joynes, James Leigh, xvi, 6, 8, 9, 62
  Biography, 7, 8, 9
  Adventures of a Tourist in Ireland, 8
  Socialist Catechism, 8
Justice, 7, 53, 62, 63, 66, 67, 68, 69, 69n, 125, 223

Kerr, Charles H., xvi, 193, 194, 218n
Knowlton, Charles, 32
  Fruits of Philosophy, 32
Kropotkin, Prince Peter, xvi
  Appeal To The Young, xvi

Labour Elector, 223
Labour Gazette, 77
Labour Leader, 156
Labour Monthly, 53
Labour Party, xv, 53, 114, 125, 156, 157, 164, 165, 166, 167, 168, 169, 170
Labour Press Society, Manchester, 71, 222, 223
Labour Representation Committee, xv
Lancashire, xv, 134, 145, 146, 175
Land League, 204
Larkin, James, 218n
Laws and Resolutions of Women's Rights 1632, 172
Lee, Henry William, 69n

Leeds:
  Arts Club, 156
  Peace Crusade Women's Branch, 156
  Royal Society for the Prevention of Cruelty to Animals, 156
  Trades Council, 155
  Women's Suffrage Society, 155, 156
Lemon, T.S., 6
De Leon, Daniel, xvi, 192, 218n, 224
  Reform or Revolution, 224
  Two Pages From Roman History, 224
  What Means This Strike?, 224
Liberal Party, xii, xiv, xv, 1, 2, 3, 90, 92, 94, 95, 96, 101n, 120, 127, 130, 148, 149, 151, 155, 169, 190, 200, 222
Libraries, 118
Liebknecht, William, 92, 101n
Liverpool, 1
Lloyd George, David, xv
London, xv, xvi, 32, 36, 41, 45, 46, 54, 59, 70, 98, 101n, 122n, 151, 163, 184, 195
  Bermondsey, 139
  County Council, 41
  Deptford, 41
  Dulwich, 1
  Grosvenor Square, 101n
  Hammersmith Mall, 60
  Holborn Town Hall, 63
  Hyde Park, xvi, 45
  Lambeth, 46
  Limehouse, Dodd Street, xiii
  Rathbone Place, Wheatsheaf Restaurant, 8
  Rose Street Club, 125
  School Board, 33, 115, 122n
  Southwark, 139
  Strand, 62
  Trafalgar Square, xiii, xiv
  Walworth, 63
  West Ham, 115
  Westminster Palace Chambers, 62
London School of Economics and Political Science, 1

London Society of Compositors, 114, 115, 116
  Socialism and Trade Unionism, 114
Lowell, James Russell, 52n
Luther, Martin, 162, 175n

MacDonald, James, 6
MacDonald, James Ramsey, 43, 222
Machinists' Society, Leeds, 155
Maguire, Thomas, 155
Margate, 180
Malthus, Thomas Robert, 31, 45, 52n, 138
Malthusians, 29, 31
Manchester, xvi, 1, 71, 85, 97, 98
  Margaret Street Hall, Openshaw, xvii
  Stevenson's Square, xvi
Mann, Tom, xiv, 69n, 122n
  Biography, 70–1
  Don't Shoot Leaflet, 71
  Socialists' Program, 70, 71
  What a Compulsory Eight Hour Working Day Means to the Workers, 70
Marryat, Captain Frederick, 32
Marryat, Ellen, 32
Marshall, Professor, 129
Marx, Eleanor, *see* Aveling, Eleanor Marx
Marx, Karl, ix, xi, xii, xiii, xvi xviiin, 9, 48, 53, 54, 59, 64, 86, 92, 101n, 125, 126, 129, 135, 143, 149, 191n, 213, 218n, 221
  Capital, xiii, xvi, 43, 59, 64, 126
  Communist Manifesto, xi, xii
  Wage Labour and Capital, xvi, 8
Mattison, Alfred, 155
May Day, 68
Mazzini, Gustav, 125
Mexico, 196
Mill, John Stuart, 18, 25, 26, 31, 43, 45, 48, 49, 50, 52n, 64, 77, 78, 174
  Autobiography, 45
Milton, John, xvii, xixn
Modern Press, 2, 223
Money, Sir Leo Chiozza, 190
Morley, John, 36, 81, 84n, 91, 101n
  Life of Cobden, 36

Morris, William, xii, xiv, xvi, 1, 6 7, 9, 53, 59, 60, 61, 62, 63, 85 92, 101n, 102, 168, 223, 224, 225
  Biography, 59, 60
  Defence of Guinevere, 61
  Dream of John Ball, 61
  Earthly Paradise, 61
  How I Became A Socialist, 59
  Life and Death of Jason, 61
  Monopoly, or How Labour Is Robbed, xvi, 102
  Socialism Made Plain, 1, 2
Morris and Company, 59
Motley, John Lothrop, 210
Murray, James, 6, 62

National Charter Association, xi
National Debt, 4, 5
National Reformer, 32, 101n
National Secular Society, 101n
National Union of Women's Suffrage Societies, 156
  West Riding Federation, 156
Nationalisation, 71, 98, 147
  Banks, 5
  Factories, 13
  Housing, 119, 150
  Land, 4, 5, 83, 90, 95, 97, 150, 210
  Mines, 13, 57
  Post Office, 13, 25, 26, 57, 97
  Railways, 5, 13, 25, 57, 62, 97, 150
  Shipping, 13·
  Telegraphs, 13, 57, 97
Netherlands, 210
New York Sun, 201
New York World, 197
New Zealand, 165, 172, 173
Newcastle-on-Tyne, 81
Nicaragua, 196
Nightingale, Florence, 174
Nineteenth Century, 62, 125
Northampton, 101n
Northwich, 85
Norway, 196
Nottingham, 1

O'Brien, James Bronterre, 128
Operative Bricklayers' Society, 116

Our Corner, 8, 33, 53
Owen, Robert, xiii

Paine, Thomas, xii, 175n
Palestine, 101n
Pall Mall Gazette, 8, 53
Paris Commune, 125
Parliament, xii, xiv, xv, 34, 56, 57
   63, 73, 74, 83, 89, 91, 94, 109
   112, 114, 118, 126, 154n, 164
   166, 169, 174, 175n, 176n, 193
Patterson, Emma, 155
Pearson, Karl, 159, 163, 171, 175n
Pensions, 119
People's Charter, 1, 43
Physical Culture Commission, 151
Plutarch, 160, 175n
Pollitt, Harry, xvii, xviiin
Positivists, 43, 49
Progress, 8

Quakers, 155
Quelch, Harry, 62, 69n

Radicals, 2, 10, 34, 41, 44, 49, 90,
   94, 155
Ramsay, William James, 221
Reade, Henry Musgrave, 85
Reade, Winwood, 221
Reeves, William, 102
Reform Bill 1832, 2, 6n, 57
   1884, 169
Revolution, 17, 30, 31, 44, 66, 89,
   148, 208, 209, 210, 212, 213,
   215, 217, 224
   French, 30, 36, 90, 134, 191n, 211,
   215
   Russian: 1905, 195; 1917, 126, 166,
   193
Ricardo, David, 64, 69n, 135
Roberts, William Prouting, 32
Rosebery, Lord, 148
Rossendale, Lancs, 175
Rossetti, Dante Gabriel, 62
Rowland, H.W., 6
Royal Commission on Housing, 150
Royal Commission on Labour, 73
Russia, 34, 62, 130, 141, 153, 166,
   193, 195, 196

Czar, 74, 75
Moscow Windau-Rydinsk Railway,
   195

Salisbury, Lord, 84n, 92, 101n
Salt, Henry S., 9
Scandinavia, 202
Scheu, Andreas, 6, 64, 69n
Scotland, 89, 151
   Aberdeen, 71, 73, 84
   Edinburgh, 1, 193, 224
Second International, 156
Shaftesbury, Lord, 146, 166, 168,
   175n
Shaw, George Bernard, xviii, 8, 32,
   41, 53, 177, 221
   Biography, 53, 54
   Man and Superman, 53
   What Socialism Is, 53, 54
   Widowers' Houses, 53
Smith, Adam, 64, 69n, 117, 135
Smith, Mary, 174
Snowden, Philip, 223
Social Democratic Federation, xii, xiii
   1, 2, 8, 9, 33, 53, 135, 136, 150,
   151, 194, 218n, 221, 223, 224
   Battersea Branch, 70
   Lancashire, 60, 62, 63, 114
   Scottish District Council, 224
   South Salford Branch, 85
Social Democratic Party, xv, 127
Socialist, The, 194, 218n, 224
Socialist Labour Party, 193, 194, 213,
   216, 217
Socialist Labour Press, 194, 218n,
   224
Socialist League, xiv, 1, 2, 9, 53, 59,
   102, 224 – 5
   Leeds Branch, 155
Socialist Party of America, 122, 192
South America, 183, 221
Spence, Thomas, xii
Spencer, Herbert, 35, 40n, 148
State and Church, xvii, xviii
Stead, William Thomas, 32
Stopes, E.C., 171
Strikes, 121, 122, 141, 200, 202, 203, 214
   Bryant & May Match Girls 1888,
   xiv, 33

Docks, 1889, 70, 224
Dublin, 1913, 192
Mannigham Mills, Bradford,
  1890–91, 155
Street Cars, New York, 202
Transport 1912–13, xv
Weavers at Alverthorpe, 1889, 155
Weavers at Wilsons in Leeds 1888,
  155
Suffrage Movement, xv
Suffrage, Women's, 33
  Australia, 173
  England, 174–5
  Finland, 174
  France, 174
  Germany, 174
  New Zealand, 172, 173
  Petitions, 174, 175
  Tasmania, 173
  United States of America, 173, 174
Summerville, Mrs, 174
Sunday Chronicle, 85,86, 219
Swedenborgians, 44
Swinburne, Algernon, 61
Switzerland, Geneva, 156

Tasmania, 173
Taylor, Helen, 6, 62
Tennyson, Alfred Lord, 61
Textile Workers' Congress,
  Blackpool 1914, 156
  Milan 1904, 156
Theosophical Society, 33
Thompson, Alex M., 85
Thompson, William, xiii
Tibet, 152
Tillett, Benjamin, xiv, 122n
Today, 8
Tories, 2, 69n, 90, 92, 95, 96, 101n,
  112, 120, 127, 130, 148, 151, 169
Trade Union Congress, 101n, 114
Trade Unionism, 94, 95, 114–22,
  140, 164, 168, 175
Trinidad, 153n
Turkey, 62
Turner, Benjamin, 155
Tweedmouth, Lord, 148
Tyler, Watt, 210, 218n

Union of Democratic Control, 156
United States of America, xii, 81,
  122, 129, 130, 131, 138, 139,
  140, 144, 145, 146, 152, 153,
  155, 158, 162, 163, 169, 172,
  175n, 192, 193, 194, 195, 196,
  201, 215, 218n, 224
  Colorado, 130, 146, 153n, 154, 165
  Idaho, 165
  Illinois, 143
  New York, 134, 210
  Utah, 165
  Wyoming, 165
Utopian Socialists, xii, 43

Victoria, Queen, 33, 59, 75

Waddington, Joseph, 85
Wages, 116, 139
Wales, 46
Walker, Amasa, 43, 48, 52n
War Workers National Committee,
  125
Ward, A.C., xixn
Weaver Navigation Company, 85
Webb, Beatrice (née Potter), 41, 43,
  177, 221
Webb, Sidney, 41, 43, 53, 125, 177
  Biography, 41–3
  Facts for Socialists, 41
  History of the Durham Miners, 43
  *Soviet Communism: A New
    Civilisation*, 43
  *What Socialism Means: A Call to
    the Unconverted*, 41
Wells, Herbert George, xviii, 177
  Biography, 177–8
  Anne Veronica, 177
  This Misery of Boots, 177
Westminster Review, 36, 64
Whigs, 2, 65, 69n, 94, 148, 151
Whitman, Walt, 155
Williams, John E., 6, 62
Women, xv, xviii, 92, 122n,
  155–76
  Parish District Councils, 175
  Poor Law Guardians, 175
  Rural District Councillors, 175
  Urban District Councillors, 175

Women's International League, 156
Women's Provident and Protective
  League, 155
Woods, Samuel, M.P., 93, 101n
Work Women's Society for Leeds
  Tailoresses and Textile Workers,
  155

Yorkshire, xiv, 146, 174, 175
  Colne Valley Election, 1907, 223
  Halifax, 85
  West Riding, 156
Yorkshireman, The, 85

Zetetical Society, 41